Miniature and Dwarf
GERANIUMS

Best Wishes

OTHER GARDENING BOOKS PUBLISHED BY CHRISTOPHER HELM

An Anthology of Garden Writing
Edited by Ursula Buchan

Conifers
Keith D. Rushforth

The Conservatory Handbook
Ann Bonar

The Cottage Garden Year
Roy Genders

Creating a Chinese Garden
David H. Engel

The Flower Show
E.D. Wearn

Growing Begonias
E. Catterall

Growing Bulbs
Martyn Rix

Growing Chrysanthemums
Harold Randall and Alan Wren

Growing Cyclamen
Gay Nightingale

Growing Dahlias
Philip Damp

Growing Fuchsias
K. Jennings and V. Miller

Growing Hardy Perennials
Kenneth A. Beckett

Growing Irises
G.E. Cassidy and S. Linnegar

Growing Lilies
Derek Fox

A Handbook of Annuals and Bedding Plants
Graham Rice

The Handbook of Soft Fruit Growing
Ken Muir and David Turner

Hardy Geraniums
Peter F. Yeo

Hebes and Parahebes
Douglas Chalk

The History of Gardens
Christopher Thacker

Plants for Problem Places
Graham Rice

The Rock Gardener's Handbook
Alan Titchmarsh

The Winter Flower Garden
Sonia Kinahan

OTHER BOOKS BY HAROLD BAGUST

Miniature Geraniums (1968)
Menorca (1971)
A History of Stow-on-the-Wold (1979)
London Through the Ages (1982)

Miniature and Dwarf
GERANIUMS
(Pelargoniums)

Harold Bagust

CHRISTOPHER HELM
London
TIMBER PRESS
Portland, Oregon

© 1988 Harold Bagust
Line drawings by David Henderson
Christopher Helm (Publishers) Ltd, Imperial House, 21–25 North Street, Bromley,
Kent BR1 1SD

ISBN 0–7470–0218–5

A CIP catalogue record for this book
is available from the British Library

First published in North America in 1988 by
Timber Press
9999 SW Wilshire
Portland, Oregon 97225, USA

Library of Congress Cataloging-in-Publication Data

Bagust, Harold.
    Miniature & dwarf geraniums (Pelargoniums)

    Rev. ed. of: Miniature geraniums.
    Includes index.
    1. Miniature pelargoniums.   2. Dwarf pelargoniums.
I. Bagust, Harold.   Miniature geraniums.   II. Title.
III. Title: Miniature and dwarf geraniums (Pelargoniums)
SB413.G35B3   1988   635.9′33216   88–2125
ISBN 0–88192–110–6

Typeset by OPUS, Oxford
Printed and bound in Great Britain by
Biddles Ltd, Guildford, Surrey

Contents

List of Colour Plates   vi
List of Figures   vii
Acknowledgements   viii
Foreword *Percy Thrower*   ix
Introduction   1

1. Geranium versus Pelargonium   5
2. Growing Media   11
3. Pots: Clay or Plastic?   19
4. Potting and Re-potting   23
5. Propagating   33
6. Grafting   59
7. Feeds, Fertilisers and Watering   63
8. Pests and Diseases   75
9. Heating Methods   99
10. Alphabetical List of Varieties   111

Hardiness Zone Maps   147
List of Suppliers of Miniature and Dwarf Geraniums   150
List of Geranium (Pelargonium) Societies   156
Index   157

List of Colour Plates

1. 'Karen'
2. 'Red Pearl'
3. 'Mont Blanc'
4. 'Mimi'
5. 'Bridesmaid'
6. 'Golden Chalice'
7. 'Sunbeam'
8. 'Monica Bennet'
9. 'Spitfire Cactus'
10. 'Melissa'
11. 'Cheiko'
12. 'Bird Dancer'
13. The first single yellow, raised by Sam Peat
14. 'Sunstar'
15. 'Beacon Hill'
16. 'Friary Wood'
17. 'Algenon'
18. 'Freak of Nature'
19. 'Golden Ears'
20. 'Deacon Bonanza'
21. 'Falkland Hero'
22. 'Love Storey'
23. 'Formosum'
24. 'Frills'

List of Figures

2.1	Watering a plant in a dried-out soil-less compost	12
2.2	Enlarged diagram of a root-hair	16
3.1	Cotton-reel 'mallet'	20
3.2	Base of a normal clay pot	22
3.3	Base of a modern plastic pot	22
4.1	(a) Jiffy-7 before soaking; (b) Jiffy-7 in use when fully expanded	25
4.2	Peat pots in strips or gangs	26
4.3	Potting-on	27
4.4	Transferring to a new pot	28
4.5	Roots can be sheared by manually compressing the soil	29
5.1	Taking a 'nodal cutting'	36
5.2	Narrow hard stem which has been short of water will not root easily	38
5.3	Peat 'plug' widely used in the USA	42
5.4	(a) Cuttings rooted in pure water after three weeks; (b) bloated and brittle roots produced by rooting in water	43
5.5	Pot-up when roots are just showing through the walls of the peat pot	45
5.6	Basic electric propagator	47
5.7	A tray of damp sand between the seed tray and the heated panel	47
5.8	Cross-section of a heated bench	48
5.9	Layout of a cable in a heated bench	49
5.10	(a) Centre of flower; (b) details of pollen grain	51
5.11	Transfer the pollen from anther to stigma	52
5.12	(a) Pollen grains deposited on stigma, pollen tube extended; (b) details of pollen grain	53
5.13	Immature and ripe seed	54
6.1	Grafting	60
6.2	Transpiration reduced by placing grafted shoot in a jam jar	61
6.3	Budding procedure	62
7.1	Self-watering for stock plants	69
7.2	Another self-watering method	70
7.3	Drying out a plant that has been over-watered	71
8.1	Mice often gnaw through the main stem	79
8.2	Pygmy and common shrews are very beneficial	80
8.3	Small circles of orange spores on undersides of leaves indicate Geranium Rust	87
8.4	(a)-(f) Photographs of rust-infected leaf of 'Karen'; (g)-(l) photographs of a healthy leaf of 'Karen'	89-94
8.5	A rust spore settled over the aperture of a stoma	95
8.6	The correct way to strip rusted leaves from an infected plant	96
8.7	Aerial roots sometimes develop above soil level in damp conditions	97
9.1	Guaranteed to kill all Geraniums and many other plants	101
9.2	Electric fan heater for a greenhouse	103
9.3	Greenhouse paraffin heater	104
9.4	Adjust the angle of the polythene until the drips run down	107
9.5	The 'Thermogem' bottled gas greenhouse heater	109

Acknowledgements

Since the publication in 1968 of my first book *Miniature Geraniums* I have corresponded and had personal contact with Geranium growers, both amateur and professional, in many parts of the world, and have derived much help and advice (and not a few plants) from them.

I am particularly indebted to Henry and Jean Llewellyn of Sydney, Australia, Frank and Jocelyne Coates of Crabbes Creek, Australia, Fred and Alice Bode and Carol Roller of California, USA and Faye Brawner of Oregon, USA, all of whom have made me and my wife very welcome during our several visits and with whom I have had many discussions and (sometimes) arguments.

To Percy Thrower who again kindly provided the Foreword, and also the late Reverend Stanley Stringer, Sam Peat, Neil Jamieson and Bill Starmes. I am also grateful to Professors A.M. Kofranek and O.R. Lunt of the University of California; Dr Jeffery Bagust of Southampton University; Chris Hawkins and the Department of Biology, Southampton University; and Dr John Gay of the Department of Botany, Imperial College, London.

Finally, my thanks are due in no small measure to my four sons who have devoted months of patient time and effort teaching the old man the intricacies of the computer — which *they* all mastered in minutes.

Foreword

Percy Thrower, MBE, VMH, ND.Hort.

Never was the Geranium more popular than it is at the present time, and quite understandably when we realise the range of bright colours Geraniums can provide for so many months of the year in the garden, the greenhouse or even on the windowsill. My wife enjoys Geraniums in full flower throughout the twelve months of the year in the sun-lounge.

One wonders why there has not been more written about this wonderful plant, and for this reason I felt privileged to be asked to provide a Foreword for this book on Miniature Geraniums. This is a much more explicit edition than the first book, which sold throughout the world and is still in demand today, as a result of which the author, Harold Bagust, was invited to lecture to the International Geranium Society in Los Angeles and San Diego and to the Australian Geranium Society, as well as broadcasting on the subject in various parts of the world.

Harold Bagust has covered the subject in great detail and describes not only the best methods of cultivation and the know-how of growing these charming plants to perfection, but also gives us the most up-to-date list of varieties and suppliers.

On reading through the pages and appreciating the many illustrations and photographs we realise there is a lifetime's experience behind these writings passed on to us in a pleasing and easy-to-understand manner. In this book we see the love of a true gardener for his precious plants.

I am sure this revised and updated edition will prove to be an even more popular and valuable book, much in demand by the many thousands of Geranium lovers world-wide — I believe it is still the only one written specifically on Miniature Geraniums, and it has my best wishes for the success which I am certain is assured.

FOR AUDREY

Introduction

When *Miniature Geraniums* was first published in 1968 it became an overnight success; it was, and I believe still is, the only book devoted entirely to its subject and has been circulated in every English-speaking country in the world. Following several reprints I was asked to revise and update it in 1980 but after supplying the amended manuscript and new photographs to the publishers, there was a devastating fire at the printers and everything was lost.

Business commitments have prevented my re-writing until now, and the weather in recent summers has made good photography difficult in the limited time available, but now in retirement I have more time to concentrate on growing and writing, and I hope that my many correspondents will feel that the following pages have been worth waiting for.

It is surprising that after nearly 20 years the original edition is still available on most library shelves, and according to the Public Lending Rights returns was taken out by over 1,000 readers in 1986. In addition I know that first editions are much sought after as witness occasional advertisements in Gardening Journals sometimes offering as much as £10 for a copy in good condition — and this for a book which cost only 12/6 (62p) when new.

Parts of it have been plagiarised on several occasions, in particular my reference to 'Solanum tuberosum' as the correct name for the humble potato, but I regard this to some extent as a form of flattery, and the reproduction of some of the sketches in certain books and articles would seem to emphasise their suitability for the purpose intended.

The present edition has been completely revised and re-written with numerous additions and deletions to bring it into line with modern methods and varieties. All the photographs of varieties are new and in most cases from my own collection, other people's work being acknowledged when used.

As before, those nurseries I have listed at the end of this book are all specialists I have had personal contact with and whose products are normally of a very high standard. The omission of a particular nursery or supplier should not be taken to imply that they or their plants are inferior, it usually means that I have not had a chance to visit them.

Although I have been interested in Geraniums since about the age of four, and grown them commercially and as an amateur over the best part of 50 years, it was only in 1952 that I first discovered Miniatures at a Horticultural Show in the south of England. At that time there were less than a dozen varieties in general cultivation, very few nurseries listed them, and none specialised to the extent of growing nothing else. But by 1968 it was normal to find a Miniature Section in the catalogue of almost every genuine Geranium specialist nursery, and although very few ever grew Miniatures exclusively, there were several who regarded Miniatures as a major proportion of their business.

The oil crisis of the early 1970s, coupled with rapid inflation and the introduction of VAT on plant sales, resulted in the demise of thousands of small nurseries, many elderly growers refusing to be saddled with the extra

1

paperwork involved in VAT, coupled with gardeners (many of whom were pensioners) refusing to pay it. Those small nurseries who managed to survive the next ten years or so (mostly family-owned and run) are today in a fairly stable position, but the production of the several million Geraniums purchased by the general public every year is now mainly centred in the large wholesale growers who are interested in mass-producing only six or eight of the most popular varieties which are distributed to garden centres over a wide area for over-the-counter retailing. The number of nurseries actually growing the Geranium plants they sell can now almost be counted on the fingers of one hand — the ones I have listed are among those few.

It has been said that the first thing every Englishman attempts to grow in a newly acquired greenhouse is a tomato plant, and it takes between one and three years for him to discover that they are more nuisance than they are worth. There is no doubt that the flavour of a home-grown, freshly picked tomato is far superior to any bought in the local supermarket, but costwise there is little in it and they are very time consuming. To grow from seed requires a greenhouse temperature of about 70°F (21°C) throughout the coldest months of the year, and ready-grown plants are expensive and not always of very good quality. If they are to be grown in a greenhouse they need to be planted in good soil or growbags (more expense), and if outside planting is undertaken they will have a very short season and suffer from the vagaries of the British climate.

They take up a lot of room in the greenhouse and the regular removal of the side shoots is essential on most varieties if fruits of a reasonable size are required. They must be sprayed regularly to persuade the fruits to set, and dusted against a wide range of pests. After all this, they mature at a time when tomatoes are at their cheapest in the shops, and as the season progresses the yield increases as shop prices fall. Finally, at the end of the season, there still remains a few hundredweight of small green tomatoes suitable only for preserving, and the family indicate after only the first two weeks that they can stomach no more chutney-based dishes.

After this experience the gardener, in a fit of despondency, abandons tomato production and begins to develop a collection of plants with the apparent intention of covering the full range of the planet's natural and hybrid plant life until, by the close of the second year of 'mixed greenhouse cultivation' it gradually occurs to him that not only will his 6 x 8ft (1.8 x 2.4m) greenhouse probably be inadequate for his ambitions, but neither will his entire garden, even were he able to enclose it completely in glass.

So it usually happens that the entire contents of the greenhouse are distributed among (often unwilling) neighbours and relatives together with the remaining jars of chutney from three years previous, the benches cleared, cleaned and re-painted, and a fresh start made with a subject which is more easily controllable — and it is at this point, or so I believe, that great numbers of amateurs have turned to Miniature Geraniums.

Initially they appear to have every advantage over most other pot plants, being very easy to grow, simple to propagate, provide masses of colour throughout the year for the minimum of attention, require only to be kept frost free during the winter, and never get out of control in the greenhouse or indoors. First impressions are confirmed by the end of the season, and it is very seldom that any gardener who has been introduced to Miniature Geraniums ever considers abandoning them for another type of plant.

The purpose of this book is exactly the same as for the earlier editions — to assist the newcomer to the world of Miniature Geraniums to know his plants and the conditions under which they will give the most satisfaction; to solve some of the few problems which the amateur gardener may encounter from time to time; and to provide this information in a way that will both entertain and instruct the reader.

As a commercial grower of Geraniums for many years, producing over half a million plants per annum of which total about 25 per cent were Miniatures, I can claim to write from experience. My plants were exported to almost every country in the world including Australia (where I was told no plant imports were allowed) and behind the Iron Curtain (where an exchange of goods was arranged since cash transfers at that time were not permitted). My company exhibited at horticultural shows all over England for several years, and was awarded dozens of medals and certificates including all the major awards at the Chelsea Flower Show (excepting the Large Gold which is only awarded to the very large exhibits usually staged by the Local Authority Parks Departments or the big wholesale growers).

Every method suggested and system used has been tested and approved by both amateur and commercial growers. This is not a book of gimmicks but all the latest techniques are examined and discussed, and there is no attempt to blind with science. There is nothing in this book that an ordinary literate gardener will be unable to understand, no method described that he will be unable to follow.

Harold Bagust

1 Geranium versus Pelargonium

What is a Miniature Geranium? The plant we normally refer to as a 'Geranium' is in fact a Zonal Pelargonium, and those plants we often hear called 'Pelargoniums' are in reality Regal Pelargoniums. Ivyleaf varieties (sometimes mistakenly called 'Climbing Geraniums') are in fact Ivyleaf Pelargoniums and as they are incapable of climbing without assistance 'trailing' would perhaps be a better description.

All are members of the Pelargonium family (the true Geranium is something quite different) and for several years there has been a small but vociferous group of devotees hell-bent on getting the public to refer to the plants by their correct botanical names, and their greatest achievement came about when they succeeded in changing the name of the old Geranium Society to the present clumsy and ostentatious 'British Pelargonium and Geranium Society' (BPGS), against the wishes of most of its members.

Until then membership of the Geranium Society was increasing steadily every year and it stood at a little under 2,000 at the time of the vote. Since that disastrous evening membership has never reached the 2,000 mark and on several occasions has fallen to less than 1,000. It follows that any society attracting such a small percentage of Geranium growers is scarcely in a position to make an impression on the ingrained habits of the mass of the British public who obstinately insist upon referring to the plants as 'Geraniums'.

The Australian Geranium Society, (AGS) as the International Registration Authority (IRA) for *Pelargonium*, finds itself in a terrible quandary for the IRA insists on the use of the word 'Pelargonium' but the AGS is well aware that to drop 'Geranium' from its title would probably result in the demise of the society within a few years. Almost everyone in Australia knows the plant as a 'Geranium' and the IRA is facing an uphill task if it intends to convert the average Aussie to 'Pelargonium'. Terms used in the USA are similar — 'Geranium' for Zonal and Ivyleaf Pelargoniums, 'Regal', 'Show' or 'Lady Washington' Geraniums for Regal Pelargoniums. Except in academic circles I have never heard the word 'Pelargonium' used in France, Belgium, Luxembourg, Germany, Spain, Portugal or Italy, and since the earlier editions of this book sold almost world-wide it would be foolish to entitle it anything other than 'Miniature and Dwarf Geraniums'. If fifty or sixty million people are convinced that the plant they are buying is a 'Geranium' and need to know how best to cultivate it, they are not likely to buy a book entitled 'Pelargoniums'.

In the first edition of *Miniature Geraniums* I drew the reader's attention to the fact that the correct botanical name for the humble potato is *Solanum tuberosum* but we seldom see them so labelled in greengrocers' shops or supermarkets. This phrase has been so copied and plagiarised by later authors that I am tempted to provide them with another — how often have you heard a shopper ask for a pound of *Lycopersicum esculentum*, a close relative of *Solanum tuberosum* and almost as popular. Try it on your local nurseryman next time you want a tomato plant.

So in order to avoid confusion I shall continue to call Zonal Pelargoniums 'Geraniums' — the name by which most people know them — and I am sure that even my friends in the many societies spread all over the world will forgive me for the pin-pricks.

Miniature and Dwarf Geraniums as described in this volume are the naturally short-growing varieties which vary in height from about 2in to 8 or 9in (5 to 23cm); the F_1 and F_2 hybrids which have to be chemically dwarfed are not included. In 1966, the British Pelargonium and Geranium Society attempted to differentiate between the terms 'miniature', 'dwarf' and 'semi-dwarf' and set up a series of committees to establish the rules, and their classification was accepted by two of the main Geranium specialist growers in Britain who attempted to put the system into practice. Unfortunately plants do not oblige by falling neatly into man-made categories, and the environment to which they are subjected can radically alter the rate of growth and ultimate height, and my old friend Frank Parrett of Cobham, Kent confided that it was one of the worst moves he had ever made commercially when he began listing his plants separately as 'Miniature', 'Dwarf', 'Semi-Dwarf', etc. So often a plant which can be expected to grow to 8in (20cm) on the nursery will make less than 6in (15cm) under the customer's conditions, and vice versa, with the result that the nurseryman gets involved in reams of correspondence and complaints from irate customers convinced that they have been sold the wrong plant, or that it is a poor specimen.

Rather than fall into this trap, all plants in this book are described as 'Miniatures or Dwarfs' generally, but consistent habits are noted so that readers may have a guide as to what may be expected from a plant under average British conditions. Measurements must always be approximate and are taken from the surface of the soil to the highest growing shoot, excluding flowers which may often be held on long stems well above the foliage. The fact that variations in the size and habit of a plant are to some extent dependent upon local conditions can be confirmed by comparing the growth of plants in the south of England with similar varieties in the north. I have seen a plant of 'Minx' over 3ft (1m) in diameter growing in Southern California whereas in Britain it is unlikely to exceed 8in (20cm) at most.

Whilst on the subject of size, it is interesting to note that two of England's leading hybridisers of Miniature Geraniums managed to produce almost simultaneously an extremely tiny plant. Miss Mary Campbell of Brighton, East Sussex raised the variety 'Chico' which has a very small salmon-pink flower and leaves seldom larger than ¼in (5mm) in diameter, and the

Reverend Stanley Stringer of Occold, Suffolk raised 'Vega' with leaves about ⅜in (7mm) in diameter and a fairly large flower in proportion to the size of the plant, in a shade of orange with a large white eye. Both varieties normally stay below 3in (75mm) in height, both are compact and low-growing, and difficult to propagate; although very attractive novelties, they are best avoided by the beginner. They are referred to here as 'Micro-miniatures', and for those who are keen to try them (and any other very tiny varieties which may be developed in the future) it is best to keep them at a temperature of around 60°F (15°C) and scrupulously clean at all times; any rotting vegetation in the centre of the plant will quickly bring about its collapse. It is some years since I saw either of these varieties listed in any catalogue so it is possible they have been lost, but there could well be a handful of devoted amateurs still holding a few plants in their collections.

Most gardeners make their first acquaintance with Miniature and Dwarf Geraniums either by being given a plant by a friend or by purchasing one or more from a nursery, perhaps during a personal visit or even buying from a mail order catalogue. Best results can only be expected from those nurseries which are specialists in Geraniums and Pelargoniums, and have been growing them as a speciality for several years. Even then it is best first to write for a few catalogues, partly to compare prices, although price is not (or should not be) the main consideration, but also to discover which and how many varieties are offered. There is no point in travelling 100 miles (160km) to a nursery to find upon arrival that they carry only six Miniature varieties — or it is early-closing day.

Nurserymen's catalogues are seldom great literary works of art. For years I have tried to convince my friends in the trade that the catalogue is the foremost salesman they have and as such should receive very careful consideration — all to no avail, most of them still use the same Foreword or Introduction they started with ten or even twenty years ago, with the result that when they need to include some new vital information in the Foreword (such as a change of opening times) nobody bothers to read it.

But this is a matter which rebounds only on the nursery and its owner; far more important to the prospective buyer is the 'small print' including the Conditions of Sale; these must be read carefully in order to discover just what is being offered. One concern I know of waits until an order (with cash) has been received before even taking a cutting, then after it has rooted out it goes with its fellows in a brown paper envelope. Reading the catalogue, their plants appear to be cheaper than those of their rivals until you realise that you are paying almost as much for a rooted cutting as you normally would for an established plant, and I doubt very much whether some of the more delicate varieties would stand the journey in such a youthful condition.

Look out for the exaggerated claims which cannot easily be verified — 'established 150 years', 'largest stock of Geraniums in England', 'more gold medals than any other firm', 'probably the finest Geraniums in the south of England' — the use of the word 'probably' has become a fashion in the advertising world almost equal in popularity to 'new'; if you substitute 'far from' for 'probably' on every occasion you read it you will usually be nearer the truth.

Bear in mind that catalogue descriptions often tend to glorify the subject, and may well be used to boost the sales of a variety which is stocked in abundance whilst quietly overlooking its faults. And don't be put off by faulty spelling or bad grammar in nurserymen's catalogues; some of us are poor ignorant clodhoppers and the preparation of a catalogue requires many months of earnest endeavour and chewing of pencil-ends. George Russell, the raiser of the glorious Russell Lupin and one of the greatest hybridisers of all time, could barely write his own name and so far as I am aware was never seen with a collar and tie upon his person. I had the very great privilege of meeting him just once before the war at his allotment at Codsall, West Midlands a very modest and unassuming gardener and a great 'man of the soil'. Remember, plants grow in soil not books.

Miniature and Dwarf Geraniums are most likely to be purchased growing in or 'ex' (a nurseryman's expression meaning 'knocked out of') 2½ or 3in (6 or 8cm) pots, and if well established can be immediately potted-on into 3½ or 4in (9 or 10cm) pots using a John Innes No2 or No3 Compost or one of the numerous soil-less mixtures now available. If carefully watered and placed in a position free from draughts but well ventilated, in a temperature of not less than 45°F (7°C) with maximum sunlight they will flourish — and basically that is all there is to it. In the following chapters I shall explore the finer details in greater depth but remember that all types of Geranium are easy to grow with the application of a little common sense, and Miniatures are no different in this respect.

Many varieties are now used for bedding or special displays outdoors, particularly as border plants in flowerbeds for which they are well adapted. For maximum effect they should be planted in groups of the same colour, and if a backdrop of dwarf conifers can be provided the effect will be enhanced. When Percy Thrower was Parks Superintendent at Shrewsbury in Shropshire, the flowerbeds in the park were usually edged with a solid border of 'Madame Salleron' and although this variety never flowers, the silver and green domes of lemon-scented foliage made a wonderful setting to complement other flowers in the beds.

For those with no garden there is enormous pleasure to be gained from growing Geraniums in a window-box or balcony-trough, and for this purpose I would suggest the Dwarf varieties as being most suitable and easy to manage. Ideally a window-box or trough should be no less than 8in (20cm) deep and the same width if possible so that the plants are provided with a reasonable root-run if planted directly into the box or trough, anything less will require more careful management, especially watering. You can, if you prefer, retain the plants in their original pots and simply sink the plant and pot into the box or trough, packing round with damp peat or soil. Peat is lighter, of course, but must always be kept damp — once it has been allowed to dry out it will be difficult to get it to re-accept water.

Plants grown indoors must be given maximum light if they are not to become etiolated. The light from a north-facing window will be inadequate for good growing, it must be south or south-west facing, and the plants turned 90° every day to prevent 'leaning'. If you wish to use your greenhouse plants for house decoration, bring them into the house for a few days (preferably not more than three) then replace them with a fresh batch from the greenhouse. By this constant rotation you can bring colour to the gloomiest of rooms without affecting the plants to a significant degree.

In Britain, most Miniature and Dwarf Geraniums are grown in heated greenhouses and it is mainly to the owners of such structures that this book is directed although much advice is of a general nature and can be applied to most situations. There can be few more versatile plants; I have seen Miniature Geraniums growing successfully in every possible type of protected cultivation from a plastic garden cloche to a magnificent conservatory built in the last century by Joseph Paxton. When Stanley Stringer first began hybridising he had only a tiny plastic-lined lean-to attached to the end of his garage behind the vicarage at Occold, unable to accommodate more than one person at a time, and although he soon acquired several garden frames and a large cedarwood greenhouse, it all began in a very modest way.

The use of Miniatures in flower arrangements usually requires the employment of the long-stemmed varieties where the flowers are carried well clear of the foliage, although it may often be possible to use some of the shorter types in the forefront. I have seen the flowerheads used in bouquets for the bridesmaids at a wedding, incorporated into a wreath at a funeral, and even worked into a canvas and frame to produce a 'living picture'. They have also been used for 'well-dressing' in Derbyshire and Gloucestershire. As Gervas Huxley once remarked 'If you can't grow Geraniums you had best abandon growing altogether and stick to bingo'.

2 Growing media

The material in which pot plants are grown is usually called 'compost' in Britain but this term is also used when referring to the humus produced from rotting leaves and other vegetation in the 'compost heap'. Between the wars experimental work at the John Innes Institute resulted in the introduction of the famous John Innes Composts — an attempt to produce a high quality product to a standard range of formulae as a substitute for the great variety of growing media then marketed by almost every nurseryman, large or small, as his own product — many derived from the soil dug from a corner of his nursery and 'sterilised' in an old copper behind the potting shed.

Whilst the John Innes Composts were a great stride forward, the basic ingredient is still sterilised well-rotted loam, and since loams will vary from area to area, indeed from one part of a garden to another, it follows that there is no such thing as an identifiable standard John Innes Compost. Today most J.I. Composts are sold in sealed plastic bags marked with the contents, but it is a fact that the compost from a Fenland area will bear little resemblance to one from say Devon or Bedfordshire. The Devon loam will normally be the reddish soil found in that part of the country with a high iron content and little clay, whereas the Fenland soil will probably have a fine sooty-black texture which tends to compact in the pot. Composts from Middlesex and Surrey usually have a high clay content. All are good, each may have been manufactured exactly to the J.I. formula, yet they are quite different and will perform differently.

In the past each gardener had his own idea as to what constituted the ideal mixture. I have known some who added cow manure to the basic loam, others straw, sheep manure, rabbit droppings, tea leaves, sugar and many other unmentionable substances. At one time, when pottery and brick kilns were more widespread, one of the favourite additives was pulverised brick dust — it had little nutritive value but was excellent for aerating and lightening heavy clay composts.

In the 1950s the University of California produced a soil-less compost from a mixture of peat and sand with chemical additives, and this was rapidly followed by other Universities with their own variations and improvements. These 'U.C. Composts', together with similar soil-less mixtures sold under a variety of trade names, have now almost completely superseded the J.I. Composts in the nursery trade, and for the nurseryman they have several

11

advantages. First they are much lighter to handle; secondly the medium is standard from batch to batch; thirdly they contain no foreign bodies or pathogens, insects or saprophytes; and finally, since nearly all commercial nurseries now use automatic watering and feeding systems, the predictable water-retention and drainage properties are an additional asset.

But for the amateur there can be disadvantages. Whereas most plants will thrive quite happily for two months or more in a J.I. Compost without supplementary feeding, in a U.C. mixture they must be fed regularly from the time they are potted if they are not to suffer from partial starvation. Then the advantages of a lightweight compost to the commercial grower can be a source of annoyance to the amateur whose plants can be blown over whenever the greenhouse is opened in windy weather, especially if he is using plastic pots and the plants have matured to a reasonable size. In addition the peat content often attracts sciarid flies (known as 'fungus gnats' in the USA) whose maggots feed on the stems of plants below the surface. But by far the greatest problem for the amateur is the drying-out of the medium, for a dry U.C. Compost is very reluctant to accept water. Most plants purchased from nurseries and other retail outlets will be found growing in pots full to the brim with compost leaving no room for normal watering, the plant having spent all its previous life on an automatic watering system. In these cases watering with a hose or watering can is quite useless, the water will simply run off the pot; if you stand it in a bowl of water it will float or topple onto its side. If you try to pot it on into a larger receptacle whilst it is still dry the centre of the root-ball will continue to repel moisture, and although eventually some new roots may grow out into the new soil, the plant is unlikely to recover from the shock it has received; if it does survive, it will never give of its best, because the original root-ball will remain dry.

Figure 2.1 Watering a plant in a dried-out soil-less compost

Numerous remedies have been suggested to overcome this problem but the only really effective method I have found is to place the root-ball (with or without the pot) into a plastic bag which should be loosely clipped around the stem of the plant about 1in (25mm) above the soil level. Carefully pour water into the neck of the bag until the soil-ball is totally immersed (the clip will prevent the plant from floating), then hang the bag complete with plant on a clothes line or anything similar and wait for the water to be absorbed, which will probably take about 24 hours. In severe cases it may be necessary to add more water and this should be continued until the root-ball is thoroughly saturated after which the plant can be removed from the bag and potted-on in the normal manner. This procedure can be repeated if the plant should again dry out, but if after soaking it is potted-on using a loam-based compost the problem is unlikely again to arise.

The John Innes Formulae

The John Innes Horticultural Institute was founded in 1904 with a bequest from a London business man of Scots descent for '. . . the improvement of horticulture by experiment and research'. The earlier 'John Innes Formulae' consisted of only two recipes, a Seed Sowing Compost and a Potting Compost, but the range has now been extended as follows.

J.I. SEED COMPOST
(for seed sowing or rooting cuttings)

2 parts well rotted loam, 1 part granulated peat, 1 part sharp washed river sand; to which must be added 2lb (.9kg) superphosphate and 1lb ground chalk or ground limestone per cubic yard (.45kg per .76 cu m).

J.I. Potting Composts (1, 2 & 3) require the inclusion of J.I. Base fertiliser, formula as follows:

(parts by weight) 2 hoof and horn, $\frac{1}{8}$in (3.1mm) grist (13% nitrogen); 2 superphosphate of lime (18% phosphoric acid); 1 sulphate of potash (48% pure potash). Giving an analysis of N:5.1, P:7.2, K:9.7 per cent.

J.I. POTTING COMPOST NO. 1
(for the initial potting)

(parts by bulk): 7 loam, 3 peat, 2 sand; to which add $\frac{1}{4}$lb (7gm) J.I. Base and $\frac{3}{4}$ oz ground chalk per bushel, or 5 lb (2.3kg) J.I. Base and 1lb (.45 kg) ground chalk per cubic yard.

J.I. POTTING COMPOST NO. 2
(for potting-on)

As for No. 1, but double the amount of J.I. Base and ground chalk.

J.I. POTTING COMPOST NO. 3
(for the final potting and for stock plants)

As for No. 1, but with three times the quantities of J.I. Base and ground chalk.

13

In my opinion a *good* John Innes Compost is infinitely preferable for amateur use, but how can one tell good from bad? There is an association of John Innes producers which claims that all its members manufacture only top-class composts exactly to formula, but in fact this is little more than a trade association whose main function is to promote the products of its members with small regard to the interests and well-being of the buying public. There are no hard and fast rules for assessing the quality of any J.I. Compost but the following points may help:

(1) Never buy a compost that is sold loose, either from a bin or a heap on the floor. It could be contaminated by insects (either flying or crawling), is an open invitation to the floor-sweeper to use as a receptacle for all kinds of rubbish, and can become an attractive toilet for cats and dogs if at floor level. The heap or bin will seldom be completely cleared, and when new supplies are added you could be served from the very stale residue of earlier deliveries.

(2) Purchase all composts only in sealed plastic bags and inspect carefully to ensure that the bag is not broken. Bags should be printed with the name and address of the manufacturer so that you know whom to contact in case of complaint. Check that the bags have been stored in a dry place — most bags are now perforated to prevent suffocating small children who may play with them, and these perforations will admit rainwater if the bags are stored in the open. Purchase only in quantities that can be used up within a month of purchase.

(3) Look for a medium brown colour indicating a reasonable clay content. Avoid bright yellow or orange composts for this indicates a high clay content which will set like rock after watering, or near-black indicating a total absence of clay and usually a very high density coupled with poor drainage. These conditions can be corrected but it will cost time and money — it is far better to shop around for a more suitable product.

(4) Take a good handful of the compost and allow it to trickle through the fingers, watching to see that there are no large stones or clods of clay in it — an occasional piece of root or fibre will not matter so long as it does not exceed about 1in (25mm) in length. The grit which is incorporated during manufacture should be no larger than ⅛in (3mm) in diameter, but a few small stones up to about ½in (12mm) are acceptable so long as they do not predominate. It is reasonable to assume that stones of 1in (25mm) and over have been added by an unscrupulous trader to increase the weight since most modern compost shredding machines riddle out stones over a certain size.

(5) Inspect carefully to ensure that no live worms or germinating weed seeds are present in the compost. Weed seeds should be destroyed during sterilisation together with all worms, insects and their eggs, and most soil-borne pathogens. The word 'sterilisation' as used in the nursery trade is a misnomer, what is meant is partial-sterilisation by which the temperature of the raw loam is raised sufficiently to destroy the 'nasties' but not so high as to render the loam into pure ash incapable of growing anything. Chemical sterilisation is also widely used to produce similar results without heat. Only

the raw loam is sterilised, the peat is added later and is naturally sterile if correctly harvested.

(6) Take a handful of the compost and squeeze it hard. When released it should break up easily into a crumbling heap — if it sticks together like a stiff pudding it is much too wet and should be rejected. Apart from the fact that you will be buying water, it is possible that much of the nutrient content could be leached out. If the mixture contains little balls of soil from ⅛-¼in (3–6mm) in diameter you can anticipate trouble. This condition results from processing a loam with a very high water content, usually from being exposed to wet weather or from the deliberate addition of extra water during manufacture to increase the weight. In such composts it is impossible to incorporate the chemicals evenly throughout the mixture, and the sands (and often some of the small grits) may have been lost.

The adulteration of either John Innes or U.C. Composts by the addition of extra ingredients is frowned upon by the manufacturers and Universities who claim the formulae have resulted from many years of experimentation. In general this argument is sound but it must be understood that these standard formulae have been developed to cover the entire range of plants grown world-wide and it is unlikely, to put it mildly, that the same formula will be ideal both for African Ground Nuts and Miniature Geraniums. All standard composts are a compromise and it must be accepted that the requirements of various plants will differ.

If you are satisfied with the standard formulae there is no reason to change; however, if you suspect there is room for improvement you may like to try a mixture I have used for many years which has yielded considerable success both in commercial production and on the show bench. A compost consisting of 75 per cent John Innes and 25 per cent U.C. produces a formula better balanced for the requirements of the Pelargonium family, will not dry out so easily as pure U.C., provides a heavier and therefore more stable base for the plant and gives a more open compost than pure J.I.

Do not use ordinary unsterilised garden soil for pot plants. All garden soils house a variety of insects, worms, worm eggs, weeds and weed seeds, and all manner of fungi spores and pathogens. A sterilised compost is a form of insurance against future problems and well worth the small extra outlay.

If you live near the coast never try to save money by using sand from the shore to incorporate into your compost even though it appears to be perfectly clean and free from contamination. Seashore sand is guaranteed to kill any houseplant it comes into contact with, and it will have a similar effect upon garden plants if added to the soil.

Very little advantage will be gained by adding spent mushroom compost to the mixture for the Pelargonium family. By the time the mushroom grower discards it almost all the nutrients have been extracted and all that remains is the bulk. By adding this to your mixture you are simply diluting the nutrient content. Spent mushroom compost incorporated into garden soil will lighten heavy soils and, by regular application, will result in a much more friable loam in a few years, but it cannot be recommended for use in pot culture.

15

The addition of animal manures to pot plants will result in rampant soft growth and large fleshy leaves produced at the expense of flowers. In the garden the same will apply — Geraniums set into soil rich in animal manure will grow leaves like rhubarb, and although yielding lots of fleshy cuttings, flowers will be scarce. The use of animal manures in the culture of Miniature and Dwarf Geraniums can not only distort the growth pattern of the plant, but the excess nitrogen may alter the colour of the flower.

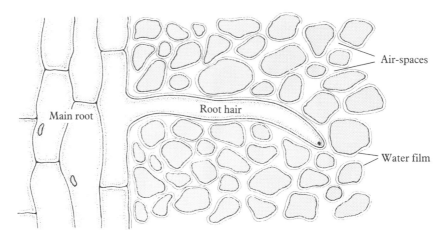

Figure 2.2 Enlarged diagram of a root-hair, showing soil particles coated with a film of water, air-spaces and developing hair with nucleus at the tip

Incorporating a proportion of Vermiculite into the compost is said to increase its water-retaining properties. This could be advantageous when U.C. composts are being used but can result in an over-wet medium when used with any soil-based composts. Except in severe drought conditions every tiny grain of soil and sand is coated with a thin film of moisture which is transported to the growing plant via the invisible root-hairs — invisible, that is, except with the aid of a powerful microscope. Figure 2 (much enlarged) illustrates one such hair penetrating between the grains of soil. For the sake of clarity it has been simplified; in nature the root-hair would be in much closer contact with the soil-grains. It will be obvious from the diagram that an apparently dry soil can still contain enough moisture to keep a plant in good condition, and the visual examination of the compost at the surface of the pot can be misleading.

Oxygen is just as important as moisture for the well-being of the plant, and air-spaces in the compost allow the root-hairs to take up both elements — this is why adequate drainage is essential. A compost which packs down solid after watering will contain a greatly reduced number of air-pockets and the plant will suffer. The U.C. composts, containing a high proportion of sand, have excellent drainage and therefore very good oxygen content; the J.I. composts are normally very well balanced, but if found to be too compact the addition of 20 per cent Perlite will yield a more open mixture, even some extra coarse sand will help. Ash from a coal fire cannot be recommended because it is normally so fine that it can only aggravate the problem.

In the garden the soil is aerated by the natural action of man's great ally, the earthworm, and farmers are well aware of the fact that the more worms they have to the acre the more fertile the land. Unfortunately we have to discourage worms in flowerpots because they multiply at an alarming rate resulting in a potful of worms and very little compost. Should you discover a worm in a pot carefully remove it and return it to the garden. Worms should never be killed, they are among the most beneficial creatures on this planet — in the right place.

It is normal in the USA and some other parts of the world to describe maggots and grubs as 'worms'. The worms I am describing above are earthworms not maggots.

3 Pots: clay or plastic?

Before the last war the only plastic material in general use was 'Bakelite', a brittle synthetic resin invented by Dr Baekeland, who died in 1944. It was usually a mottled brown colour, used mainly for the production of cheap moulded containers and such items as radio cabinets for the mass markets.

Great strides forward were made in the development of thermo-plastics during the war, and soon after the cessation of hostilities we began to be bombarded with a variety of plastic products ranging over a wide field from rainwear to plumbing and sanitary ware, and it was not long before the horticultural trade attracted the attention of the manufacturers.

In the early 1960s the plastic pot was very much a new 'gimmick' and was scorned by the great majority of British gardeners. It was brittle, badly designed, often only obtainable in the most violent of colours and more expensive than the clay variety.

Today, the manufacture of clay pots is reduced to a tiny fraction of the total pot production, and very few clay pots are now made in England; those that are on sale come chiefly from France and Italy apart from those hand-thrown by a few enthusiasts with back-garden kilns.

I have always preferred clay pots for their aesthetic appeal — to my mind no plastic pot has yet been designed to compare to the form and feel of clay whether in white, cream or terracotta. But the disadvantages of clay over modern plastic are too many to be disregarded by the commercial grower, and I have used nothing but plastic for the past 20 years.

We have to accept that prices for plastic pots are considerably cheaper today than for a clay equivalent and this must be a major consideration, but there are others not the least of which is weight coupled with bulk, and breakages. The plant itself has no preference, clay, plastic, paper or glass; it is the treatment provided by the grower that decides whether or not it does well or badly. Some gardeners swear by clay, others use nothing but plastic with equally good results — so what are the facts?

Until the early 1960s, I was growing entirely in clay pots but as the prices became more competitive we began to change over to plastic pots on the nursery and immediately ran into trouble, for the treatment of plants growing in clay must be totally different to those in plastic pots. The first problem arose over watering. At that time the watering was performed by a team of women starting at one end of the nursery and gradually working their way to the other end, by which time (during the summer months) it was necessary to start again at the beginning. Automatic watering systems were then in their infancy and part-time labour plentiful and cheap. But with a mixture of plastic and clay pots on the benches we soon found that those in the plastic pots were dying off with stem rot through over-watering, and we never did manage to educate the ladies into watering only those plants which needed it; they were paid for watering and that is what they were going to do.

It became obvious that we must either revert back to clay or go over entirely to plastic. We therefore conducted a series of experiments using groups of both kinds of pots, but giving the plastics exactly half the quantity of water as the clays, and after six months the plants were indistinguishable in either size or quality. Consequently we disposed of our entire stock of clay pots and by the end of 1964 there was scarcely a clay pot to be found on the nursery.

One has to agree that the main reason for the popularity of plastic pots among commercial growers is economic — few can afford the luxury of employing a man to scrub pots before re-using, and a box of 1,000 4in (10cm) plastic pots can easily be carried by a young girl without assistance whereas a similar quantity of clays will need a forklift truck to shift them. However, it does not automatically follow that the same advantages apply to the amateur grower with often less than a total of 200 pots to care for and whose time is not charged out at union rates.

Whether your preference is for clay or plastic, it is essential to avoid a mixture of both kinds, for although the resulting complications may be well within *your* capabilities, trouble must result as soon as you accept help with watering whether it be due to holidays, sickness or business commitments.

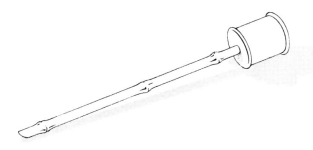

Figure 3.1 Cotton-reel 'mallet'

In days past the old gardeners equipped themselves with a small mallet made from a wooden cotton reel fixed to a cane, and this was used to tap the side of a clay pot, and from the resulting 'ring' or 'thud' our ancestors were able to judge when water was required. Unfortunately this highly scientific method cannot be used with plastic pots and many were the complaints I received in the past from elderly gardeners still using the cotton-reel mallet and attempting to get a plastic pot to 'ring'. The other main complaints, in

20

order of popularity, were 'the soil stays too wet' and 'the plant cannot breathe through the pot'.

I am afraid I have come to regard the latter argument as just plain nonsense — whether a plant is grown in plastic or clay has no effect upon its breathing habits. Some years ago I planted some rooted cuttings of Ivyleaf Geraniums one each to a wine bottle. Each bottle was filled to within 1in (25mm) of the top with compost to ensure that the risk of overwatering would be reduced to the minimum, and the plants were then left to grow normally in one of the greenhouses. No drainage hole was provided and there was no possibility of the plant's roots 'breathing' through the glass, the only special treatment the bottles received was to ensure that they were never exposed to full summer sunlight because of the risk of the roots being scorched (all the bottles were of clear glass). All the plants thrived and flowered normally until, whilst I was in California, one of our more enlightened assistants decided that they were not getting sufficient water through the narrow neck apertures and lowered the entire batch into a tank to soak for a few hours. By the time I returned some weeks later nothing could be done to save them, although I did find one he had overlooked and took it with me to several lectures afterwards to demonstrate the point.

To the complaint that 'the soil stays too wet' I can only reply that this is the fault of the waterer, not the plastic pot. Plants in plastic pots will require almost exactly half the water needed by a similar plant in clay, and far from being a disadvantage this is one of the great benefits of using plastic, for surely watering is among the most boring of all chores and presents so many difficulties during a hot summer, especially to the enthusiast who has to be away from home all day.

For anyone interested in exhibiting plants at Horticultural Shows plastic pots are essential. A dirty pot will lose marks, and one session of scrubbing clay pots clean enough for the showbench will be sufficient to ensure that all plants for future showing will be grown in plastic unless you have masochistic tendencies. From time to time one reads statements from persons who should know better that 'plastic pots are all right up to about 6in (15cm) but plants will not do well over that size'. More nonsense. I have taken plants up to the 18in (46cm) pot size and have never had the slightest trouble, in fact I exhibited four plants of 'Deacon Bonanza' in 18in (46cm) pots at the Chelsea Flower Show in 1971 and was awarded a Silver Medal.

Plastic has yet another advantage over clay to my mind, in the superior drainage arrangements. Most clay pots have either one hole in the centre of the base or a couple of small holes punched through the sides of the pot towards the bottom, whereas a modern plastic pot will usually have a number of holes radiating from the centre of the base which is slightly elevated on small lugs to assist further the escape of excess water. In recent years the clay pot manufacturers have added more variety to the shapes and colours available, but they cannot compete with the range offered in plastics which come in all manner of designs and colours (some of them, incidentally, quite nauseating).

Clay or plastic, the final choice is one which only you can make, the plants do not care either way, but avoid mixing them if you can. If you must have

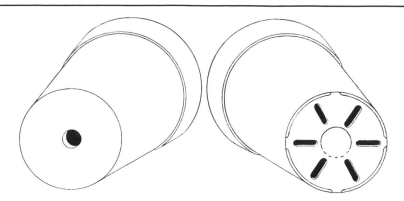

Figure 3.2 Base of a normal clay pot   **Figure 3.3** Base of a modern plastic pot

some of each in the same greenhouse or conservatory, separate them so that all the plastics are together on one bench and all the clays on another — this is the only way you can hope for success, and you will still need to exercise considerable care if you are to avoid killing off those plants in plastic by over-watering or ruining those in clays by starvation.

Plastic pots can be used straight out of the packet or box, but clays must always be soaked overnight before being brought into use to prevent the clay sucking the moisture out of the compost. If you wish to re-use a plastic pot it is best to immerse it in a weak solution of Jeyes Fluid for an hour or so before planting; a clay pot must first be scrubbed inside and out until every trace of soil and algae has been removed (special pot brushes are obtainable for this purpose), then soaked overnight in a weak solution of Jeyes Fluid. When soaking any type of pot in Jeyes Fluid always ensure that the pot is fully immersed in the liquid — Jeyes Fluid can stain pots slightly and if part of the pot is not covered by the fluid it will dry a slightly different colour to that which was submerged.

If you intend exhibiting a plant in a clay pot make sure the pot is thoroughly scrubbed clean before setting the plant in it, then cover the pot with black plastic sheeting so that no algae can form on the walls. The sheeting can be removed before taking the plant to the show and avoids the necessity of cleaning a pot containing a fully grown plant.

22

4 Potting and re-potting

New techniques and modern equipment have made it possible for plants to be sold in the pots in which they have been grown on the nursery, whereas in earlier years it was the custom to remove the pot from the root system so that it could be re-used. The plant was then either wrapped in newspaper or placed into a 'transport pot', a plastic or paper container which held the soil loosely around the roots. Today labour costs are too high to permit this practice to continue, and the gardener benefits from the plant suffering less root disturbance.

Miniature Geraniums are usually supplied in 2½ or 3in (6 or 8cm) pots, and if well rooted should be left to recover for a few days then immediately potted-on into larger pots. Anything less than an inch (25mm) upgrading will present difficulties and probably result in large pockets of air between the side of the pot and the root-ball, and there is no advantage in increasing the size more than one inch (25mm) at this stage. Years of growing and showing Geraniums (large and small) have proved to my satisfaction that best results are obtained by increasing pots sizes by 1in (25mm) stages, and I particularly recommend this for Miniatures. However, I must in all fairness point out that growers and authors are not in unanimous agreement over this detail, and John Cross, the author of *Pelargoniums for All Purposes*, is one who considers that there are advantages in going straight from a 3in (8cm) pot to a 6 or 7in (15 or 18cm) pot. However, since he is not referring to Miniatures perhaps we are not entirely in disagreement.

Considerable damage can be caused to the plant at this stage by incorrect treatment, and it will be found advantageous to follow the method detailed in the remainder of this chapter in every particular. It is impossible to over-emphasise the importance of keeping root-disturbance to the absolute minimum; the correct procedure will enable the plant to grow on without check or stress but bad methods will show immediately in a distressed and ailing plant.

For those unfamiliar with the terms I should explain that 'potting-up' means transferring a seedling or rooted cutting from the propagating bed into its first true pot, and 'potting-on' is moving a plant one stage on into a larger pot. So 'potting-up' is the first move and all moves from then on are 'pottings-on'.

Seedlings

Seedlings should be potted-up as soon as the first true leaves have developed. The cotyledons which first appear above the soil are not true leaves and any disturbance at this stage will almost certainly destroy the plant.

Have a pot of compost ready-filled and slightly firmed, and make a small hole in the centre of it, with a pencil or similar implement, not more than 1in (25mm) in depth. Gently water the seedling with lukewarm water, then ease it out of the compost with the aid of a plant label or perhaps the handle of a teaspoon, trying all the time to keep the tiny root system intact with as much compost adhering to it as possible. Transfer it immediately into the pot prepared for it, enlarging the hole to receive it according to the amount of compost you have been able to retain around the roots, and setting the seedling into the compost at the same level as it was in the seed bed. A few gentle taps on the bench will be sufficient to settle the compost around the tiny stem; do not compress with the fingers or the roots will almost certainly be damaged.

Water very carefully and sparingly with lukewarm water, place the plant in partial shade for ten days or so, and it will grow away without check. So-called 'damping-off' of seedlings is usually caused by damage to the stem or root system at potting-up, nearly always by the vigorous compression of the compost in the pot to firm the plant, and no amount of spraying or dusting can restore damage caused in this manner.

Rooted Cuttings

Rooted cuttings do not need such careful and delicate handling as seedlings but the same general principles apply. First prepare the pot by placing a small quantity of compost in the bottom so that the base is covered by a thickness of at least ½in (12mm). (Don't waste time and effort 'crocking' the pot, this idea has been abandoned by commercial growers for at least 30 years, see Potting-on, p. 27.) Gently water the cutting in the propagating bed with lukewarm water before easing it out with a spoon or small trowel with as much of the compost adhering to the roots as possible. Transfer it immediately into the pot and adjust the compost level in the base so that the cutting, when finally potted, will be set at the same level as it was when growing in the propagating bed. Centre the cutting in the pot then gently trickle compost all around it until the pot is filled *up to the rim*. Tap it gently on the bench three or four times to settle the compost, then water carefully with lukewarm water. The level of the compost will now have dropped to a little below the rim of the pot and be sufficiently compressed to support the plant. An excess of water will allow the cutting to fall about, so only water sparingly. Compressing with the fingers will almost certainly damage the root system which the plant will have to restore before it can make any progress, and encourage the entry of pathogens.

Cuttings grown in Jiffy-7s (see page 41) suffer much less root disturbance and are easier to handle than those rooted loose in propagating beds or several to a pot, but they still need to be carefully handled if optimum results are to be obtained. I like to set Jiffy-7s 40 to a standard seed tray — this ensures that they are close packed and therefore unable to fall over or move around — it also makes maximum use of the heated propagator if one is being used. Jiffy-7s must never be allowed to dry out and before potting-up it is best to give them a gentle watering with lukewarm water. Ideally the roots should be just beginning to penetrate through the netting so that after potting they continue to thrust outwards into the new compost without noticing any change. In practice it is more usual for the roots to be rather more developed and for almost the entire surface of the netting to be penetrated by roots. Some gardeners seem to think that the more roots there are outside the netting the better the plant but in fact this is not so, for most of the visible roots will die and have to be replaced by the plant. The invisible ones still within the netting will be those that will grow away and replace the visible ones.

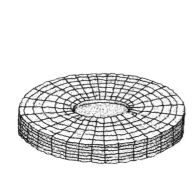

Figure 4.1 (a) Jiffy-7 before soaking;   (b) Jiffy-7 in use when fully expanded

Nearly all roots easily visible to the naked eye are little more than anchoring roots, the feeding roots sprout out from these, can only be seen by most people with the aid of a microscope or very strong magnifying glass, and from these grow the root-hairs which are the actual feeding roots, quite invisible without a powerful microscope and very easily damaged or destroyed. Potting-up always has some effect upon the feeding roots and all the foregoing instructions can only help to minimise this effect; by the use of Jiffy-7s the problem can be almost entirely overcome and the plant potted-up with no noticeable check to its progress.

Even so, there is no magic about it; much care and common sense is required to obtain the best results. The plant in its Jiffy-7 should be separated from its fellows and removed from the tray before the roots have had a chance to penetrate the adjacent Jiffy-7 or real damage will result. It should then be set into the pot and the soil-level below it adjusted to bring it up to the correct level — so that the top of the Jiffy-7 is just below the top of the pot. Centre it in the pot then trickle compost around it until it is up to the level of the rim. Tap on the bench three or four times to settle the compost, then gently water with lukewarm water and place in semi-shade for ten days or so until well established.

Seedlings or cuttings set into plastic and polystyrene multipot trays must be treated exactly as those loose-rooted in propagators or several to a pot. They grow well in the potlets but the problems commence when one tries to get them out without damage to the root system — almost impossible in my experience — even when a peg board is supplied by the manufacturer so that the tray can be placed upon it and the pegs forced upwards to eject the plants. I found that the roots of the cuttings I grew under this system penetrated the polystyrene walls of the potlets and when the ejector-peg was pushed up the hole in the base it simply ejected the stem of the cutting, shearing off most of the roots which remained attached to the walls. Those made of the very thin plastic which can be distorted to eject the plant are slightly better in my opinion, but most of the compost around the roots will be lost as the plant is removed unless it has a high clay content to enable it to remain intact.

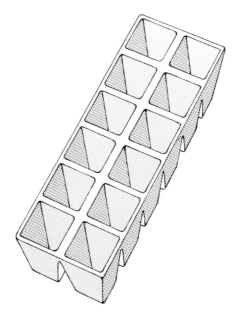

Figure 4.2 Peat pots in strips or gangs are ideal for cuttings of Miniatures or Dwarfs

Peat pots are almost as good as Jiffy-7s in my opinion for raising seedlings or rooting cuttings, and some gardeners prefer them. However, soaking them and filling with compost is not as simple as the manufacturers would have us believe because the chosen medium almost always has to be packed down into the pots by hand if the required consolidation necessary to support a stem is to be achieved — and this can easily result in the sides of the peat pot being ruptured and allowing the compost to escape. But with reasonable care they are excellent and will provide the same results as a Jiffy-7 but without the restraining netting. They should be potted-up in exactly the same manner as for Jiffy-7s but it is essential to ensure that the peat pot never dries out or the roots will be unable to penetrate the walls, so it is best to give them a thorough soaking before potting commences.

Even after more than 20 years since their introduction to British gardeners there are still a few who refuse to use the Jiffy-7 because the netting 'strangles the plant' in their opinion. This, of course, is not the case and it can be proved by the many commercial nurseries who use them for the mass production not only of Geraniums but of many other types of plant also, not only in Britain but almost world-wide. The roots will penetrate the net with case and you can easily satisfy yourself on this point by taking a plant rooted in a Jiffy-7 and planting it out in the open garden in June — when you come to lift it before the winter frosts you will still be able to see the original Jiffy-7 in the centre of a great mass of roots, all of which have been produced in spite of the netting.

Should you find that a pot plant is not doing well after potting-on, and that upon knocking it out of the pot after a month or two the roots have still not penetrated through the netting, the fault lies not in the Jiffy-7 but in your compost — roots will not grow out into a hostile environment so change the medium and all will be well. Never remove the net either before or after rooting, it can do nothing but harm.

Potting-on

Most Miniatures will be quite happy in 3 or 3½in (8 or 9cm) pots for several months, especially if they are regularly fed with a liquid fertiliser, but the time will come when the pot will be full of roots and it will then be necessary to consider potting-on. Whether a plastic or clay pot is used makes no difference to the method, which is still based upon disturbing the root-system as little as possible.

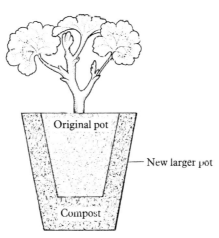

Figure 4.3 Potting-on

First water thoroughly with tepid water and allow to drain. Then take a pot 1in (25mm) larger than that which the plant presently occupies and put ½in (12mm) of compost in the bottom (again no crocking, please). Place the plant in its pot centrally into the new pot so that there is an even space all around and adjust the depth of the compost in the outer pot so that the rim of the inner pot is at the same height as the outer; with a spoon or tiny trowel carefully pack the space between the pot walls with compost and ram down firmly with a suitable stick or knife handle. The compost should be moist enough to stick together when compressed in the hand but not so wet as to be gummy. Carefully twist the inner pot about half a turn whilst pressing down slightly, then lift out slowly and the outer pot should then be nicely lined with ½in (12mm) of compost.

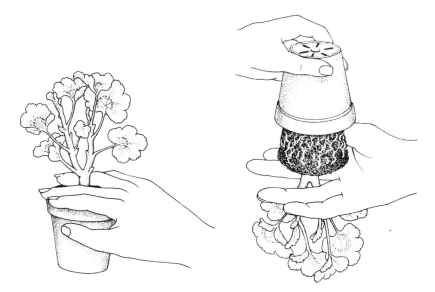

Figure 4.4 Transferring to a new pot. (a) Place the hand over the top of the pot; (b) invert and the plant will slide out of the pot

Meanwhile the plant is still in its original pot undisturbed. It has already been well watered and drained so is ready to be transferred into its new home. Place one hand over the top of the pot so that the stem of the plant protrudes between the second and third fingers, invert the pot and the plant, with soil-ball complete, will slide into the palm of your hand; it is then a simple matter to lower it gently into the cavity prepared for it in the centre of the new pot. A gentle tap on the bench to settle it and the job is done without the plant noticing a thing.

It is often said that a plant will shed many of its leaves as a natural consequence of re-potting but this need not be so. If any leaves are shed it is a fair indication that the methods used were faulty; it is quite possible to re-pot any member of the Pelargonium family without the loss of a single leaf if the foregoing instructions are carefully followed.

Sometimes when transferring a plant from a clay pot it will be found that some of the fine roots have penetrated the terracotta walls just sufficiently to prevent it sliding out when inverted. To overcome this a gentle tap on the bench may be needed after it has been watered and drained. The plant will suffer a severe set-back if it is dry and bashed on the bench several times to extract the root-ball, and quite often the clay pot will disintegrate leaving most of the roots clinging to the broken pieces.

I entirely disagree with the practice recommended by some writers and TV gardening 'experts' of breaking up the soil-ball and spreading the root system among the new compost. This can only result in the death of the tiny root-hairs and unnecessary damage to the main root structure followed by an immediate shedding of much of the foliage whilst the plant uses its energy in re-establishing the root system. The same writers usually recommend firming the soil by pressing down with the fingers and this again can be disastrous, for any remaining undamaged roots will probably be sheared from the stem by excessive pressure — a few taps on the bench is all that is needed.

Figure 4.5 Roots can be sheared by manually compressing the soil

Another bright idea which fills me with horror is that of making vertical cuts down the sides of the soil-ball with the aid of a razor blade or sharp knife after removing it from the pot. This is said to force the plant to produce new root growth, but of the 30 or so plants on which I tried this experiment all but one died of Blackleg within two months. I have no hesitation in stating that in my experience the less the soil-ball is disturbed during re-potting the greater the chance of success.

Many readers will have noted my remarks regarding the inclusion of 'crocks' in the bottom of a pot before inserting the plant, and perhaps an explanation is necessary at this point. 'Crocking' is a horticultural term used to describe the placing of several pieces of broken clay pot or stones in the bottom of the pot before filling with compost — I have not 'crocked' a pot for more than 30 years, nor have most commercial growers. In my opinion it makes not the slightest difference to the health of the plant, certainly it does not affect the drainage unless you are potting into pure yellow clay, and as for keeping out worms, earwigs, etc. I consider this suggestion too ludicrous to warrant discussion. However, whilst on the question of drainage it should be remembered that plants will always push out a few roots through the drainage holes in the base of the pot, and it is possible for the hole in the base of a clay pot to become completely blocked in this way with the result that the soil will become waterlogged and the plant collapse. (Plastic pots are seldom so affected since they normally have several large holes or slits spaced all around the base.) So if you are using clay pots take a pencil or knitting needle and push it up the hole in the base to a depth of about 1in (25mm) four or five times a year to prevent a total blockage.

Re-potting

Miniature Geraniums are usually quite happy in a 4in (10cm) pot as their final home, but those that grow a little larger (dwarfs and semi-dwarfs to revert to the BPGS classifications) will probably need to go up to 5in (13cm). All must be regularly fed with a diluted fertiliser once they have reached their maximum pot size, but should continue to bloom and flourish for several years in a good environment. A few of the miniature Fancyleaves do best in smaller pots — say 4in (10cm) as a maximum, even for stock plants, and I have never taken any of the micro-miniatures above 3½in (9cm).

When a plant has been in the maximum size pot for several years the soil or potting medium will eventually become exhausted and will have to be changed, even with regular feeding, for the chemical ingredients in the feed leach at different rates and the soil will finally become so out of balance that plant growth will visibly alter. In these cases the plant tissues become hard and woody, the leaves smaller and the flowers undersized and puny with often a distinct change of colour. Re-potting will then have to be undertaken with all the risks that implies.

There is no perfect method of re-potting a plant — any plant — however you do it that plant is going to suffer a severe set-back, all you can hope for is a reduction of the shock to the minimum. In this case the plant must not be watered before commencing, in fact the soil-ball should be fairly dry — and this is where a plastic pot scores against clay, for it is necessary to knock the plant out of its pot, and you will find that the root-ball is withdrawn more easily from plastic than from clay.

Once out of the pot gently tap the soil-ball on the bench a few times so that the soil begins to fall away from the roots, then manipulate the roots to encourage more soil to fall and continue until most of the roots are bare and visible and no more compost can be removed. At no time should the roots be cut or broken, the plant has enough to cope with without any extra aggravation.

Clean and prepare the old pot by placing about ½in (12mm) of fresh compost in the bottom, seat the plant upon this then gently begin to scatter new compost into the pot, tapping it on the bench every now and then to ensure that the compost gets well down among the roots. When the pot has been filled to the brim, give it a few final taps on the bench then a thorough watering with tepid water and place in partial shade for two weeks or so.

Most if not all of the feeding roots will have died during this operation but there is no way of avoiding this that I know of, but with luck the plant will show signs of recovery within a month and go on to give every satisfaction for a further four or five years before a duplicate operation becomes necessary.

Another method which some gardeners advocate is to submerge the entire soil-ball in a bucket of tepid water, then gently manipulate the compost away from the roots whilst keeping the foliage clear of the water. Less damage to the fine roots is said to be caused by this method and I can see the reasoning behind it; unfortunately the survival rate among those plants I subjected to each method was identical, although I have to admit that I have only tried a comparison using about 20 plants — not really enough to reach a positive conclusion.

Root-pruning of Miniature Geraniums cannot be recommended in any circumstances, it lays the plant wide open to the entry of pathogens often present in the compost, especially when the compost has been in use for some time. If it is unavoidable, cut the selected thick roots back to about half their length with a razor blade or very sharp knife — do not use secateurs which tend to crush the woody material — treat the cut ends with a fungicide making sure that they are all thoroughly coated before setting the plant into new compost.

When a plant has spent the summer bedded out in the garden in good soil, it will sometimes be found upon lifting it in the autumn that it has spread its root-system far beyond the radius of its foliage, so that it can no longer be accommodated in the pot which housed it originally. If it will go into a pot one or two sizes larger there is no problem, it is only when the root system is so developed that it will not go into a reasonable size pot that root pruning should be considered, and only then if the plant is in perfect health. Most plants (except the micro-miniatures) will benefit from spending the summer planted out in the garden, but do take a few cuttings from each in July so you have replacements for possible losses when the plants are lifted before the winter frosts.

5 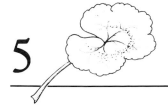 Propagating

Most gardeners like to experiment with methods of increasing their stock of plants. A few are not successful and regard the whole business as a form of black magic, but the great majority find it so easy when growing Geraniums and Pelargoniums that lack of space soon becomes a major embarrassment.

Perhaps the easiest, and to many gardeners the most satisfactory, way of producing new plants is by taking vegetative cuttings from an existing healthy parent plant. By this method it is quite possible to produce a new plant (but not a new variety) and have it in flower within three or four months on average, but when growing from seed one can wait for up to 18 months before a flower is produced and even then it is quite impossible to forecast just what the flower will be like, whereas any plant produced from a cutting will usually be an exact replica of its parent. There are a few exceptions — the F_1 and F_2 hybrids come true from seed and can be induced to flower in about five months if grown in a constant temperature of 70°F (21°C), but the range available is limited mainly to singles and most have to be chemically treated to force them to 'break' and produce a bushy compact plant. Any attempt to retain them (or to save seed from them) for a second season will result in disappointment, even cuttings taken from them will yield very poor plants, and the seed often reverts to an inferior single red. There *are* occasions when a cutting will show a variation from its parent — I have had one instance when 'Red Pearl' produced a pink flower on one of its cuttings, which I named 'Pink Pearl', but this happening is so rare that I intend to ignore it for the purposes of this chapter.

The most successful time to take cuttings in the British isles is during the months of July and August when the plants are in vigorous growth, although quite good results are possible during the rest of the year if the correct equipment is available such as a warm greenhouse with heated propagating bed or electric propagator. Unfortunately, the plants are in full flower during the best months for propagating and many gardeners are loathe to cut a plant which is in full display, and make the common mistake of waiting until October or November before cutting when the plants are lifted from the open ground and brought inside for the winter. It is usually fairly easy to take one or two cuttings from a plant in full flower without any noticeable effect upon the display; there are often a few shoots growing inwards which are best removed anyway in order to increase the ventilation in the centre of the plant, and these can be used as cuttings.

The treatment of Miniature and Dwarf cuttings is basically identical to that for all other members of the Pelargonium family. The fact that the vegetative matter is scaled down in size does not mean that it is any more delicate, and in general you can apply the same methods to Miniatures and Dwarfs as you already use for their larger brothers. If your present methods are proving satisfactory I would suggest that you stay with them; I am certainly not wishing to start a crusade, neither do I believe that I alone know the secret of success with cuttings, but if you are losing more than about 10 per cent your methods must be suspect and you may like to consider changing to one of the systems detailed in the following pages, some of which are in general commercial use by the major wholesale and retail growers in Britain and overseas.

Although an increasing number of Miniatures and Dwarfs are now used by amateurs for garden borders and bedding schemes, by far the greater number are grown throughout the year under some form of protection (such as a greenhouse) or indoors on a sunny windowsill, and the following comments apply mainly to these. Most Miniatures and Dwarfs are bushy by nature and grow far too dense for their own well-being. If left unattended the centre of the plant will become so crowded that air movement is minimised and conditions are created under which fungus spores, botrytis, moulds and rusts can develop, and very soon the plant will begin to rot from the centre outwards, and once this rotting gets established it is very difficult (often impossible) to control.

For most varieties an initial 'ventilation operation' is best performed towards the end of March or early April when vigorous growth is apparent after the winter, followed by a second thinning about mid-June or early July, and a final cut in October to ventilate the plant prior to the close conditions which can be expected during the winter months. The July cuttings will be found to be the best for reproduction purposes in most varieties, but some of the denser growing cultivars such as 'Granny Hewitt', 'Kleine Liebling', 'Orion' and 'Urchin' will benefit from even more frequent cutting. It is neither necessary nor desirable to prune the very slow-growing varieties such as 'Silver Kewense', 'Gwen', 'Fairy Storey', 'Golden Flute' and 'Golden Chalice', in fact you may consider yourself very fortunate if you are able to secure one cutting a year from any of these varieties, and they *must* be taken during July for a reasonable chance of success. Furthermore, it is important to inspect these plants (and any similar slow-growing compact Miniatures) at regular fortnightly intervals to ensure that the centre of the plant is free from dead leaves and flowerheads — and use a pair of tweezers to remove any debris, fingers can do much damage.

In general Miniatures and Dwarfs are more susceptible to botrytis than the larger members of the family because the dense growth restricts the air circulation, so it is essential that the plants are kept clean and any dead flowerheads removed promptly. Overcrowding on the greenhouse benches will have a similar effect, and once botrytis gets a hold it can destroy all the plants in the greenhouse in a very short space of time and will be very difficult to eradicate. It need never bother you if a high standard of cleanliness and ventilation is maintained.

I am frequently asked whether one should remove Geranium leaves which are beginning to yellow or are showing signs of damage, and it is unwise to give a simple yes or no without actually seeing the plant concerned and knowing the degree of yellowing or damage and the general condition of the plant. Normally I would say that it is best to allow any leaf still showing a trace of green to remain upon the plant, for so long as chlorophyll is present the plant is deriving benefit from the leaf. This advice although perfectly sound for bedding Geraniums needs modifying when Miniatures and Dwarfs are being considered and one must be more ruthless if the risk of botrytis is to be kept to the minimum; not only do I recommend removing all damaged and discoloured foliage just as soon as it is noticed but I would suggest that any leaves growing into the centre of the plant should also be removed, even though in excellent condition, in order to keep the centre of the plant open. And remember, when a flowerhead is finished remove the stem as well as the dead head.

Propagating by Cuttings

Cuttings should be taken only from healthy stock for it is almost certain that any disease suffered by the parent plant will be transmitted to the cuttings even though the shoots may appear to be unaffected for some time. Almost all the characteristics of the parent plant will be transmitted to the offspring, good and bad, so use only the very best plants for cutting material. Considerable benefit will be derived from applying a high-nitrogen liquid feed to the parent plant twice a week for the two weeks prior to cutting, and lightly shading the plant for two or three days to reduce the rate of transpiration. If the parent plant has been allowed to dry out, do not take cuttings from it until at least four days after bringing the moisture-content of the soil back to normal. A cutting taken from a limp plant has a reduced chance of survival, so try to ensure that the plant is sparkling and crisp with health and all the stems are plump with sap. It is best to take cuttings early in the morning before the sun rises too high and the rate of transpiration begins to increase. Cuttings of Miniature and Dwarf Geraniums taken before 6 am on a July morning have the best possible start in life and should begin to develop a root system within 14 days.

Geraniums are among the most tolerant of plants and it is possible to achieve success with many types of vegetative cutting, but for the beginner (in fact for all without specialised equipment) it will be best to stay with the normal commercial methods which have been proven over the years and leave the gimmicks (such as leaf-axil cuttings) until more experience has been acquired.

When taking a cutting of an ordinary Regal or Zonal Pelargonium (Geranium) in Britain it is usual to cut about 3–4in (8–10cm) off the tip of a strong-growing shoot (in warmer climates the cuttings are often much longer). This gives a cutting of about the correct size and, more importantly, will force the parent plant to bush out from all the nodes below the cut. This is where the treatment for Miniatures and Dwarfs differs, for most of them are naturally very self-branching and our efforts must be aimed towards reducing the congestion in the centre of the plant rather than trying to increase the bushiness. This is done by removing entire shoots from the point where they are attached to the main stem, or if they arise straight from the soil from an underground union they must be cut off clean at or below soil level. It may sometimes be necessary to cut the complete centre out of a plant where it is very congested, and this will yield quite a crop of cuttings. When a cutting has been taken from the side of a main stem, make sure that a very sharp knife or razor blade is used and that no stump is left to rot back. If the centre has been cut out of a plant make the cut at an angle of 45° so that any water will tend to run off, and in all cases dress the wound with a fungicide powder.

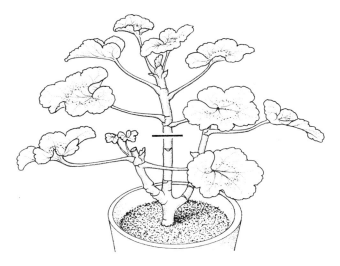

Figure 5.1 Taking a 'nodal cutting'. (a) Cut just above an outward-facing node;

Roots are produced more freely at nodes (leaf joints), and a cutting which has been trimmed back to a node is termed a 'nodal cutting'. Those cut half-way between nodes and left untrimmed are called 'inter-nodal cuttings' and are not recommended when dealing with members of the Pelargonium family with very few exceptions (some of the Ivyleaf Geranium varieties will root inter-nodally but they usually take longer to do so). All Miniature cuttings must be treated as nodal cuttings and the stem cut back to within ⅛in (3mm) of the node or severe losses will result. If a cut is made half-way between two nodes with no trimming, the stems of both the plant and the cutting will begin to decay from the cut both outwards and inwards and there is no guarantee that this decay will be halted when the node is reached. Not only can the cutting be lost but the parent plant may also be destroyed.

There are some who believe it is best just to tear a shoot off the parent plant, for 'this is the way it happens in nature'. This may be so, and in general I am all for following natural methods as far as is practicable, but one

36

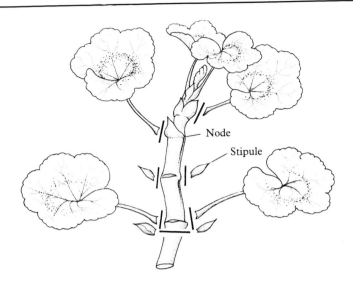

Node

Stipule

(**b**) remove surplus leaves and stipules and trim base of stem;

(**c**) the cutting ready for inserting into the rooting medium

must remember that nature is very extravagant and is quite prepared to waste 1,000 or more seeds in an effort to grow just one plant, whereas we are seeking 100 per cent success. It is possible to purchase a surgical knife with spare stainless steel blades for those who are fanatical about these things, but for most of us a sharp knife or stainless steel razor blade has to suffice (preferably the latter, for it is impossible to sharpen a knife to the same degree). This will give you the greatest chance of success and cause the minimum of damage to either cutting or plant.

The length of cutting taken will vary according to the variety. A cutting from 'Granny Hewitt' may be as much as 2in (5cm) long after trimming, although one from 'Red Pearl' will seldom exceed 1in (25mm), and in the case of 'Gwen', 'Golden Flute' and 'Golden Chalice' ½in (12mm) is about as long as you can expect. The size is not really important so long as the wood is not too hard and the stem has several nodes down its length. Except in the case of the very rare varieties mentioned above, cuttings shorter than 1in (25mm) are generally more trouble than they are worth and the mortality rate is very high. It is best to allow the shoot to remain upon the parent plant until it has lengthened to a more usable size.

Figure 5.2 A narrow hard stem which has been deprived of water will not root easily

You will sometimes read that shoots to be used for cutting material should be of 'ripe' wood. This is a fallacy — the harder and riper the wood the more difficult it will be to root; the young green shoots are the most vigorous and will root faster. Sometimes when a plant has been deprived of water for a long period then saturated, the shoots develop narrow hard stems at the base but fatten out with more lush growth towards the tip. These thin hard stems seldom produce roots so if using this kind of material for cuttings trim off the hard portion and prepare your cutting from the softer part of the stem.

Again, one may read 'take cuttings from a shoot which has not flowered'. This may be good sense when propagating Regal Pelargoniums but quite the opposite where Miniature and Dwarf Geraniums are concerned, for most produce flowers in abundance and it will be almost impossible to select stems which have not borne a flower or a flowerbud. It *is* preferable to cut to a leaf-node when trimming the base of a cutting rather than a flower-stem node, but this usually presents no difficulty.

Sterilisation of the blade between cuts is easily achieved by having a container of diluted Jeyes Fluid beside you on the bench as you take your cuttings, and returning the blade to the liquid between cuts. For several years past I have tried to transfer viruses from plant to plant by the use of unsterilised knives and also by injection, without result, so I am less than convinced that viruses are spread this way. However, it will do no harm to play safe, and if the plant to be cut is infected with botrytis, pythium or blackleg it will be a waste of time taking cuttings from it anyway.

Having separated your cutting from the parent plant it must now be prepared for insertion into the rooting medium, and this is done by removing most of the foliage from the stem, leaving only a few leaves at the top and by cutting the base of the stem square and close to a node. The amount of foliage to be retained will have to be decided in the light of your own experience and conditions, for much depends upon the environment in which rooting is to be attempted. If all the foliage were to be left intact upon the cutting most of it would drop of its own accord and the resulting mass of decaying vegetation would provide ideal conditions for the spread of botrytis; alternatively, if every trace of foliage were to be removed the cutting would have very little chance of survival. In a growing plant moisture is transpired through the foliage and replaced via the root system; an unrooted cutting has no root system and until such system is developed, the foliage, by continuing to transpire, will debilitate the cutting. In an attempt to circumvent this the cutting will shed most of its leaves, retaining only those it is able to support until such time as new roots develop and are able to restore the circulation.

Ideally we should anticipate just how much foliage the cutting will shed naturally and remove the surplus, but this calls for a degree of judgement which cannot be expected from a beginner, so we have to compromise. At the top of the cutting will be several small leaves still only partially opened. Allow these to remain together with the two nearest fully-developed leaves, but remove all others. After the cutting has been inserted into the rooting medium, keep a daily watch and remove any leaves that show signs of decay — at no time should a decaying leaf be allowed to remain lying across the cutting nor in contact with any part of the stem, it should be instantly removed and burned. If you are successful the first time and no extra leaves are shed by the cutting, experiment a little further next time and allow two more leaves to remain upon the cutting. In this way you will rapidly learn just how much of the foliage should be stripped off when preparing a cutting.

With the cutting suitably prepared, the next step is to dip the cut end into one of the Hormone Rooting Powders for about one-third of its length. This increases the speed of rooting and reduces the risk of infection through the open cut. I am well aware that it is quite possible to root Geranium cuttings successfully without the aid of rooting powders, especially for cuttings taken during the month of July, but the percentages of losses will be reduced when they are employed and will adequately justify the small extra expense. Several manufacturers offer these powders for sale under a variety of trade names, and each appears to be advantageous when dealing with a particular type of plant, but in my experience that marketed in Britain by Boots under their own name is the most suitable for the Pelargonium family, and it is significant that this is the product widely used by those commercial growers of Geraniums in Britain who are still propagating from cuttings.

Dip the stem of the cutting into the powder, make sure it is well coated, shake off the surplus and the cutting is ready for inserting into the rooting medium. Cuttings are best planted immediately after removal from the parent plant, and certainly within the hour. The old idea of leaving them to wilt for 24 hours is definitely harmful in the case of ordinary Geraniums, and usually fatal if applied to Miniature and Dwarf varieties. The disappearance of many of the lovely Zonal and Regal Pelargonium varieties which were widely grown during the Victorian period is largely due to this idea of wilting cuttings, and you may be fairly certain that any writer or broadcaster who advocates this method today is extracting his 'knowledge' from an outdated encyclopaedia and has little or no actual experience of growing.

No special compost or medium is required to root any member of the Pelargonium family if the cuttings are taken during the month of July in Britain. At this time of the year they will root in soil, sand, peat, moss, or even pure water. However, commercially it is not economic to use such a variety of media since commercial propagation has to be a continuous operation throughout the year and successful rooting must be predictable and consistent.

If you prefer to use soil get the John Innes Seedling Compost and add to it about 20 per cent pure washed silver sand, mixing well. There are numerous soil-less composts on the market which are excellent for rooting and need no preparation other than watering, and there are also a few mineral products which I have experimented with, with varying degrees of success. Basically the medium should be sterile, fairly open in texture, well drained but with sufficient water retention to create the correct environment for the roots to develop. I am not happy with pure Vermiculite for it retains the water too long for the good of the cutting and therefore often encourages rotting. It is true that it can be mixed with silver sand, peat or soil, but this is just making extra work. I prefer to use a product which is immediately acceptable to the cutting — and if possible, straight out of the bag.

Whichever medium is to be used the method will be very similar (with two exceptions which I will deal with separately). Fill the receptacle with the chosen medium, tap it gently on the bench to settle it, water thoroughly, allow to drain for half an hour then insert the cutting to about half its length, gently firming (but not compressing) the medium just enough to support the stem. Firming the compost around the stem is most important because a cutting that can flop about will never root, and if the cutting has been inserted into a previously dibbled hole there may be a gap left around the stem which could fill with water and result in the stem rotting.

Nearly all commercial growers now use one of the peat-based soil-less composts for propagating, and on the whole I have found these to be superior to soil for the initial rooting. Since its introduction in the 1960s I have been very impressed with Fison's Levington Compost for rooting all Geraniums and Pelargoniums. I have used it extensively and have had very few failures; J. Arthur Bowers' Compost is equally good. Both of these are soil-less composts and variations of the original University of California formulae.

Methods will have to be modified slightly if Jiffy-7s or pure Perlite are being used, as follows.

The Jiffy-7 is a pellet of compressed Norwegian peat with additives, contained in a fabric net. When purchased it will be a disc about 1½in (4cm) in diameter by perhaps ¼in (5mm) thick, but after immersion in water it expands to nearly 2in (5cm) in thickness. It is essential for the peat to absorb its full quota of water before a cutting is inserted and the amount it will accept depends to some extent upon the age of the pellet and the conditions under which it has been stored prior to purchase. A batch of fresh pellets will take up their full requirement of water in about ten or fifteen minutes, stale or badly stored ones may have to be soaked overnight before they are usable. This has no effect upon the viability of the pellet, just a bit annoying if you have little time to spare.

When ready for use the soaked Jiffy-7 should feel soft and pliable when gently squeezed; if it still has a hard centre it needs longer in soak. After removing from the water set the Jiffy-7s into a seed tray and allow to drain for an hour or so before using. I use 40 to a standard seed tray — 8 down, 5 across — this makes for a close fit and ensures that they cannot move once the cuttings have been inserted. If you use the smaller half-trays you will have to reduce the number accordingly.

A hole should now be dibbled in the centre of each Jiffy-7 and the cutting inserted. Gently squeeze the peat around the stem of the cutting to firm it, label it, and the job is done. Of all the rooting systems available I confess this is the one I prefer. Each cutting is individually rooted in its own potlet, by peering down between the potlets it is possible to see when they are rooted, and they can then be potted-on with the absolute minimum of disturbance to the young root system. At no time should any attempt be made to remove the netting — it is a fallacy to assume that the net will 'strangle the plant', the roots will grow through it without the slightest difficulty if conditions outside the potlet are suitable — if they do not, they have encountered a hostile environment and the compost you have used for potting-on must be suspect.

More recently, Horticultural Perlite has been recommended for rooting cuttings. This is a type of volcanic rock in granular form obtainable in several grades from fine to coarse. It is completely sterile and inert and extremely light and easy to handle. The product is best retained in its plastic bag and water inserted through a small hole cut in the top until it is thoroughly wetted. Not only will this make it easier to pack into a seed tray or pot but it will prevent any dust getting into the atmosphere. After packing the seed tray or other chosen container and slightly compressing the Perlite the cuttings can be inserted as with other media. Great care must be taken to avoid breaking the stems when inserting, and firming Perlite is not easy, but it

41

remains warmer than other media and this offers some compensation for the extra effort required. When the cuttings are rooted they must be potted immediately into J.I. No. 2 or 3 for the Perlite contains no nutrients, and do not try to shake the Perlite off the rootlets — they will be brittle and delicate and easily broken off by rough handling. Try mixing 50 per cent Levington and 50 per cent Perlite rather than pure Perlite, this produces much less brittle roots, firms around the stem better, and will provide enough nutrient to last the cutting for at least three weeks before potting-on becomes essential.

Pure washed river sand is almost as sterile as Perlite until it is contaminated by poor storage methods, and suffers from almost the same problems without the advantages of being light and warm. If you want to root cuttings in it the instructions concerning Perlite (above) will apply almost without amendment. Cuttings also root well in a 50/50 mix of Perlite and sand.

The thin-walled vacuum-formed plastic moulded potlets ganged to fit a seed tray (the Vacapot is one example) are much better to work with; after a light watering the rooted cutting will slide out of the pot without damage, and with care the potlet can be used again if properly sterilised.

The 'plugs' widely used in the USA for rooting are excellent for Miniature

Figure 5.3 Peat 'plug' widely used in the USA

and Dwarf Geraniums. They are manufactured from peat compressed into a small elongated cone about ¾in (2cm) square at the top, tapering to about half that width at the foot, and about 2in (5cm) deep. They are usually supplied in moulded plastic trays holding 80–100 and are used in much the same manner as Jiffy-7s.

Rooting Miniature and Dwarf Geranium cuttings in pure water is possible but there are many problems. With bedding Geraniums there is no difficulty in keeping the foliage clear of the water; if the cuttings are bundled together and inserted into a jam jar the heads will remain above the jar whilst the cut ends dangle nicely in the water. Keeping Miniature and Dwarf cuttings clear of the water is a different matter; it can be done by cutting a paper collar to fit around the stem so that the head protrudes above the paper whilst allowing the cut end to reach the water below. Personally I don't think it is worth the trouble especially since the roots produced will be bloated with water, very brittle, and liable to break off as soon as they are potted. If you want to

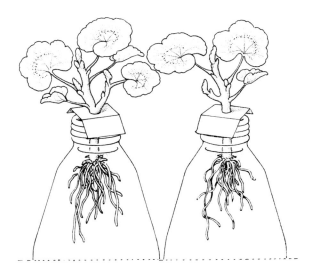

Figure 5.4 (a) Cuttings rooted in pure water after three weeks;

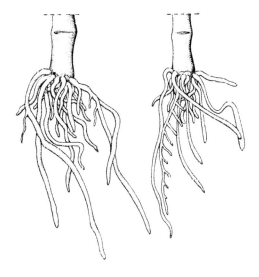

(b) bloated and brittle roots produced by rooting in water

43

experiment with rooting cuttings in water use a narrow-necked bottle for the water-receptacle and only set one cutting per bottle — if you try to get four or five into a jam jar the paper will get damp and the whole lot will gently descend into the depths.

The latest craze appears to be the marketing of a clear gel for rooting cuttings of all kinds. It is one of the most expensive methods yet devised but quite acceptable for use with all kinds of Geraniums including Miniatures and Dwarfs, if one bears its limitations in mind. First let me say that there is no need to purchase the very expensive proprietary branded products, you can buy a Nutrient Agar from almost any chemist and mix it yourself simply by boiling a little of the powder in water in an ordinary saucepan for a few minutes until it is thoroughly dissolved, it will set as it cools and is then ready for use. The density of the resultant gel can vary from almost solid to near liquid according to the ratio of agar to water; if it is too thin it will not support the cutting, if too thick the roots will be torn off as you take the cutting out of the agar for potting.

It will be necessary to arrive at the correct consistency by trial and error. Begin by adding a tablespoonful of the agar to one pint (0.5 litre) of water, then adjust as necessary to reach the right density. You cannot add more agar to the mixture once it has been boiled; if it is not to your liking you will have to start again from the beginning. The roots formed will again be bloated and brittle, almost as if rooted in water, and must be treated with great care. If the agar is too dense, pulling the rooted cutting out of it will tear off most of the roots and retard the plant if it does not actually kill it. Because of this it will be best to root each cutting individually so that roots cannot intermingle, and although a wine glass will be suitable for ordinary Geranium cuttings, Miniatures and Dwarfs really need something much smaller such as a test tube so that the foliage can be supported by the lip of the tube and held clear of the gel into which the stem is set.

When seen to be well rooted it is an easy matter to slide the whole unit out of the test tube without damage ready for immediate potting. 'Nutrient Agar' is something of a misnomer for it is derived from seaweed and contains few nutrients in its natural state; it is completely sterile after boiling. All manner of nutrients can be added, but for horticultural purposes it is normally used in its natural form and relies upon the potting-on compost to provide the nutrients later.

Whichever rooting system you use avoid the old method of rooting five cuttings around the edge of a pot. This must be the cause of more failures than any other single method and I am always surprised when I see television gardening 'experts' and magazine journalists still recommending it. Anyone suggesting this method of propagating Geraniums has little or no practical experience and the rest of his advice should be very carefully scrutinised. There is no doubt that Geraniums (large and small) can be rooted 5-to-a-pot and our Victorian ancestors were adept at it, but the losses are heavy, the rooting lopsided, and the set-back suffered by the plant through roots intermingling and being torn apart before potting means that flowering is always delayed for several weeks if the plant manages to survive.

Every modern technique aims to reduce the shock to the plant caused when it is potted-up. A successful potting will result in the plant growing on with no sign of stress; if the root system has been damaged the plant will shed its lower leaves and make no further growth until new roots have grown. So it is quite simple to determine whether or not your system is correct — if your newly potted plants shed any leaves your methods are suspect.

Peat pots have been used for many years and have long been accepted as a method of striking cuttings in such a way as to avoid the set-back encountered when potting-up a tray-rooted cutting. Several types and shapes are available and I think I have tried most of them at various times. My advice is to ignore the claims of the manufacturers and try a few experiments yourself, for they are not all as good as we are asked to believe, although the best are very good indeed. One of the major faults of peat pots (in fact all peat products) is their resistance to water once they have dried out, so this must be the first consideration. Take a new peat pot and fill it with water. If the water runs straight through leaving the pot almost dry, it is going to be useless; if the water is retained for several minutes but the sides of the pot show no signs of saturation, reject it. The pot which is going to give the only satisfactory result is the one which saturates in about 30 seconds but retains the water, gradually releasing it over a period of two to five minutes.

When using peat pots for striking cuttings it is important to choose the right moment for potting-up. The ideal time is when the first root-tip is showing through the side of the pot (and this applies to Jiffy-7s also) for at this stage there will be several more roots about to penetrate and it is best for these to push straight into the growing-medium. If they are allowed to penetrate freely through the sides of the peat pot and remain suspended in space, the tiny root-hairs which are invisible to the naked eye will die, the small visible roots be damaged when the plant is potted-on, and in extreme cases the roots will grow away and link up with those in adjacent peat pots causing considerable damage when they are finally torn apart.

Figure 5.5 Pot-up when roots are just showing through the walls of the peat pot

All cuttings will have to be lightly shaded for the first week after inserting in the rooting medium to reduce transpiration, except during the winter months when transpiration is not a major problem in the British Isles. This is easily achieved by laying a sheet of newspaper or white tissue paper over the

45

cuttings during daylight hours, but it must be removed at night or during dull weather if botrytis is to be avoided.

Cuttings should be taken only from healthy, disease-free plants and stock which is not infested by aphids or whitefly, and they must be kept free of these pests at all times for they are instrumental in the spread of viruses and numerous pathogens. Several proprietary products are available for this purpose, but avoid those with a Malathion or DDT base (it is now illegal to sell or stock DDT in Britain) for these can be harmful to Geraniums.

Smokes and dusts are widely used but these will kill not only the harmful insects but bees and ladybirds also, and although you may carefully chase all the bees out of your greenhouse before igniting the smoke bomb, it is a clever gardener indeed who can round up and persuade every ladybird of the inadvisability of remaining. For this reason above all others I prefer the use of a systemic insecticide. Some are applied to the soil, others to the foliage, but whichever you choose the action is the same. The insecticide is absorbed by the plant and from then on any biting or sucking insect will be poisoned. Bees and ladybirds (ladybugs in the USA) do not suck or bite plants so are left to continue with their good work, but aphids, whitefly and some small grubs will be destroyed.

Electric Propagators

Those wishing to extend their propagating activities beyond the range of the raw beginner will require some kind of heated bed to enable rooting to continue throughout the year. There are several small electric propagators on the market ranging from the simple and inexpensive to the very elaborate and costly, depending upon the size and the variety of gadgets included, but basically the same principle is employed — the application of gentle heat to the base of the cutting.

The smaller (and cheaper) electric propagators are not thermostatically controlled and usually consist of a heated plate about the size of a seed tray upon which a tray containing the cuttings is placed. The temperature is pre-set so that there is no danger of fire, but it is often high enough to cause the tray of cuttings to dry out long before they have rooted, so that extra watering becomes essential and the risk of trouble is increased. Overheating is easily overcome by first placing a tray of damp sand on the heated plate to act as a diffuser between the plate and the tray of cuttings. Not only will this reduce the risk of the cuttings drying out, it will produce a more even and gentle heat, and the gentle evaporation of the water in the damp sand will create a slightly humid atmosphere around the cuttings and reduce transpiration.

The larger and more expensive models are thermostatically controlled, some with both soil and air thermostats. They are usually supplied with plastic domed covers, and if these are used during the propagation of Geraniums a far too humid atmosphere will be created and a great deal of rotting will be experienced. It is very easy to say 'leave the cover off' but since some of the models are controlled by air thermostats the removal of the dome will result in an increase in temperature at the bottom as the thermostat tries

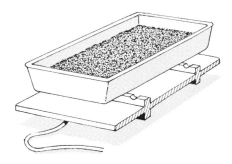

Figure 5.6 Basic electric propagator consisting of a seed tray mounted above a heated panel

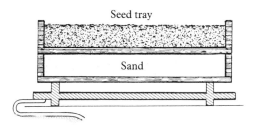

Figure 5.7 A tray of damp sand placed between the seed tray and the heated panel will ensure more even distribution of the heat and reduce drying-out

to maintain the air temperature, and again drying out will result. Make certain that any air thermostat is linked only to air-heating cables and that soil-heating cables are controlled by a soil thermostat. If both kinds are fitted ensure that they are independently switched.

Soil warming cables can be obtained to run either direct from the mains or through a transformer. The former, used commercially, consists of a heavily insulated and waterproof cable which is sealed during manufacture and cannot be cut or joined. It is sold in different lengths to suit the nursery benches and is normally buried under 2in (5cm) of damp sand. Alternatively the low voltage cable operates through a mains transformer (usually built-in) and is virtually a length of bare copper wire.

The insulated cable normally works through a soil thermostat and is in 24 hour operation; the low-voltage wire is usually switched on and off manually as required although it can be coupled to a soil thermostat. It is advisable to disconnect the low-voltage wire before working on the bench although there is no danger from the small amount of current flowing unless you have a heart condition; it is imperative to disconnect the high-voltage line before working on the bench.

Both types are equally effective and much cheaper to install than any manufactured propagator and running costs are almost identical area for area, in fact the cost in electricity for a propagating bed 3 x 5ft (1 x 1.5m) controlled by a soil thermostat at a temperature of 60°F (15°C) will probably not exceed three units per week if the greenhouse temperature in which it is installed does not fall below 50°F (10°C).

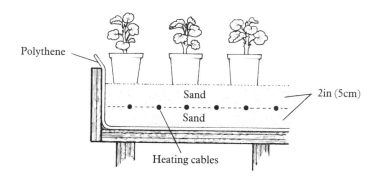

Figure 5.8 Cross-section of a heated bench

A propagating bench must be so constructed that it is well able to support the weight of the extra sand covering, but apart from that consideration any bench or part of a bench can be used. The selected area will have to be boxed in with sides not less than 4in (10cm) deep with close fitting corners. Line the bottom and up the sides with heavy-duty polythene to prevent moisture rotting the wood, then fill with sand up to a level 2in (5cm) all over the bottom and gently compress to give a fairly firm base. Arrange the heating wire or cable on the surface of the sand in loops or runs so that the strands are not less than 3in (8cm) and not more than 5in (13cm) apart, not less than 3in (8cm) away from the edge of the box at any point, and at no place does the line cross itself. If necessary the cable can be pinned down in position with handfuls of damp sand before the final layer of damp sand is spread on top of it to a depth of a further 2in (5cm). The cable is brought through the side of the box about half-way up through a hole previously drilled and connected to the electricity supply preferably via a soil thermostat, and the propagator is now ready for use.

Seed trays containing cuttings or seeds can be placed directly upon the sand which will have to be watered at intervals to keep it moist. It must not be allowed to dry out or the cable will overheat. Should you wish to root directly into the heated bed (avoiding the use of seed trays) you will need to extend the sides to allow for a further 2in (5cm) of compost and it is best first

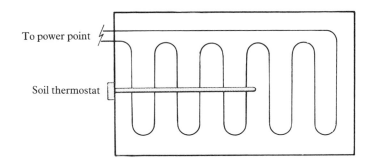

Figure 5.9 Layout of a cable in a heated bench

to cover the sand with heavy duty polythene for the compost will have to be changed every six months or so and if it has become mixed with the sand that will have to be changed also. Rooting directly into the heated bed is a clumsy, inefficient method and one best avoided in my opinion. The cable manufacturers supply full instructions for the installation of their products, and publish tables to indicate the length of cable required to serve a particular area. First decide how much bench space you wish to devote to propagating, then obtain the cable to suit before building the bench. If you construct the bench first you may find there is no standard cable made to fit it.

Instead of a thermostat you can operate the propagator through a domestic time switch set to give a two-hourly or four-hourly cycle throughout the 24 hours. This is not so economical as thermostatic control but some gardeners may prefer it. In any case, where electricity in the garden or greenhouse is concerned it is essential to employ the services of a qualified electrical engineer, if not actually to install then at least to check the work before the equipment is put into operation.

Several gardeners have shown me home-made propagators constructed from an old wooden box usually about 12 x 18 x 8in deep (30 x 46 x 20cm) with a 100-watt electric light bulb fixed into each end panel. I am told that the heat generated by the bulbs is sufficient to provide ideal conditions for a couple of seed trays placed on top of the box. I have not tried it personally, but am assured that it works. My only comment would be to make certain the thing is properly insulated and separately switched, and that the electrics are fully protected against damp.

Finally, I must mention the use of expanded polystyrene in propagating Never use it in granular form instead of sand in a propagating bed or the cable will certainly burn out. Its use in an unheated bed may raise the base temperature a fraction but not more than about 1°F (0.5°C) at the most. I have tried standing trays of cuttings on sheets of expanded polystyrene 2in (5cm) thick without base heating and there appears to be very little advantage over bench rooting without heat. However, if you wish to experiment for

49

yourself most electrical, radio and computer shops dispose of masses of the stuff every week and will be happy to give you some to try out.

Producing New Varieties from Seed

Expanding or replenishing your stock by vegetative cuttings is an excellent way of producing more plants of the same kind, but new varieties can normally only be propagated from seed, and anyone who has not tried producing his own seed has missed half the fun of growing Geraniums.

Nearly all new varieties of Miniatures and Dwarfs are produced by amateurs, for very few professionals can spare the time or the greenhouse space needed, and even when a new variety has been raised and promises to be a commercial success, it can take several years to propagate enough stock to make it marketable, during which time wages, rent and overheads still have to be paid. A few amateurs have been particularly successful — Bill Wells of Mitcham, Surrey achieved world-wide fame with some of his seedlings including the beautiful 'Grace Wells', one of the most attractive Miniatures ever raised; Reverend Stanley Stringer of Occold gave us many outstanding creations such as 'Bridesmaid', 'Orion', 'Sunstar' and 'Tapestry'; and Sam Peat of Clevedon, Avon with 'Friary Wood', 'Boudoir' and 'Creamery' — the nearest to a yellow yet raised*, but really too large to be considered as a dwarf or even a semi-dwarf.

I know of only two professional growers who specialised in raising Miniatures and Dwarfs from seed, although each also produced several ordinary varieties. Frank Parrett of Cobham, Kent was responsible for arousing more interest in this group of plants than any other person in England, and a similar position was occupied by Holmes Miller in Palo Alto, Southern California. More than 90 per cent of present-day nurseries growing Miniature and Dwarf Geraniums are growing from stock the origin of which can be traced back to one of these pioneers. Although most professional growers raise one or two new varieties themselves as a side-line or hobby (I propagated a dozen or so myself during my professional years) only Parrett and Miller raised new seedlings as their main business — and made a living out of it.

Seed is produced when pollen from one plant is transferred to another or sometimes to a different part of the same flower, an operation performed in nature by bees and other insects. This statement may well be an over-simplification but it is the principle underlying the following paragraphs.

When dealing with the species (the original plants going back centuries before hybridisation) it is true that the pollen from one plant will need to be transferred to a different plant before seed can develop, but all modern

---

*This statement needs some clarification for, in about 1986, Sam Peat raised a seedling Miniature with pure primrose-yellow single flowers. Unfortunately during a period of illness during which he spent some time in hospital it was lost. A photograph of this sensational seedling appears on Plate 13.

cultivars are many generations beyond this stage and the genes are all thoroughly mixed, so in addition to being able to fertilise other plants they can also often fertilise themselves. The permutations are endless, plant A crossed with plant B, plant A self-pollinated and the progeny crossed onto plant B, the progeny of this double-cross crossed back to one of the species, etc., etc. — all you need is a notebook and patience to provide hours of enjoyment.

I am not over-impressed with the recent and much publicised innovation of producing Geraniums from F_1 and F_2 hybrid seed. As one critic answered when asked his opinion of these, 'They are very good indeed — for the seed company'. Initially the seed is very expensive (commercial growers buy it at about a third of the retail price); its germination is erratic, often less than five out of nine seeds (the normal retail packet) germinating; for any hope of successful germination a constant temperature of about 70°F (21°C) is required; and after all this, unless you treat the plants with a chemical retardant they will often make very poor straggly specimens.

It was claimed that they would revolutionise the industry and result in the wholesalers being able to market plants at much lower prices because of the enormous savings in labour costs. In fact, I doubt whether many gardeners have benefited from any price reduction; if anything I suggest we have been subjected to a fairly steady increase in prices so that today there is no difference to the gardener in the price of a Geranium raised from a cutting or from seed. Treated as annuals they are excellent for the big wholesale growers and Parks Departments who require mass quantities of a few varieties, and who are able to balance the cost of seed and heating against expensive labour; the amateur does not have these advantages, neither is he able to offset his heating costs against his profit margin or local rates, and there are few gardeners able to afford to maintain a temperature of 70°F (21°C) day and night throughout a British winter. In any case the sheer predictability of the outcome dispenses with much of the pleasure for most of us.

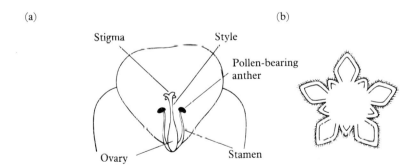

(a)   (b)

Figure 5.10 (a) Centre of flower (vertical section); (b) ovary (cross section)

Producing your own seed is exciting and very easy, and once you have raised a few plants with no assistance other than perhaps 'bee-power' you will become an addict and will most certainly wish to investigate the various methods available to you, even though at first the results may be only slightly more predictable than nature's way.

You can do very little until you have learned the composition of a flower, so, on a warm sunny day examine a newly-opened flower (singles are best until you have gained a little experience) and with the aid of a strong magnifying glass identify the various parts in co-operation with Figure 5.10. As the flower opens the anthers can be seen (these contain the pollen) attached to the stamens (short stems). At first the anthers will be sealed but as the day brightens and becomes warmer they will split, allowing the pollen grains to become visible. In the centre of the group of anthers is the short stem (style) which connects to the ovary, not easily seen at this stage, but very soon the style and stigmas will develop at the top and can then be more easily identified.

The pollen is usually produced two or three days before the style and stigmas are ready to receive it, and although the pollen is thought to have a limited life, the timing is not really critical. When the stigmas are ripe and receptive they become slightly sticky and this helps the pollen to adhere.

Several methods have been advocated for transferring the pollen from anther to stigma, and only one grain of pollen is needed to fertilise the ovary. In fact, no more than one will be accepted by the ovary. The simplest method must be by using a fine paint-brush (such as is found in a child's paint-box), coating the tip with pollen from one plant then gently transferring it to a waiting (sticky) stigma. Reverend Stanley Stringer favoured a tiny piece of cottonwool attached to a thin slither of wood or held in tweezers to achieve the same result, the cottonwool being discarded after each transfer. Sam Peat's method is carefully to remove the anthers before they can open to reveal the pollen (thus preventing self-pollination) using very fine tweezers so

(a)   (b)

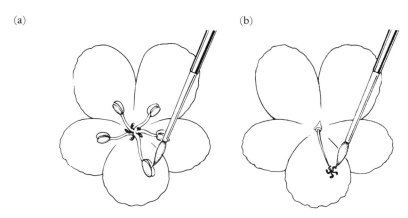

Figure 5.11 Transfer the pollen from (a) anther to (b) stigma

52

as to leave the stigma untouched, then, when the stigma is receptive and sticky, to take one pollen-laden anther from another flower and bring it into contact with the selected stigma.

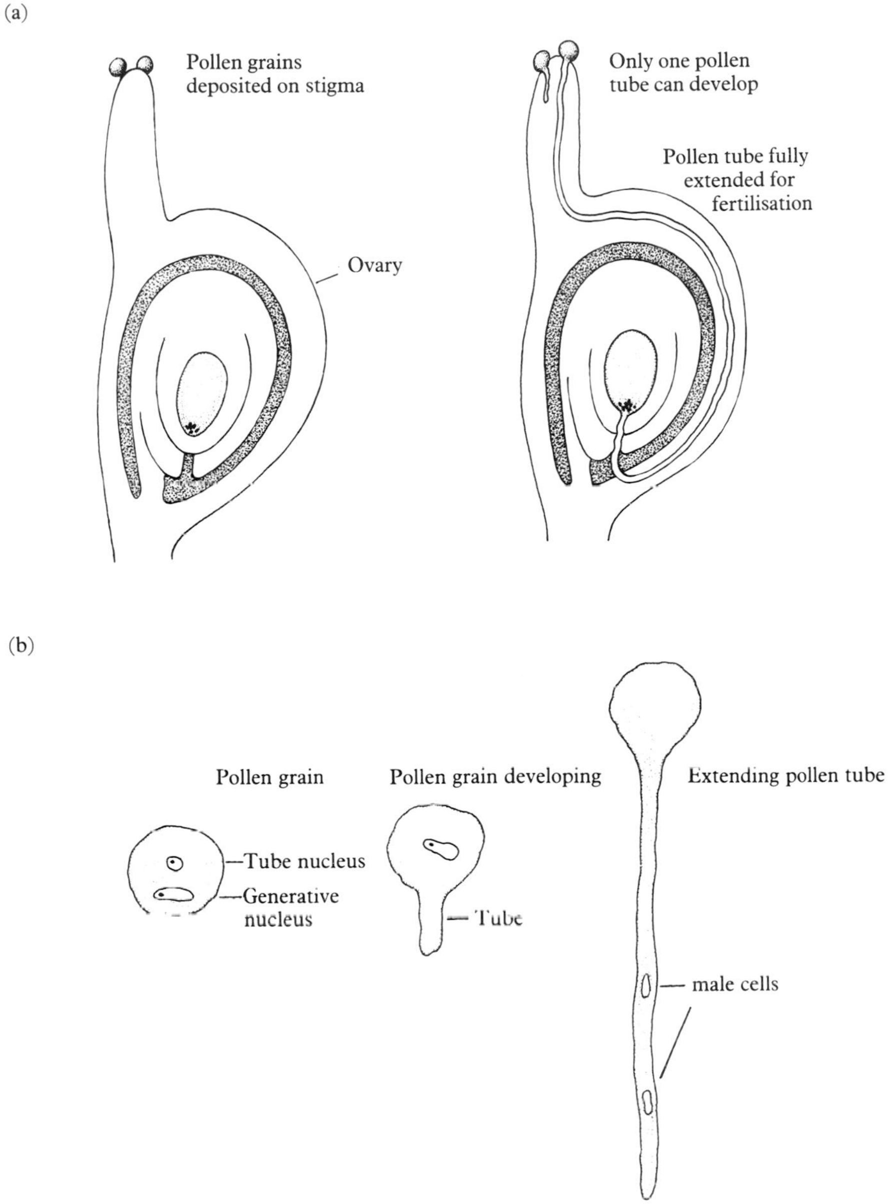

(a)

(b)

Figure 5.12 (a) Pollen grains deposited on stigma, pollen tube extended; (b) details of pollen grain

53

The 'rabbit-tail' method is where a small brush or piece of fur is applied to a flower carrying pollen, then this is brought into contact with several flowers in the greenhouse, transferring pollen indiscriminately. Not very scientific perhaps, but still lots of fun and it appeals to many because there is no point in keeping records with this method. Whichever method you employ, remember to mark the flower in some way so that you do not remove it by mistake when 'dead-heading'.

Some gardeners like to cover the flowerhead with a paper or muslin bag after cross-fertilising to prevent contamination by bees or other insects. This is quite unnecessary in my opinion for the ovary can only be fertilised by one grain of pollen — the first to reach it, no other grains will develop a fertilising tube beyond the initial stages (see Figure 5.12). Once fertilised the flower has served its purpose in nature and will soon drop its petals; this is why it is important to keep insects away from show plants until after an exhibition. The seed will gradually develop inside the seed case and, when ripe, the seed case will become detached from the base whilst still attached at the tip, and the ripe pollen tubes will curl into a feathery 'corkscrew' ready to be blown away. In nature that seed which falls upon soft damp ground will be drilled into the soil by the corkscrew untwisting as it absorbs the damp from the soil, but for our purpose it should be collected before it has a chance to disperse and either planted immediately or stored in an envelope in a dry place until required.

(a)   (b)   (c)

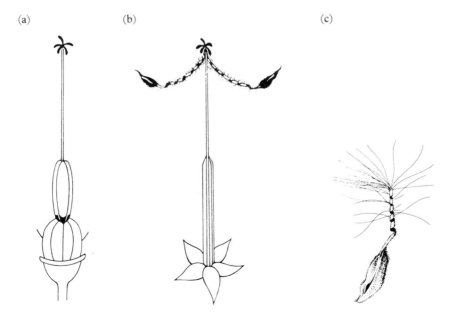

Figure 5.13 Immature and ripe seed

Bees, flies and many other insects are nature's hybridisers, and if you are interested in experimenting with new introductions you may prefer to give nature a chance before dabbling with camel-hair brushes, rabbit-tails, magnifying glasses, etc. Place all your plants together in a greenhouse, open all ventilators and doors so that insects can fly in and out of the house as they wish, and await results. By about September you should have all the seed you can cope with, and it can be sown immediately in seed trays or small pots, or kept dry in an envelope until February or March when it can be sown in a heated propagator or similar device. If you have no propagator delay sowing until April or early May when it will usually germinate without heat in a few weeks. Some seedlings will flower within about seven months of sowing if the hard seed case has been removed, others will take longer. No matter, you will be able to sow a second batch the following year and from then on you can have a succession constantly coming into flower.

Sowing Seed

The treatment of seed at sowing time involves more controversy in the ranks of the enthusiasts. In the past I have favoured nature's own method — sowing the seed complete with case, just as nature intended, and being prepared to wait the full 18 months or so usually required before expecting to see a flower. Of that 18 months it probably takes about six for the seed case to rot, and until this happens the seed cannot absorb water so no progress is possible. In the late 1960s I read a paper by a professor at the University of California in which he suggested that germination of Geranium seed could be accelerated by scarifying the seed before planting. He had carefully removed about ⅟₃₂in (0.8mm) from the tip of a seed case, and this was sufficient to allow water to penetrate and the seed to germinate. I tried this method with considerable success. Then I wondered what would happen if I detached the seed case entirely, and so, with the aid of a surgical knife and a pair of fine tweezers, removed the seed cases from 12 seeds before planting them. To my great joy they all germinated within about three weeks. Since then I have always used this method although I now soak the seeds in clean water for four hours before sowing. I find the soaking gives more even germination usually within two or three weeks at the outside. It is possible to leave the seeds actually to germinate in the water and they will do this in about the same time, especially if the water can be kept at about 65°F, (18°C) but the shoot produced will be bloated and brittle and is very easily damaged when potting-up (which will have to be done eventually). Each seed produces just one shoot and if that shoot is broken or mutilated it cannot grow another. By removing the seed case it is often possible to produce a flowering plant in about seven months from sowing the seed, but the time will vary according to conditions and the season of year.

Seeds are best sown individually in 2in (5cm) pots, Jiffy-7s, 1½in (4cm) Vacapots or similar. If grown loose in seed trays they will suffer a severe set-back when potted-up and many will be lost. Any loss is almost certain to bring on a fit of depression to the seed-raiser for there is always the chance that the one that died was the blue or yellow Geranium he had been working for, so for peace of mind grow your seeds individually.

55

After the roots have filled the pot or when they are visible emerging through the sides of the Jiffy-7 or peat pot, the seedlings should be potted-on into 3 or 3½in (8 or 9cm) pots. There is no point in taking them into larger sizes until they have flowered, for they will flower sooner if the root-run is restricted.

I prefer to use one of the soil-less composts for seed sowing, Levington, J. Arthur Bowers or Cal-Val are all equally good, but after germination it is best to pot-up using one of the John Innes Composts (No. 2 or 3), then feed regularly at every watering.

Conditions Required for the Optimum Germination of Pelargonium Seed

(1) Moisture-content will have been reduced during the ripening of the seed and until it is replenished no activity can begin. The protective seed case will prevent water reaching the seed. Until it has rotted or been ruptured or removed the seed has no access to water.

(2) Oxygen is essential to enable the seed to obtain the energy needed to promote the growth of the embryo. Seeds planted too deep can be starved of oxygen and will fail to develop.

(3) Correct temperature is important. Too low a temperature will inhibit germination whilst excessive heat will destroy the embryo. 65–68°F (18–20°C) would seem to be the optimum.

(4) Light appears to be unnecessary for the germination of Geranium (Pelargonium) seed, although total darkness is not necessary either. If covered with about ⅛in (3mm) of soil or sand they will germinate readily if all other requirements are met.

Once the new seedling has flowered you will have to decide whether it is worth retaining. You can anticipate that most of your early raisings will bear single red flowers of poor or indifferent quality and will be best destroyed, but as you progress and your methods improve the ratio of acceptable seedlings to those discarded will improve also.

The seedling may carry some of the characteristics of both parents but in different proportions (and sometimes none at all), but its habit as a seedling will be quite different to that of any cuttings taken from it. Nearly all seedlings develop a fairly thick central stem covered in masses of side shoots, and carrying a flower at the top extremity. Ignore the plant's habit at this stage and examine the flower and foliage; if these are to your liking remove a few of the side shoots (the ones towards the base are usually the first to reach a usable size) and root them in the same way as you would any other cutting. These cuttings, when rooted, will show the true character of the plant you have produced and its habit will be quite different from that of its seedling parent. You can continue to take cuttings from the seedling until its eventual demise, and as the cuttings develop into plants they too will yield cuttings which will then be true to the first generation.

Some gardeners like to cut the top off the seedling and root this without waiting for the flower to be produced; it is said that the cutting will produce a flower earlier than the parent. I have not found this to be so, but you may like to experiment for yourself.

As soon as you decide to propagate from a seedling, name it. You can then ensure that every cutting taken from it bears the same name and so avoid the possibility of confusion in the future. If you want to try some complicated crosses begin by coding the names or perhaps giving each name a code number. This will save you the chore of writing out lists of names every time you make a cross, and so long as your notebook shows the code it will be quite easy to refer back to see which plants were involved in the progeny.

Readers should appreciate that the foregoing can be little more than an outline of the principles of raising plants from seed. Those wishing to investigate the matter in greater detail should consult one of the many excellent books on the subject, such as *Plant & Animal Biology* by Vines & Rees, published by Pitman.

When *Miniature Geraniums* was first published in 1968 their popularity was only just beginning to spread from England and the USA into Holland and a few isolated areas of Europe. Today they are grown almost universally and are exhibited regularly at horticultural and flower shows as far apart as Iceland, Portugal, South Africa, New Zealand, Canada, Mexico and, of course, Australia. The lists towards the end of this book provide a guide to the enormous number of varieties available, but there are probably hundreds more which are unknown to me, and still more being raised as I write.

6 Grafting

There are occasions when grafting can be advantageous. A slow-growing variety can sometimes be improved by grafting onto more vigorous stock, or perhaps a better type of flower grown onto a particularly favoured fancyleaf stock, for instance. Most gardeners agree that the best time for grafting Geraniums in Britain is from mid-April to mid-May when the plants are growing vigorously and the light is good.

To accelerate a slow-growing variety, select a healthy, sturdy shoot, preferably 1½-2in (4–5cm) long (on some varieties you may have to go smaller) and detach it from the parent plant as for a normal cutting but severing at a point mid-way between nodes. The shoot remaining on the parent plant should then be trimmed back to an outward facing node, but the severed cutting (scion) should remain untrimmed.

Select the stock plant for its strong growth and vigour ('Stradt Bern' is good for this purpose) plus any other characteristics required. It must be in peak condition, well branched and free from disease or insects. Take a branch of approximately the same age and diameter of stem as the scion taken from the first plant and prepare both scion and stock as follows.

A very sharp knife or stainless steel razor blade is usually suggested for this operation, but I prefer a surgeon's scalpel blade which, together with its special holder, can be purchased from most artists' supplies dealers (I use those made by Swann-Morton, but there are others equally good for grafting plants).

Cut the selected branch of the stock plant half-way between nodes, removing the top portion which is no longer needed (it can be rooted in the usual way if required). We now have the stock branch with its top missing plus a scion with top but no bottom. Cut both stock and scion diagonally so that when brought together there is a node both above and below the joint, and notch them carefully so that the cuts interlock (see Figure 6.1). Bring both parts together as quickly as possible to prevent the cut surfaces drying and to reduce the risk of contamination, then cut strips of polythene about ½in (12mm) wide to make a bandage and carefully wrap around the stem from about ½in (12mm) below the join to the same above, afterwards coating the join liberally with grafting wax to ensure that all air is excluded and taking care to keep the bandage tight without disturbing the graft. Finally secure the graft by wrapping tightly with an adhesive tape such as Sellotape

59

or Scotch tape. If you attach the adhesive tape directly to the graft without first protecting it with the polythene bandage you risk damaging the graft when removing the tape. If the diameter of the stock is not an exact match to that of the scion, align them at one side, do not centre. Grafts whose diameters are totally different to that of the stock are seldom successful.

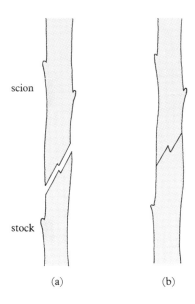

scion

stock

(a)   (b)

Figure 6.1 Grafting. (a) Cut both stock and scion diagonally; (b) joining the stock and scion

Transpiration must now be controlled or the scion will dehydrate before the graft is complete. It is not a good idea to place the stock plant complete into a plastic tent or container because the plant needs to transpire normally, we only need to restrict the loss of moisture from the scion. This can be achieved by inserting a cane into the pot so that its top is about 2in (5cm) above the tip of the grafted scion but quite close to it. Over this cane invert a clean jam jar, locating it so that no part of the stock or scion comes into contact with the glass. Some gardeners then like to seal the opening of the jar with kitchen foil but I have not found this to be necessary. However, if your plants are growing in a very dry atmosphere you may be advised to use the foil; if the condensation in the jar becomes excessive it is a simple matter to make a few holes in the foil.

The plant must then be shaded for at least three weeks and must always be protected from direct sunlight. After 30 days, raise the jam jar slightly every other day, watching carefully for any signs of the scion wilting. If wilting occurs immediately lower the jar and wait for another week before once more starting to raise it. Eventually it will be possible to remove the jar entirely but this should not be taken to mean that the union of scion and stock is complete, so maintain light shading for at least another month.

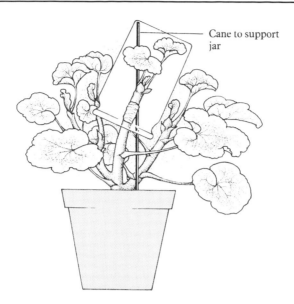

Cane to support jar

Figure 6.2 Transpiration reduced by placing grafted shoot in a jam jar

When the scion has grown ½in (12mm) or more it is safe to assume a successful graft. The adhesive tape and polythene bandage can now be carefully removed, but bear in mind that the joint will still be weaker than the rest of the stem and any rough handling at this stage can result in an irreparable fracture.

Some writers suggest grafting onto three or four shoots of the stock plant at the same time, but I prefer to limit my efforts to one only so that the stock plant is not stressed. Additional shoots can be grafted when the technique has been mastered and more experience gained, but don't expect immediate success; in the early days I was losing three out of four grafts, but by limiting myself to one graft per plant I never lost a stock plant.

Once the union is complete and the shoot is extending successfully you may like to consider rooting a cutting from it in the usual way. A plant from such a cutting should, in theory, bear some of the characteristics of each parent. In practice this does not always occur but you can expect success in most cases and anyway there is nothing to lose by experimenting.

Other types of graft can be utilised for Miniature and Dwarf Geraniums but I have found the foregoing to be the easiest and most successful. However, one of the alternatives is 'budding' which is described below.

Take a node which is showing a small shoot or bud, preferably before the bud opens to show any kind of developing leaf, and remove it from the parent plant with a small oval of bark around it. This can easily be performed by cutting an oval around the bud, about ¹⁄₁₆in (1mm) deep, then by sliding the knife under the bark the oval can be lifted clear of the stem complete with central bud.

Select a suitable branch on the stock plant and make a horizontal cut mid-way between nodes and just deep enough to penetrate the bark — the cut should be about one-third the circumference of the stem in width. From the centre of the horizontal cut make a 1in (25mm) cut downwards. It will now be possible to peel back the bark from the vertical cut sufficiently to allow the oval with bud to be inserted (make certain it is the right way up). The bark can then be drawn over so that the oval is trapped under the bark of the stem. Bandage with the polythene strip, seal the joint with grafting wax, then bind closely with adhesive tape. It is imperative that the bud is not allowed to dry out before inserting into the slit.

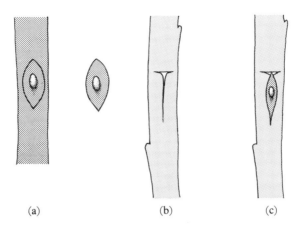

(a)   (b)   (c)

Figure 6.3 Budding procedure (a) Remove bud from parent plant; (b) make a cut in a branch of the parent plant; (c) insert bud into cut and bind with tape

Some gardeners then remove the top of the branch above the graft, feeling that this will force the graft to develop sooner; I prefer to leave it on the plant to ensure that normal photosynthesis continues in the belief that this will reduce the risk of infection and increase the bud's chances of survival. Once the bud has developed and grown to about 1in (25mm) long it will be well established and can then be treated exactly as any other shoot on the stock plant. There is a good chance that it will bear the same flower as the mother plant whilst incorporating the vigour and possibly other characteristics of the stock plant.

I am told that it is possible by either of these methods to produce a stock plant carrying several different flowers at the same time, in much the same way that multi-fruit trees can now be purchased. I have not tried it nor have I yet seen one, but I look forward to the day when such a plant is exhibited at the Chelsea Flower Show, just to see the consternation among the judges.

7 Feeds, fertilisers and watering

Feeds and Fertilisers

A sickly plant will often throw a flower in a last attempt to reproduce before it dies, and this has led to the erroneous belief in some quarters that Geraniums flower best in poor soils and under indifferent conditons. One often sees these half-starved specimens bedded out in suburban gardens in England, and they are commonplace in hot climates such as Spain and Italy where poor spindly plants with one or two small flowers flourish in the dry sandy soils of the coastal and inland areas of scrubland.

I know of one instance in a Cotswold village where it was proposed to construct a sizeable bed of Geraniums beside a small ornamental lake where the soil was particularly rich and fertile, having been used for several years by a market gardener specialising in cut flowers. The head gardener employed by the lady of the house insisted that a pit be excavated, filled with brick rubble, sand and cinders from the greenhouse boiler, and the plants bedded out in this to ensure they would 'get the benefit of a poor soil'.

Of course, we also have the other extreme; the enthusiast who spends much of his spare time following the horses, or his spare money purchasing 'well-rotted farmyard manure' from roadside sites at inflated prices and is eventually able to fill a trench with pure dung into which he proudly settles his Geraniums. His complaint to the nurseryman from whom he purchased his stock usually runs on the lines that 'they grew like cabbages but scarcely a flower all summer'. The lesson to be learnt — a plant fighting for survival in arid conditions cannot give of its best, and one enduring a surfeit of nitrates will develop lush, almost gross foliage at the expense of flowers.

For best results with outdoor plants I recommend planting in a prepared bed of John Innes No. 3 compost, then after about three weeks begin feeding with a weak liquid fertiliser at regular weekly intervals. Remove all flowerbuds as they develop until the plant is fully grown and well established, then let it flower and you will discover just what a Geranium is capable of. The same basic principle applies to pot-grown plants and those in hanging baskets and similar containers; regular feeding with a weak liquid fertiliser will produce the best results. Most successful competitors at shows have kept their plants out of flower for much of the year before allowing the buds to develop in time for exhibiting, and although the gardener who is growing solely for pleasure may consider this too long to wait it certainly proves that a little patience will be amply rewarded.

If you are already growing Geraniums and Pelargoniums (Zonal and Regal Pelargoniums to give them their correct names), you will find that Miniatures and Dwarf varieties can be grown beside them with no difficulty whether in the greenhouse, in pots or other containers, or outside in bedding schemes and borders, for they enjoy almost the same conditions and treatment. But to fully understand their requirements, it is necessary to pay some attention to the effect upon them of various fertilisers and chemical feeds.

It is essential to understand that plants can only accept food in liquid form, so if fertilisers in solid or powder form are applied they can be assimilated by the plant only when they have been dissolved into liquids. This explains why, if a plant is kept permanently dry it must die eventually, and the time it will take to die depends upon the amount of fluid stored within its tissues.

The particles of dry fertiliser which are added to the soil or which may already be incorporated into it dissolve at different rates, some very much faster than others, and with regular watering the faster-dissolving matter will often be leached out and will run off with the waste water leaving the slower-dissolving particles intact. Eventually the soil will contain a surfeit of the slower-dissolving matter and the chemical content will be out of balance. Taken to extremes the soil can become hostile to the plant, which will then resist the extension of the rooting system into the surrounding compost, so making little or no progress. Where the compost becomes hostile *after* the roots have fully developed, most of the roots will die off and when the plant is taken from the pot for inspection it will appear to be unrooted even though top development is temporarily apparently normal.

The advantages of feeding in liquid form will be obvious, for not only is the nutriment instantly available to the plant, but the type of feed can be easily adjusted to meet any special requirement which may become apparent at different seasons, and furthermore the balance of chemicals in the soil (or other growing medium) can be kept constant. Mixing such dry ingredients as bone meal, hoof and horn, dried blood, fish meal, etc. into the soil of an outdoor bed at the time of planting Geraniums is almost a waste of time and money since by the time these additives have dissolved sufficiently for the plants to be able to assimilate them, the winter is upon us and they have to be lifted. Winter snows and rain will remove almost all traces of the fertiliser by the following spring so it is true to say that members of the Pelargonium family derive almost no benefit from these dry additives although they are excellent for trees, bushes and most perennials which remain in the ground for more than one season.

Whichever type of fertiliser is used, liquid or solid, it will consist principally of three chemicals — nitrogen, phosphorus and potassium (often listed as NPK), plus trace elements (boron, copper, iron, magnesium, manganese, molybdenum, sulphur and zinc) and calcium.

Nitrogen is essential for vigorous growth and, in balanced combination with other elements, enables seedlings to grow fast enough to escape seedling blight and several pathogens. Excessive nitrogen delays maturity and produces lush and succulent growth often with weakened stems; the plant's cell walls will probably be thin and easily penetrated by pathogens. Nitrogen deficiency is important also, and it is accepted that excess favours some diseases and deficiency others.

Phosphorus promotes good root development and maturity of seeds; to some extent it is thought to help counteract an excess of nitrogen. An excess of phosphorus may reduce the plant's resistance to certain diseases.

Potassium assists in the development of the plant's structure; it promotes the thickening of the outer walls of the epidermis and general well-being of the structure resulting in increased resistance to penetration by some pathogens, particularly powdery mildews. Potassium deficiency results in an accumulation of carbohydrates and inorganic hydrogen in the plant, interferes with the natural photosynthesis and causes yellowing of the foliage margins and the formation of necrotic spots.

Calcium reduces soil acidity and may therefore have a direct effect upon some soil-borne pathogens; it can also affect host plants by adjusting the soil pH. It helps in the building of the framework of plants and is essential in the production of new cell walls. Calcium deficiency results in reduced plant growth and is thought to encourage certain root problems.

It will be seen therefore that an excess of any of the basic chemicals will produce unwelcome effects, as will a deficiency; best results can only be expected from a fertiliser correctly balanced to produce a well-proportioned, healthy plant, having a well-developed root system enabling it to yield a steady succession of flowerbuds throughout the season with no sign of stress or exhaustion. You will never get optimum results from a Miniature or Dwarf Geranium (or any other member of the Pelargonium family) by feeding it with dilute soot-water, cold tea, diluted animal manure, sugar-water, urine, or even rose-fertiliser. The perfect analysis for all Geranium liquid feeds and the only formula I can personally recommend is as follows: nitrogen 15.10%, phosphorus 2.10%, potassium 23.50%. It is the result of many years of experimentation in both laboratories and nurseries and needs very little adjustment from season to season, but it has to be accepted that conditions in distant countries can be very different from those in Britain, and an acceptable formula in Britain could need considerable adjustment before being applied in Australia for instance. In fact I know that in Southern California a 20:20:20 feed is quite normal for plants grown in their near-desert conditions.

The formula recommended in the foregoing paragraph is not easy to find ready mixed, in fact I have been unable to trace one since the withdrawal of 'Com-pel' from the market in the mid-1970s. I have overcome this problem by mixing two products from one chemical manufacturer, one with a high-nitrogen content, the other with a high-potash (the formula is always printed on the container) and thus arriving at almost the correct balance of ingredients. The method is not perfect, but good enough for most purposes, and it is important to avoid mixing the products of different manufacturers and to keep the powder dry after mixing until required for use when it must be thoroughly dissolved in clean water.

One often sees advertisements for proprietary brands of fertiliser containing the claim that 'it improves the colour of the flowers'; this of course

65

is just not the case. It is not possible to 'improve' a colour, only to alter it, and once altered it becomes a different colour. Any fertiliser with a high-potash content will alter the colour of a Geranium, some quite violently, and possibly the most startling illustration of this can be seen in the case of 'Maxime Kovalevski' which under balanced conditions is pure orange, but which, after a few applications of potash, will change to a bright scarlet not unlike 'Paul Crampel'. Variations in the formulae of feeds will also have a marked effect upon the foliage of many of the fancy-leaved varieties, such as 'Mrs Henry Cox', where the greens can be intensified until they are almost black and the reds increased in density to give stronger pigmentation and greater contrast against the base yellow. Many experienced gardeners employ their own pet formulae and concoct their own feeds as required, but when growing Miniatures and Dwarfs experimentation can be costly, and beginners would be well advised to seek instruction from one of the genuine experts before departing far from the analysis I have detailed.

Another misleading statement often seen in gardening advertisements announces that the product is 'a balanced fertiliser suitable for all plants'. This again is not possible — a fertiliser correctly balanced for cabbage will require a fairly high nitrogen content so that foliage predominates over flowers, whereas tomatoes require extra potash to produce fruit rather than foliage. It is not possible to manufacture a standard feed balanced correctly for *any* plant, at best it can only be a compromise and as such a poor substitute for the correct formula.

Manufacturers of fertilisers always provide full instructions on the label as to strength and frequency of feeding, and they usually recommend feeding at regular weekly or fortnightly intervals according to the strength of the product. One has always to balance their concern for the gardener and his plants against the profit motive, and I prefer to increase the rate of dilution so that the solution is used at quarter strength or even weaker, and then applied at every watering. This has several advantages; the cost is considerably reduced, it is not necessary to remember when to feed and when to use just plain water, there is much less risk of the foliage being scorched by an over-strong solution (and this can easily happen), and if at some time the plants have to be left in the care of another person his (or her) job will be that much easier. It is very wasteful to use a stronger solution than that suggested by the manufacturer for the plant cannot take advantage of it and the excess will simply be washed down the drain; in extreme cases a build-up of salts in the compost can have a disastrous effect upon the plant.

Watering

The pollution of rivers and watercourses has decreased slightly in recent years but they still contain enough chemical products to get into the mains water supply and adversely affect Geraniums. It is reasonable to take no chances. Rainwater is far better for Geraniums than mains water, and since this commodity forms the major ingredient of a British summer it is perhaps surprising that so few gardeners bother to collect it. Even an apartment-dweller can usually find a down-pipe from a gutter beneath which to place a bucket, and anyone with a greenhouse or garden shed has a ready-made catchment area. Many people in country areas in Britain have their water supply metered and have to pay for the water they use — if metering were more widespread over the population as a whole we would see a great improvement in the quality of Geraniums grown in the country as more people saved rainwater and money.

Excessive water is responsible for the death of more Geraniums than any disease or pest, Miniatures and Dwarfs being particularly susceptible because the small leaves have a limited area for transpiration, so the plant is less able to dispose of any excess. Very few Geraniums die from a shortage of water and there are still many gardeners who let their plants get bone dry before watering — far better than keeping them too wet, but not the way to get the best from a plant. This method is often seen in nature in places such as southern Spain, Italy and Mexico where Geraniums grow wild and almost dry out completely in the heat of the summer. By the end of the summer they have shed almost all their leaves to keep transpiration to the minimum and may appear to be little more than a few dead stems, yet within a few days of the rains coming new shoots appear, and very soon the plant is thriving again. It will never be a perfect specimen, but the prolonged drought has not killed it as many would expect.

Excessive transpiration in summer (usually only noticed in greenhouse plants) will cause the foliage to droop, but this should not be taken to mean that water is required. It usually happens when the root system is not sufficiently developed to support the volume of foliage the plant is carrying, and the plant will recover overnight. Shading against intense sunlight will overcome the problem during the daytime, and damping down the paths and benches will also be helpful. If the situation develops rapidly before there has been time to shade the greenhouse glass, a sheet of newspaper placed over the plant will serve the same purpose temporarily but it is important to remove it at night or during dull weather to avoid the risk of botrytis. Cuttings should be shaded in the same way until well rooted.

During the summer months watering is best performed in the cool of the evening, then if the foliage is inadvertently splashed the water will have a chance to dry off before any scorching can result from the action of the sun's rays through the glass, and the water will be thoroughly absorbed by the compost with less risk of its evaporating before it can benefit the plant. It is just as important to water the plants bedded out in the garden in the evening also. It is true there is little chance of leaf-scorch if water remains on the foliage, but the water will be able to penetrate down to the roots before the sun recommences the evaporation process.

The advantages and disadvantages of top or bottom watering can be argued *ad infinitum*. By 'top watering' a gardener means the application of water directly into the top of the flowerpot by hose or watering can, and 'bottom watering' means standing the pot in a receptacle containing water and allowing the liquid to soak up through the medium by capillary action. Each method has its merits and it is for the individual to make his own decision after considering the arguments.

If total saturation of the growing medium is the object then top watering is less efficient, for the water will always run to the edge of the pot and seep rapidly down the easiest route — close to the inner wall of the pot, with the result that those roots nearest to the wall will get most of the water whilst those towards the centre remain dry. This point is easily proved. Take a really dry plant and give it a thorough watering with a can or hose, then knock it out of its pot and examine it. You can easily follow the path of the water down the inside of the pot, and if you break open the soil ball you will find it still quite dry.

You may sometimes hear elderly gardeners declare that as soon as the roots of a cutting reach the wall of the pot the progress of the plant is accelerated. This is quite true, but it has little to do with an inherited passion for walls implanted in the cutting at birth, it is simply due to the fact that if the cutting is being top-watered more nourishment becomes available to it the moment the roots reach the wall and moisture. Top watering usually means that only the outside inch (25mm) or so of the compost is being actively used by the plant, so in a 5in (13cm) pot the plant is getting the benefit of only just over half the compost. On the credit side top watering changes the air content of the compost as the water progresses downwards, and air is equally important for the well-being of the plant.

Bottom watering is normally achieved by standing the plant in a dish of water and waiting for the liquid to be absorbed by the compost, and this is where the difficulty arises — how much water — how often should the contents of the receptacle be replenished? No plant likes to have its feet permanently in water (except bog plants), alternatively if the liquid applied is insufficient it can result in only the bottom inch (25mm) or so of compost being of benefit to the roots.

There *is* a method of watering which is completely foolproof but really only suitable for use with stock plants or plants which can remain unmoved for a year or two. It can be used for an individual plant or for a group according to the size of container to be used. Take a metal or wooden tray of suitable size with walls not more than 2in (5cm) high. Line it carefully with heavy-duty black polythene taking the plastic up over the sides and securing to the outer surfaces, making quite certain there are no holes or gaps through which water can escape. In the centre of the plastic-lined tray place an ordinary house brick (several if you wish to accommodate more than one plant) making certain that the bricks do not come nearer to the edge of the tray than about 2in (5cm) at any point, and immerse the bricks in clean water for at least two hours before using. Next cover the brick or bricks with pieces of old flannelette sheeting (wool will not do) ensuring that the entire surface of the brick is covered and that there is sufficient fabric over for the edges to hang down into the water all around. The fabric must be thoroughly soaked with water before being laid over the bricks, and I like to use a double thickness to ensure an even capillary action. If you have to purchase *new* flannelette it will have to be boiled before using to break down its natural resistance to water. Now fill the tray with water (including diluted feed if you accept my advice) and the capillary action will keep the fabric permanently damp. The plants can never be watered to excess because the bricks on which they stand will be at least 1in (25mm) above the surface of the water, and if someone pours too much water into the tray it will simply run over onto the floor.

Before placing the plants upon the raised bricks it is important to cut the base out of the flowerpot with a sharp knife so that the entire base of the soil-ball comes into contact with the damp fabric, and I usually give the plant a little water before placing it to give it time to settle before the roots get into the fabric. Once placed the plants cannot be moved without losing all those roots which have penetrated the fabric, a shock from which it will suffer for many months before recovering — the reason why this system is unsuitable for show plants.

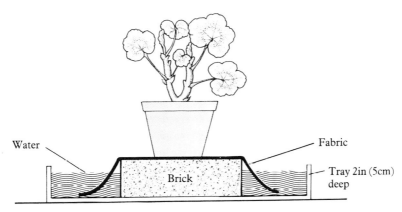

Figure 7.1 Self-watering for stock plants

There are several proprietary brands of fabric sold for this purpose but they are very expensive and in my opinion not so efficient as flannelette. All fabrics will develop algae very quickly and begin to look very unsightly. There are chemicals available to kill the algae but they also kill or severely damage Geraniums. To overcome this you can either place a sheet of black polythene over the plants, cutting slots for the foliage to penetrate, or, as I do, cut a second sheet of black plastic slightly larger than the total area of the tray and place it on top of the bricks *before* placing the plants, then cut a disc out where you wish the plant to sit. In this way the fabric is completely covered with black plastic except where the plant sits, and not only is the fabric protected from daylight and the formation of algae restricted, but all the water and feed in the tray is also covered so evaporation is reduced as is the risk of contamination.

This method allows the plant to take up just as much liquid as it requires and no more. On a hot day when transpiration is high it will need much more water than on a dull day, and it will adjust the uptake to meet its needs. There is an additional benefit to the keen greenhouse owner in that no temporary helper can over-water the plants, and if he has to be away all day it is an easy matter to fill the tray in the morning knowing that it will last all day — possibly several days if the container is large enough and the weather dull.

Another foolproof method of watering uses the same basic principles as the foregoing, somewhat simplified, but is still unsuitable for use with show

69

plants. It abandons the use of fabric and the plants do not have to be located in fixed positions. Take a clean empty pot one size larger than that in which your plant is growing and put about 1in (25mm) of coarse gravel into it, next put a ½in (12mm) layer of horticultural grit followed by 1½in (4cm) of silver sand. Place the plant in its pot inside the larger pot, and fill the space between the pot walls with horticultural grit or sand. When the complete unit is placed in a tray of water the moisture will rise by capillary action to feed the roots which will rapidly penetrate into the damp sand. No top watering should be applied once the plant is established or the compost will become saturated. The formation of algae on the surface of the compost can be prevented if some horticultural grit is scattered on top of the pot.

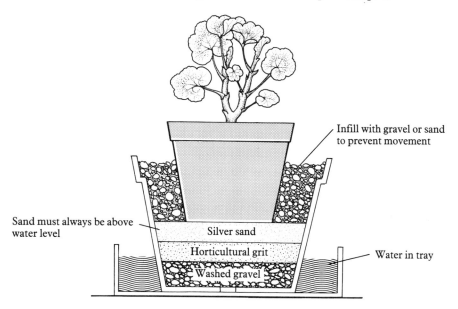

Infill with gravel or sand to prevent movement

Sand must always be above water level

Silver sand

Horticultural grit

Washed gravel

Water in tray

Figure 7.2 Another self-watering method

For the system to be successful the water level must never be higher than 2in (5cm) so that the silver sand is always slightly above the water. If the bottom is cut out of the plant's pot before it is placed on the silver sand more even rooting into the sand will be obtained. Clay pots are unsuitable for this system.

But to revert to ordinary watering methods by hosepipe or watering can, there is no easy rule-of-thumb which can be applied, and if one suggests the use of common sense, over-watering will nearly always result since few people in my experience ever believe that they can be guilty of this error.

The idea that whenever a plant looks sickly or has just been received after a long journey in adverse conditions it must 'need a drink' is the cause of a great number of plant losses. A Geranium which has been in an enclosed parcel for several days after leaving the nursery should be immediately unwrapped and stood in an airy place with slight shading for a few days — on no account should it be watered unless the roots are absolutely bone dry, a very unlikely possibility. The plant cannot benefit from watering at this stage because most of the tiny invisible feeding roots will have been destroyed or detached by movement during the journey, the visible roots are mainly anchoring roots and until these once more get a firm hold on the compost no more feeding roots will be developed, so quiet undisturbed rest is the first requirement coupled with shading to reduce transpiration. After three or four days it should be possible to pot-up the plant without any further reversal, but even then water sparingly until it is well established, after which the watering will have to be adjusted to suit the plant. Remember plants are individuals — if 2oz (57g) of water is correct for 'Betsy Trotwood', a similar amount could well be fatal for 'Fairy Storey'.

If a plant fails to thrive, faulty watering must be suspected with over-watering as first favourite. In this case the foliage will become dull and rather darker than that of a healthy plant, with a tinge of yellow appearing around the edges as the condition progresses until eventually the entire leaf yellows and drops off. By this time the roots will have started to rot and the damage will progress until the entire root system is destroyed and the stem becomes visibly affected as the rot creeps upwards. Once rotting is visible above soil level the plant is doomed and should be destroyed immediately, nothing more can be done for it. However, if signs of over-watering are noticed early enough, the plant may be removed from the pot, all the old soil washed off then re-potted into fresh compost of the correct consistency. There is no doubt that this treatment will give the plant a severe shock from which it may not recover, but to leave it to soak in a saturated compost is certain death.

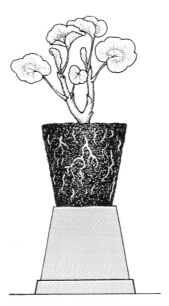

Figure 7.3 Drying out a plant that has been over-watered

71

Another way, if you notice the problem early enough, is to lift the plant with its soil-ball complete, out of the pot, then reverse the pot on the bench and stand the soil-ball upon it. In this way it is free of the water-retaining influence of the pot walls so that it can dry out much faster, and it is elevated above the level of other plants on the bench and will therefore enjoy better air circulation. I cannot say that this method always works, it depends how soon you take action, but I have been able to save quite a few friends' plants by its use.

Where a shortage of moisture in the compost is the cause of the plant's sickly appearance, the symptoms will be rather different. The leaves will be smaller than usual and in extreme cases may have a ring of dried tissue around the edges which will gradually spread inwards until the entire leaf is crisp and dry, and a golden brown in colour. If the plant is growing in a damp atmosphere (but its roots are dry) the dried foliage may begin to decay, and in this case the colour will be a rather dirty grey and it will lose its crispness. The stipules will be the first to dry off long before the leaves show any signs of distress, and any flowerbuds that develop will turn brown and crisp before they open. In fact the stipules are a very good indicator of watering efficiency for they act as a guide and enable you to correct your methods before the plant suffers seriously from faulty watering. If the stipules are green and lush right up the plant from bottom to top it is almost certainly being over-watered; if they are crisp and brown it is lacking in water; the ideal condition would seem to be when those stipules towards the top of the stem are green, gradually getting drier and crisper as they progress downwards, until finally those at the bottom are just dry enough to be detached easily from the stem without effort.

As soon as you notice the stipules half-way up the stems beginning to dry off, slightly increase the watering and you will have no further trouble. If the drought condition has progressed and the foliage is affected several other changes will have taken place in the plant and full recovery will only be achieved after prolonged and careful treatment — any attempt to rush things may result in the loss of the plant.

First, all feeding must stop and only plain rainwater be given until signs of recovery are well advanced. Whatever quantity of water the plant is receiving, begin by doubling it and continue watering at that rate for two weeks. Increase again by half and continue for a further two weeks. During the progress of this treatment the plant should be lightly shaded to reduce transpiration or further problems will arise. By now there should be signs of new growth appearing at the top of the main stem, and if this is so continue watering at the same rate until two new leaves are fully developed. If no signs of new growth are visible again increase the water, this time by 25 per cent and wait for a further two weeks, after which the plant will either be showing signs of recovery — or be dead. Once you have two fully opened healthy leaves you can restart the feeding programme and the plant will quickly return to normal, but feeding too early can kill it, so if in doubt wait a little longer.

One of the side effects of a plant becoming too dry is that the tissues harden and lose much of their natural suppleness. If the roots are then flooded with water it surges up the stem, the cells are unable to expand rapidly enough to accept the water and burst, resulting in groups of tiny unsightly scars on the undersides of the foliage, a condition loosely termed 'cell-burst'. It is very prevalent in Ivyleaf Geraniums but can also be seen occasionally on Miniature, Dwarf and Bedding Geraniums. It is not a disease or a virus and cannot be transmitted to other plants, it is simply a sign of faulty watering methods. Leaves affected can never recover but may be left on the plant without danger until their useful life is over.

It is not easy for an amateur to maintain the correct soil-moisture level without the aid of a soil moisture meter, and since these are quite expensive most of us have to wait for a birthday or Christmas before hints can be dropped in the right quarter with any hope of success. A cheaper form of soil-moisture tester has recently been marketed in the form of a pack of little printed cardboard slips about an inch (25mm) or so long with a pointed end. The instructions claim that when inserted into the soil of a pot to a depth of about ½in (12mm) the colour will indicate whether or not the plant needs watering — green means it is damp enough, yellow water is needed.

I cannot vouch for other plants but it is certainly of little use on Geraniums. The penetration of the soil is so slight that only the top ½in (12mm) registers — so the indication can be that water is required when the main soil-ball is saturated but the top is dry, a condition which applies quite often. On the other hand, when a plant is bone dry, a small application of water, insufficient for the plant to derive more than passing benefit from it, will be more than enough to change the colour of the indicator to bright green to inform the gardener that the plant needs no further water. Unless a soil-moisture meter (whatever type or make) is fitted with a probe to enable a reading to be taken from a point at the centre of the root-ball it is quite useless in my opinion and a complete waste of money when dealing with any member of the Pelargonium family.

When the moisture content is correct the compost will be reasonably compacted but will contain a considerable proportion of minute air pockets necessary for the proper functioning of the plant's chemistry, and it is because these air pockets are so important that you may hear it said that Geraniums should be allowed to dry out thoroughly before further water is given. The other reason is that over the years nurserymen have come to realise that it is quite useless telling most members of the gardening public to avoid over-watering, for almost every individual is confident that this is one crime of which he or she is entirely innocent, and the fact that all their plants died last year is due entirely to the bad stock which was supplied. In desperation he says 'let them thoroughly dry out between waterings', confident that not one in a thousand will follow his advice, but hoping that they may at least be persuaded thereby to reduce the watering just a little. The Americans have an expression 'greenhouse dry' which is used to describe the point at which pot plants have dried out sufficiently to warrant further watering, but unfortunately the phrase has never been defined so we are no better off. After a few years' experience you will probably be able to assess the plant's watering requirements by weight, for a wet compost is heavier than a dry one; meanwhile one of the simplest aids in the greenhosue for a beginner is a pair of scales which should enable him to remove at least some of the guesswork.

8 Pests and diseases

Aphids

Miniature and Dwarf Geraniums, together with the larger varieties, suffer from very few pests and diseases if they are grown under reasonable conditions. Whether in garden or greenhouse the chief pest in Britain is the aphid (greenfly) which pierces the outer skin of the young shoots and sucks the sap, and in so doing transfers viruses and pathogens from plant to plant. Several species of aphid can live on Geraniums but fortunately they are all very slow moving and easy to deal with; however, as with most problems, prevention is better than cure.

Aphids are soft-bodied insects usually found in groups or clusters initially on the growing tips, but as they multiply at a prodigious rate, they can rapidly expand their feeding area until almost every part of the plant is covered by a seething mass of greenfly. Both adults and nymphs take the sap from the plant often causing the leaves to curl, and at the same time excrete a type of honeydew on which grows a black, sooty fungus.

In the past the cheapest and one of the most effective aphid eradicators was nicotine, applied either as a liquid spray or as a smoke; it had the added advantage of being a natural plant food. Unfortunately its use is now banned since it has been found to be a source of cancer in humans, consistent with other nicotine-based products.

Many alternative 'smokes' are now marketed but I have yet to find one as efficient as nicotine, and it is essential to get complete and rapid control if damage is to be avoided. One of the modern systemic insecticides would appear to be the best alternative, applied early in the season either as a fine spray or drench. The chemical is taken up by the plant through the roots or absorbed into the system through the leaves (or both) and from then on each insect gets a dose of poison with every bite taken. The treatment needs to be repeated every five days for the first month after which it can be reduced to once a fortnight.

If a spray is used the temperature should be not less than 65°F (18°C) when spraying commences, the plant must be thoroughly coated with spray, every leaf treated on both surfaces until the liquid runs off and into the soil. Try to avoid spraying in the evening or the plants will remain damp all night and this will encourage botrytis.

Nature's own greenfly controller is the ladybird (ladybug in the USA), the small round carnivorous beetles, often brightly coloured and spotted, which devour large quantities of aphids. It is said that an adult ladybird can consume eight times its own weight of aphids in a day, and many gardeners collect them in matchboxes from the hedgerows and transfer them to their own plants with excellent results. Unfortunately even this degree of gluttony cannot normally cope with the aphids' rate of reproduction; the shelter provided by greenhouses and conservatories allows greenfly to reproduce steadily throughout the winter months, and by the time the ladybirds emerge from hibernation they are faced with a near-impossible task.

When applying systemics, read the label on the bottle and follow the instructions carefully. Most systemics will kill not only aphids but all sucking and biting insects including whiteflies and a variety of thrips. They are completely harmless to bees, wasps, hoverflies and ladybirds, and unfortunately they appear to have no effect upon caterpillars.

Although the systemic insecticides do not kill ladybirds it is possible that they could be affected by eating a poisoned aphid, although I have had no confirmation of this to date, and certainly no ladybird will ever consume a dead aphid. But for those who are concerned about harming ladybirds the old method of washing aphids off the plants with a powerful jet of water into which enough soapsuds has been added to give a good lather can be quite effective if carefully applied. (Don't take the easy way out and use a washing-up liquid — these vary as to the chemical content and some can scorch the foliage.) After spraying with the soapy solution leave for about 20 minutes then spray again with clean water and the aphids will drop off the plant and, being very slow moving, many will starve before they can regain the feeding grounds above, and in this way the numbers can be controlled at a level at which the natural predators (ladybirds) have a better chance of coping. It is advisable to dry the plant after spraying with an electric fan heater or hair dryer, but the plant should never be nearer than 6ft (1.8m) away from the heat source and must be rotated at intervals to obtain even drying and to prevent scorching of the foliage.

Ants

Ants can be a nuisance. They are quite harmless to Geraniums in themselves but tend aphids in herds in order to 'milk' them of the 'honeydew' fluid they secrete. Not only will they protect the herd as far as they are able, but they are quite capable of transferring the aphids from plant to plant or from one part of a plant to another where the shoots are more lush in the way that a farmer selects the best meadow or part of a meadow for his cattle, moving them on as the sward is depleted.

The best control for ants was DDT until its use was made illegal, now we have to be content with the branded 'Ant Powders' to be found on the shelves of nurseries and garden centres. It is almost impossible to eradicate ants from the garden, but in the greenhouse a measure of control can be achieved by sprinkling ant powder liberally around the plants on the benches. By far the best control is to destroy the aphids, the ants then have no interest in the plants.

Whitefly

The greenhouse whitefly (*Trialeurodes vaporariorum*) is controlled by smokes and systemic insecticides as mentioned above and even the raw beginner will have no difficulty in identifying this pest. Similar to a very small moth, less than ⅛in (3mm) long, they attack the plants in hordes, taking off in a cloud of white whenever the plant is disturbed. Early treatment is essential or the plants will be ruined by the sooty deposits which are almost impossible to remove. Ladybirds are ineffective against whitefly and smokes appear to give only limited control. A systemic insecticide is the only worthwhile control and the cheapest over the season. Sprays or aerosols using a malathion-based formula can kill or severely damage Geraniums.

Slugs and Snails

If your plants are growing on sand benches you may have trouble with slugs, and occasionally snails will travel up the glass and move along the benches to the plants. Slug and snail damage usually occurs first at or just above soil level but they will soon devastate the foliage if not treated early. Both are night feeders and tend to rest during the day in a concealed hiding place.

Snails can often be found on the underside of large leaves or on the pots, and can be easily picked off. Slugs, however, will retire into the soil or under the pot where it is difficult to find them during daytime. If you care to take a torch into the greenhouse at midnight you can enjoy an exciting hour or two hunting the creatures, but for those of us who prefer more scientific measures a few small heaps of slug bait or slug pellets will account for most of the culprits within a day or two.

Before using any type of slug bait make quite certain it is placed beyond the reach of children and domestic animals, and if set in the garden it should also be protected against rain. A safer alternative is to place a dish of beer close to the plants (you may need several on a long bench) and this will attract slugs from 2–3ft (60–90cm) around. Whether they are poisoned by the beer or simply inebriated and fall into the liquid in a drunken stupor has yet to be ascertained, but they are certainly killed. The same system can be used in the garden but in this case I prefer to use jam jars to hold the beer, sinking them into the soil so that the rim is just above soil-level. In both cases the beer needs renewing at least once a week if the traps are to remain effective. One correspondent informs me that the blackbirds in his Devonshire garden have discovered these traps and can be seen fishing for beer-marinated slugs every morning.

Caterpillars

Caterpillar damage is not restricted to night-time and many species carry on eating throughout the day. Methods of eating vary according to the species, some begin at the edge of the leaf and continue all round in ever decreasing circles, others make holes in the leaf between the ribs, whilst others just keep eating with no apparent consistent pattern. Their destructive capacity is enormous — I have seen a sycamore tree stripped within three days by a plague of caterpillars moving steadily from branch to branch and leaving only the bare skeletons of leaves in their wake, so you can imagine the effect upon a Geranium which is host to two or three of these pests.

In the garden the birds (those still sober) will take most of them, the rest can usually be controlled by dusting with a proprietary chemical product such as derris, but in the greenhouse the only really effective control is by hand picking them off the plant before despatching them to join their ancestors. Caterpillars develop from eggs laid by butterflies and moths, so if you can keep your greenhouse free from these you will not be bothered by their progeny. This can be achieved fairly simply by netting the ventilators and doors with a fine curtain net; the butterflies and moths will be unable to pass through the net, therefore no eggs on plants and no caterpillars to hatch.

Mice

Mice can wreck the entire contents of a greenhouse almost overnight and are particularly fond of Geraniums; it is the larger plants that usually come in for their concentrated attention and it is only after these have been thoroughly investigated that the Miniatures and Dwarfs are attacked. Damage from mice is easily identified; the stems are gnawed through just above soil level and the plant is felled as a lumberjack fells a tree. In order to survive, all rodents must wear down their teeth on hard wood (or something similar) and for this reason it is always the older woody stems that are attacked — very annoying because these are the established plants, usually in their second or third year and at the peak of their productivity.

For some reason a mouse (or possibly a family of mice) often appear to become addicted to one particular variety of Geranium and will return to it night after night until it is completely wiped out, ignoring adjacent varieties. Traps baited with milk chocolate set close to the area attacked will gradually eliminate the pest but you are unlikely to destroy every one and those surviving may well transfer their attentions elsewhere in the greenhouse.

In any case the trapping of these small animals is to me utterly repulsive, so often the trap does not kill outright and the creature is left to die a slow and painful death. In the past it was probably preferable to baiting with poisons which took several hours or sometimes days to kill, but now we have very fast-acting poisons, so fast in fact that a mouse taking a grain of corn treated with the poison dies within seconds, and usually has no time to move from the spot where he took the grain. Naturally these poisons are lethal not only to mice and rats but also to domestic pets, they are also toxic to humans, and for this reason they are not obtainable by the general public and are not on sale in the shops. If you are plagued by rodents you must contact your local council offices and ask the Public Health Department to send round a Rodent Investigator and Elimination Operative, who will arrive suitably attired in protective clothing and place little trays of the treated grains in strategic positions in the greenhouse. There was no charge for this service the last time I used it, but times change and today you may have to pay something.

Figure 8.1 Mice often gnaw through the main stem

On one occasion I thought our cat would solve the problem, so we put his basket in the greenhouse among the plants on the bench, made him comfortable for the night and left him to it. Whether he and the mice came to an arrangement or he was just overfed and too lazy to hunt there is no way of knowing, but in the morning I found Thomas fast asleep in his basket surrounded by fallen plants, and not a dead or injured mouse in sight.

During the day one of the lady assistants let out a scream and pointed to the back of one of the long benches where she had seen a mouse lurking. Puss was sent for and placed on the bench where the mouse was last seen. At first he seemed a bit puzzled, glanced around for a minute, then sat down and began washing. We waited with baited breath. He had finished both front paws and raised the near-side rear into licking position when, with tongue fully extended, he froze. The mouse was quietly moving down the back of the bench between the plants oblivious to the danger he was approaching. Puss did not move, he still had one leg cocked in the position necessary for soaping. He waited until the mouse was about three feet past him, then, regretfully postponing his ablutions, he retracted his extended leg and carefully and silently assembled his body into the hunting position. All the time his gaze had not left the mouse which continued slowly on its way, and now the cat lowered himself so that his face was down on the bench as he attempted to slide forward to achieve a better position for the pounce.

Unfortunately as he did so he brushed against a plant, and the noise of it falling alerted the mouse, who immediately scuttled off down the bench with puss in hot pursuit. With no need for further concealment or caution the cat's only thought was to catch the mouse, and the plants suffered in consequence. Within seconds plants were flying in all directions as the cat-and-mouse game continued up and down the bench until the mouse finally escaped down a hole in the floor, over which Thomas kept guard for the next two days but in

79

vain. Most of the plants were undamaged, but many of them had to be re-potted and a few were broken, but the chaos in the greenhouse for those few minutes was a talking point among the staff for weeks afterwards. The cat was rushing up and down trying to catch the mouse, three men were attempting to catch the cat, and four girls were screaming their heads off whilst trying to be first through the door, their skirts tightly clasped around their knees.

The moral of this true story is keep your cat out of the greenhouse if you value your plants — not only will it chase mice, but almost anything that moves including spiders and flies.

Frogs and Toads

Frogs and toads are harmless to plants and a toad in the greenhouse can be of enormous benefit if it can be persuaded to stay, for they feed upon slugs and a variety of small creatures which can be harmful to plants. You are unlikely to see one if you have slatted benches or those made of metal, but they are often attracted to sand benches and will burrow into them during daylight hours coming out at night to search for food. They can be handled carefully, but if distressed will emit a foul-smelling fluid, not toxic to humans, but distinctly unpleasant. Sometimes they make quite unusual pets.

Common and Pigmy Shrews

Shrews are occasional visitors and are very beneficial. Similar in appearance to a mouse and about the same size but with a darker coat and longer nose, they are not easily confused because they are normally quite indifferent to human presence. In order to survive they need to eat several times their own weight of food every day, so almost nothing can divert them from the important business of eating. They will take anything and everything from slugs, snails, worms, ants, woodlice and hairy caterpillars to small fledglings which have fallen from the nest; they will even eat each other if the opportunity occurs. Fortunately they are not vegetarians so plants are quite safe.

Figure 8.2 Pygmy and common shrews are very beneficial

It is unwise to handle a shrew without strong gloves. They are very attractive little creatures, not unlike a tiny mole with an elongated nose, and easily caught, but they will not stop eating and will immediately transfer their attention to your hand when you will discover that they are fitted with an excellent set of dentures custom-made for the purpose. A bite is not dangerous but it can be quite painful and very disconcerting when the shrew shows no sign of disengagement. If you wish to move the creature to another position in the greenhouse (perhaps where there are some slugs) it is best to scoop it into a flowerpot for transfer, but do release it immediately — remember it cannot survive long without food.

Sciarid Flies (Peat Flies or, in the USA, Fungus Gnats)

These are tiny black flies similar and related to the fruit fly and mushroom fly, and either emanate from or are attracted to damp peat in which they lay their eggs. In a greenhouse the eggs hatch within a few days into minuscule maggots which feed on the roots at the base of a cutting or mature plant.

When a plant which seemed perfectly healthy suddenly begins to look sickly and sheds its leaves from the base upwards, pull it out of the compost and examine the base of the stem with a magnifying glass. At first you will see only roots but after watching quietly for about 30 seconds some of the tiny white 'roots' will begin to move — these are the maggots of the sciarid fly. In advanced infestation the inside of the stem from the base upwards can be an oozing mass of grubs with the main stem tissue completely eaten away. Control at the maggot stage is almost impossible and infected plants should be immediately burned. Prevention consists of eliminating the flies from the greenhouse by the use of smokes as for whiteflies but at intervals of three days for five applications or until no further flies are seen. Covering the compost in the pots with a layer of grit will prevent the flies laying their eggs therein, but once the eggs have been laid in the peat the plant is doomed.

Viruses

Miniature Geraniums suffer very little from diseases, and if they are purchased from a reputable specialist nursery the risk of disease is usually negligible. A great deal of American and European stock develops a virus after a few months in Britain and it is essential to purchase plants from a British nursery which quarantines its imports for at least six months before using them for propagating, or one which obtains its stock only from reliable British raisers. Plants or cuttings must never be brought into Britain from abroad unless accompanied by a current Certificate of Health issued by the country of origin. Without this certificate any import of plants is illegal and could result in the infecting and possible loss of the entire contents of the importer's greenhouse. Seed can be imported without restriction or risk to stock.

Viruses come in a range of effects and it must not be assumed that every variation of the foliage is due to a virus. Geranium viruses usually appear as varied patterns of yellowing on the leaves — spots, rings or pale green or yellow veins. They do not always affect every leaf on the plant and can sometimes disappear as the plant matures. Symptoms can also appear suddenly on a mature plant previously thought to be quite clean, so you will see that they are not easy to diagnose accurately without scientific apparatus and knowledge.

Net Virus

Net Virus (otherwise known as Yellow-net Vein) produces a yellowing of the veins of the foliage and persists all the year. It is usually most noticeable on the younger leaves and tends to fade as the leaves mature. Non-malignant, it is often encouraged particularly in Ivyleaf varieties such as 'White Mesh' and 'Crocodile'. The virus is almost impossible to transmit by any means other than grafting. There is no cure.

Leaf-curl Virus

Crinkle or Leaf-curl Virus shows as yellowing spots which appear mainly during the winter months on the small leaves at the growing tips. The spots turn brown as the leaves expand causing considerable distortion and curling. There is no cure; infected plants should be burned.

Tobacco/Tomato Ringspot Virus

Tobacco and Tomato Ringspot viruses are thought to be related. They appear as necrotic spot lesions on the leaves of young plants but the symptoms usually disappear as the plant matures and the virus descends to the roots. Very difficult to identify, especially as infected plants appear to develop with no visible disability once the initial spots have gone. Because Geraniums can host these viruses they should never be grown in the same house as either tomato or tobacco plants, in fact all members of the Solanum family must be suspect.

All plants showing symptoms of virus infection should be destroyed, and they must never be used for propagating purposes.

Bacterial Blight

Perhaps the most serious disease affecting Geraniums is a vascular wilt called Bacterial Stem Rot or Bacterial Blight; its scientific name is *Xanthomonas pelargonii*. When a plant is infected the leaves wilt from the centre and droop, they may fall off the plant immediately or hang down for a week or more before dropping. Before these symptoms become visible the bacteria will have infected the main stem from within and this will now develop into the condition commonly known as stem rot. The condition progresses until the rot spreads right up the stems and only the extreme tips still bear leaves. Occasionally the plant will throw what appears to be a clean shoot besides the dying main stem. This may survive and flower for several weeks or even months but eventually it will die. Cuttings taken from an infected plant, although apparently sound, will not root but will develop stem rot from the base upwards. It is thought that the bacteria reproduce faster under warm conditions but at 65°F (18°C) and over the symptoms are suppressed; it is said that it can be controlled to some extent by the application of sodium nitrate. Apparently the nitrogen does not eliminate the pathogen but increases the plant's resistance to enable it to survive; this view is opposed by others who claim that an excess of nitrogen encourages the spread of the bacteria. Overhead watering will assist the spread of Bacterial Blight as will setting cuttings several to a pot or directly into a propagating bed, but there is no doubt that the most usual vector is the whitefly. There is no cure, infected plants must be burned.

Verticillium Wilt

Verticillium Wilt (*Verticillium albo-atrum*) is a soil-borne fungus which can survive in soil and other composts for long periods until a suitable host appears. It can be controlled only by correct sterilisation of the medium so it is important to purchase only those products which are guaranteed to have been subjected to a genuine and approved process of sterilisation. The symptoms of Verticillium Wilt are so similar to those of Bacterial Blight that it is almost impossible to distinguish them without laboratory assistance, and plants infected with either should be immediately removed from the greenhouse and burned.

Culture-indexing

Some years ago the University of California had considerable success with culture-indexing for the control of viruses in Geraniums. It is not possible to describe in detail the complicated laboratory procedures here, but briefly, a thin slice of stem tissue is tested under the microscope for the presence of either Bacterial Blight or Verticillium Wilt, those cuttings showing a positive reaction are discarded whilst the negative ones are rooted and used as stock plants. By this method clean stock was produced in the laboratory and used for propagating, and the method was widely adopted by wholesale growers in the USA. Unfortunately the details were not fully implemented by some growers who wrongly assumed that once they had purchased culture-indexed stock they would be free from virus for ever. In fact culture-indexed plants lose some of their natural resistance to infection, and can very quickly become re-infected if raised on a 'dirty' nursery. Only first generation culture-indexed cuttings can be guaranteed clean and then only for their first season.

Pythium (Blackleg)

Blackleg, the disease of Geranium cuttings, is caused by the Pythium fungus. Although it can attack mature plants it is seen most frequently in propagating beds where cuttings are loose-rooted or in pots with the cuttings set five or more to a pot. The fungus attacks the base of the cutting travelling rapidly up the stem and causes total collapse very quickly — often within a week or ten days of the initial infection. Occasionally a cutting will be attacked after several roots have developed, but in most cases it is destroyed whilst still unrooted. Pythium is seldom seen among cuttings individually rooted in small pots or Jiffy-7s, but in a propagating bed it can destroy 100 per cent of the contents if left to rampage for a week or more.

Once infected a plant or cutting is incurable and should be burned. An infected propagating bed should be cleared and thoroughly disinfected with diluted Jeyes Fluid before being re-used. Bottom heat reduces the spread of the fungus; excessive watering promotes it.

Oedema

Oedema is a condition brought about by faulty culture; it is not a disease or the result of parasitic activity. The undersides of the leaves develop small pimply blisters which turn brown as they mature and enlarge into corky scabs (ivyleaf varieties are particularly susceptible). Oedema is the result of the plant being allowed to get too dry so that the epidermis hardens; when the plant is flooded with water the leaf-cells are unable to expand to accommodate the extra liquid and burst, leaving unsightly scars. Once scarred the leaves will remain marked for life, but new shoots will be unaffected and remain so unless subjected to the same faulty treatment.

Control is obtained by careful watering, spacing plants on the benches to permit plenty of air movement between them, and good ventilation.

Botrytis

Botrytis is caused by the fungus *Botrytis cinerea* which lives on dead and dying tissue. It can attack flowers, foliage and stems of both old and young plants, especially if damaged or in a damp environment with restricted ventilation. Crowded, damp flowerheads are an ideal breeding ground for the fungus, or a fallen petal coming to rest on a leaf, two leaves in close contact, or even a small puddle left on a leaf after watering. Botrytis is distributed by spores carried through the atmosphere by air currents and once it becomes established in a greenhouse it is very difficult to eradicate. Open wounds where leaves have been detached, the severed ends of shoots after cuttings have been taken, even the places on the main stem of the plant from which flower stems have been detached are all liable to infection from the spores.

Every greenhouse has its complement of Botrytis spores and constant vigilance is required if it is to be controlled. Good ventilation coupled with adequate spacing of the plants is the first requirement, followed by the immediate removal of all rotting or damaged material — flowerheads, foliage, etc. — from benches and floors. Water must be kept off the foliage and flowerheads, and all dead and dying leaves removed from the plants before they can begin to rot. Every plant should be inspected on a weekly basis. After this hygiene routine has been carefully followed all the plants should be given a light dusting with a fungicide, repeated at fortnightly intervals.

Geranium Rust

Geranium rust (*Puccinia pelargonii-zonalis*) was unknown in Britain until the early 1960s since when a great deal of nonsense has been written and spoken about it — quite recently I was infuriated to see one of the presenters on south-west television display an infected leaf to viewers with the advice 'It is not harmful, just pick it off and the plant will be OK', implying that no further effort is needed for total control. Unfortunately such is not the case.

In the early days, even the Ministry of Agriculture was guilty of misguided statements. One pamphlet stated that Geranium Rust only affected the area south of a line drawn from Bristol to the Wash, and another that it came to Britain first in 1965 being blown across the channel from France on the salt-laden winds. Our cousins in the USA were not much better informed, one American professor claimed that rust spores need to over-winter on English Oak in order to survive, a theory I was easily able to disprove much to his annoyance. Actually the overwintering of Geranium Rust involves the production of a different type of spore, a subject rather too complicated for inclusion in this non-technical volume.

I first saw rust on a consignment of cuttings from Australia back in 1963, and again in one of the Local Authorities' Parks Departments in 1964, and I am sure others will have seen it even earlier. By 1966 when I first went to California the nurseries there were so badly infected that they were desperately changing from open-field culture to growing in vast greenhouses where effective control was easier to achieve. The situation rapidly deteriorated to the extent that the US Government finally quarantined all Geranium nurseries until they could prove they were 'clean'. Today, nearly all Geranium-growing in California is under glass or plastic except in parts of the Los Angeles area where atmospheric pollution is so dense that the spores cannot survive.

Most reputable specialist growers in Britain quarantine all imported stock for at least six months before releasing it to the public or using it for propagating, and it was this policy which prevented the rapid spread of rust in Britain in 1963. All infected plants were burned and the remainder isolated for a further year before being released. Whether the major outbreak on the south coast in 1966 was caused through airborne spores from the Continent or, as I suspect, through travellers bringing infected material back with them from holidays abroad we shall never know, but the facts are that infection on a massive scale was reported from Kent, Sussex and Hampshire, and within a very short time it had spread nearly 100 miles (160km) up the country.

In common with most other responsible Geranium growers at that time I was most concerned to prevent an outbreak in my own nursery and made enquiries as to the recommended control measures to be taken. I soon discovered that the trade was in a state of utter confusion — every cure suggested by one nurseryman would be immediately condemned as useless by the next, and the Ministry publications simply added to the confusion, among other errors referring to the Irenes as Regals.

Business commitments obliged me to visit other countries on average three or four times a year, so I began investigations abroad in areas where rust had been known for several years longer than in Britain. In all I have studied the problem in France, Luxembourg, Belgium, Portugal, Spain, the Balearic Islands, California, Mexico and Australia, and have been able to discuss methods with growers on the spot and to compare the successes they have claimed.

Geranium Rust is fairly widespread in Europe and until the mid-1960s was largely ignored by officialdom. When eventually it was recognised and action instituted the authorities were panicked into costly and largely ineffective programmes based upon completely false premises. The system used in Belgium will serve to illustrate the point particularly since this method was (and may still be) widely followed in other European countries.

Whether infected or not, every nurseryman in Belgium is required by law to take his entire stock of Geraniums to the State Laboratory in his district where they will be subjected to treatment by immersion in hot water for a period of several hours, the length of time depending upon the temperature of the water but usually being between 48 and 96 hours. The treated plants are then collected and returned to the nursery from whence they came, and a certificate of health is issued by the Ministry Inspector which permits the nurseryman to continue in business for another year.

In theory this might seem to be an excellent system, but in practice it is little more than a farce. In experiments conducted for me at Oxford University it was found that very few plants survived this treatment, and those that did had their natural resistance to the disease reduced to the extent that they were immediately re-infected upon exposure to rust spores.

Seldom, in my experience, is it possible for a commercial Geranium nursery to transport its entire stock to the laboratory in one load, so in practice the first infected load is delivered then the lorry goes about its normal business for two to four days carrying infection wherever it goes. It then collects the sterilised plants for replacing in the nursery, which is teeming with infected plants awaiting treatment, where the sterilised plants are immediately re-infected. The system does nothing to reduce the rust problem; in fact, it is a certain way of perpetuating it. I know of not one Belgian nursery that has been cleared of Geranium Rust by this method since its institution but a great number of nurserymen have lost a lot of money through plants failing to survive the treatment, and several have now abandoned the production of Geraniums entirely.

It was during a visit to southern Spain in 1967 that I first realised just how efficient a parasite it is, for rust is not a killer. In the area covering a hundred-mile (160-km) radius from Malaga it seems that every individual Geranium is saturated with rust, but although yellowed and unsightly the plants continue to survive year after year entirely without treatment. It is true that the lower leaves fall off but that is to be expected in a dry climate such as this; none the less the plants continue to produce clean growing points and throw the normal amount of flowers consistent with the inferior varieties indigenous to the area. This part of Spain has one of the lowest rainfalls in Europe and the wet season is usually confined to little more than a month of the year, thus disposing of the theory that Geranium Rust cannot survive for more than eight days without water — in the Malaga area it often manages quite successfully for eight months or more of absolute drought.

Another theory which received the blessing of the British Pelargonium & Geranium Society, when first advanced, is that certain varieties are immune,

1. 'Karen'

2. 'Red Pearl'

3. 'Mont Blanc'

4. 'Mimi'

5. 'Bridesmaid'

6. 'Golden Chalice'

7. 'Sunbeam'

8. 'Monica Bennet'

9. 'Spitfire Cactus'

10. 'Melissa'

11. 'Cheiko'

12. 'Bird Dancer'

13. The first single yellow, raised by Sam Peat

14. 'Sunstar'

15. 'Beacon Hill'

16. 'Friary Wood'

17. 'Algenon'

18. 'Freak of Nature'

19. 'Golden Ears'

20. Most Deacons can be regulated by the pot size — this is 'Deacon Bonanza' in an 18 inch (46 cms) container; 'Audrey' is 5ft 9ins (175 cms). (Photo: Sam Peat).

21. 'Falkland Hero'

22. 'Love Storey'

23. 'Formosum'

24. 'Frills'

in particular they quoted 'King of the Boars' and its progeny. 'The Boar' and 'The Prostrate Boar'. Now I have never grown 'King of the Boars' so I am not in a position to pass judgement upon its resistance to rust, but I do know of one nursery with infected stock of 'The Boar' and of two others carrying rusted stock of 'The Prostrate Boar', so yet another theory is disproved.

Miss Campbell of Brighton spent the later years of her life studying Geranium Rust and it was she who claimed to have spotted rust spores 'travelling up the sap of a plant' with the aid of a reading glass. This was not possible, of course, for rust is a fungus not a systemic disease and must be treated as such.

Before rust can be controlled its life cycle must be understood, and the following is a brief outline of that life cycle in non-scientific terms.

Rust spores are carried on air currents, on clothing and on infected plants, they are constantly in the air in infected areas and will rapidly contaminate all Geraniums within a wide radius of any infected plant. Most parts of the British Isles can support the spores, but in general the cleaner the air the heavier the infection. Rust is seldom seen in central London or cities such as Birmingham where the concentration of atmospheric pollution is at its worst.

When a rust spore settles on a leaf it immediately begins to grow a tiny shoot or leg with which to enter a stoma. Once into the stoma the spore begins to reproduce at a furious rate, distorting the epidermis (the skin covering the leaf-surface) until the blister is so packed with tiny spores that the retaining epidermis ruptures and the spores are released into the air to alight on another host. The stomata are the tiny tubes which are distributed over the underside of the leaf-surfaces to enable the plant to breathe and thereby feed upon the atmospheric gases.

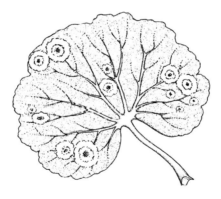

Figure 8.3 Small circles of orange spores on undersides of leaves indicate Geranium Rust

Spores of Geranium Rust are usually seen as a circle of bright orange dots but sometimes take on a more brown tinge. They are most visible on the underside of the foliage and are at their densest on the older leaves and

87

stipules, and it often seems to be the pale-green leaved varieties which suffer first. The ripe spores are discharged in the form of a fine dust very similar in appearance to snuff or finely ground ginger.

Control of Rust

It will be obvious from the foregoing that merely picking off infected leaves as they develop will only aggravate the problem and hasten the spread of the spores.

The first requirement for effective control must be regular inspection of the plants so that any infection is detected at the earliest possible moment. When a rusted plant is discovered, close all ventilators and doors to restrict air currents and avoid rapid movement which could increase the dispersal of the spores. Take a clear plastic bag several sizes larger than the plant and gently slide it down over the plant and pot until both are totally enclosed, close the bag around the pot without disturbing the plant and take it outside, well away from the greenhouse.

Now place the entire unit into a much larger clear plastic bag and, with your hand inside, secure the neck of this bag around your wrist with an elastic band so that it is reasonably airtight. You can now begin to strip the infected leaves off the plant, depositing them into the outer bag whilst still keeping the plant contained within the inner bag. No spores can escape into the atmosphere because the elastic band is sealing the neck of the larger bag around your wrist. When every visibly infected leaf has been removed, withdraw your hand holding the plant still in the inner bag, leaving all the rusted leaves in the outer bag which should then be sealed and burned.

The plant should next be dusted with a fungicide making certain that every part of the plant is coated including the surface of the soil and the pot. Repeat the dusting at weekly intervals for the next month, then if no further signs of rust have appeared it can be reduced to a monthly treatment.

Geranium Rust on plants growing in the open garden is almost impossible to control; no amount of spraying or dusting can prevent fresh spores being transported from other infected areas by air currents. The Californian growers spent millions of dollars trying to find a cure and finally had to abandon the project as quite hopeless. Some slight reduction of the problem is possible by burning all the infected plants at the end of the season without taking any cuttings from them, but this will not prevent next year's newly-purchased plants being subjected to the attentions of peripatetic spores.

The treatment suggested above for dealing with an individual infected plant, or even a few, in a greenhouse can hardly be applied when the entire house is contaminated. In this case it will be necessary to carry every plant out of the greenhouse to a position at least 40ft (12m) away (and by every plant I mean not only Geraniums but every plant of any type or species). The greenhouse should then be completely closed and thoroughly sprayed with a wettable sulphur-based fungicide. A fine spray producing a droplet no larger than 40 microns must be used, larger droplets have been found to be ineffective, and the greenhouse thoroughly saturated — glass, walls, benches and floors. Repeat the treatment after five days, keeping the greenhouse closed and choosing a time when the temperature is not below 65°F (18°C).

Figure 8.4 (a)-(f) Photographs of rust-infected leaf of 'Karen'; (g)-(l) photographs of a healthy leaf of 'Karen'. (All photographs taken by the Scanning Electron Microscope of the Department of Biology, Southampton University)

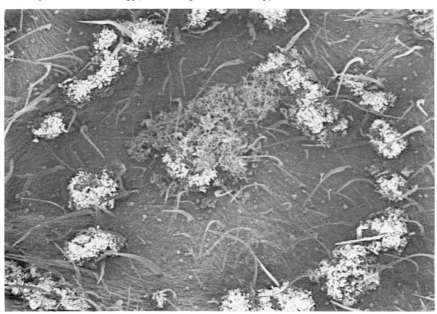

(a) Lower leaf surface. Rust spot and outer ring of infection. Magnification × 30

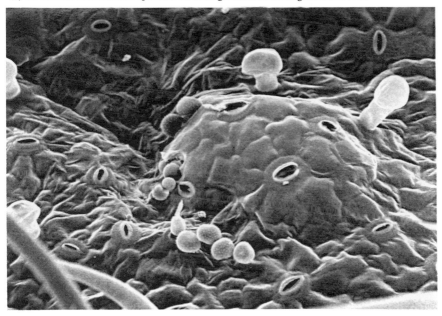

(b) Lower surface. Rust spot just at the moment of rupturing — the first few spores have escaped from the split in the epidermis. Magnification × 300

89

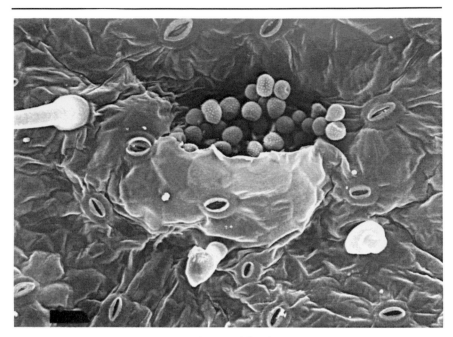

(c) Lower surface. The epidermis has now burst enabling the spores to escape.
Magnification × 300

(d) Lower surface. Ripe rust spot with the epidermis torn and spores about to be dispersed into the atmosphere. Magnification × 100

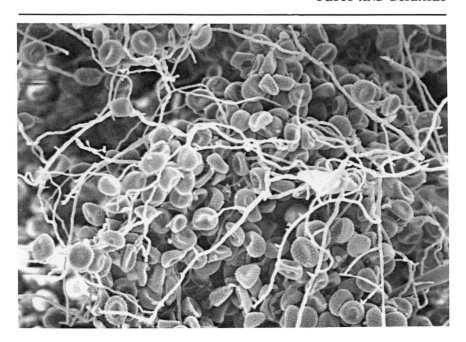

(e) Lower surface. Close-up of central rust spot showing spores and mycelium strands. Magnification × 300

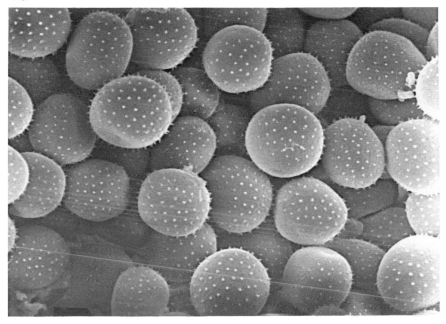

(f) Rust spores enlarged × 1000

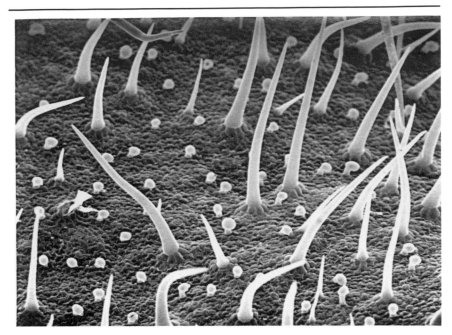

(g) Lower surface of leaf showing leaf hairs in different stages of growth. Magnification × 100 (Note: stomata are barely visible at this magnification)

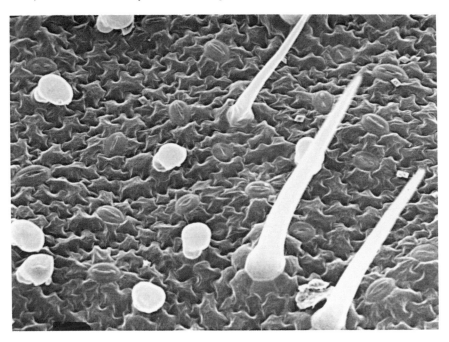

(h) Lower surface as above; stomata clearly visible — closed. Magnification × 300

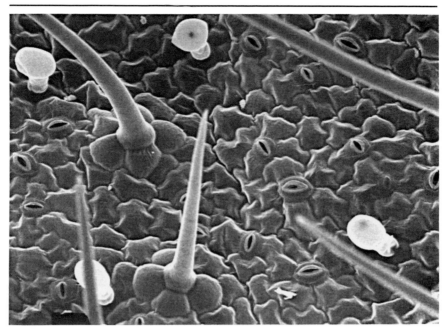

(i) Lower surface as (h); stomata open. Magnification × 300

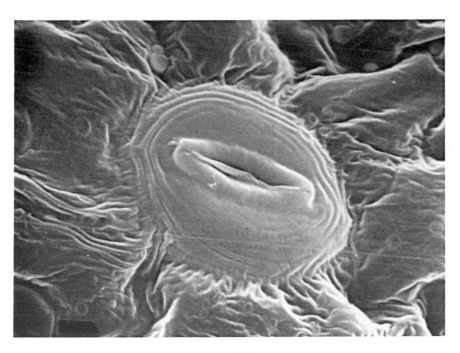

(j) Lower surface; stoma closed. Magnification × 3000

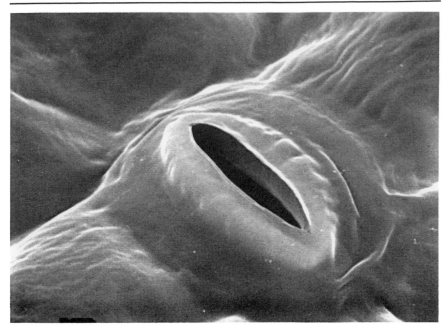

(k) Lower surface as (j); stoma open. Magnification × 3000

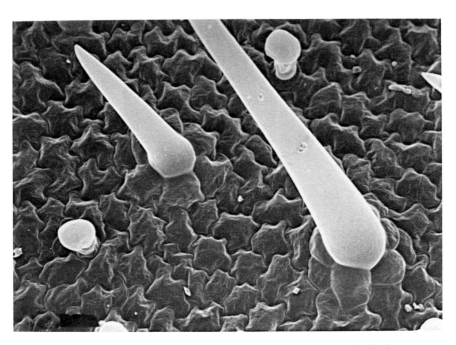

(l) Upper surface; no trace of stomata at this magnification (× 3000) on upper leaf surface

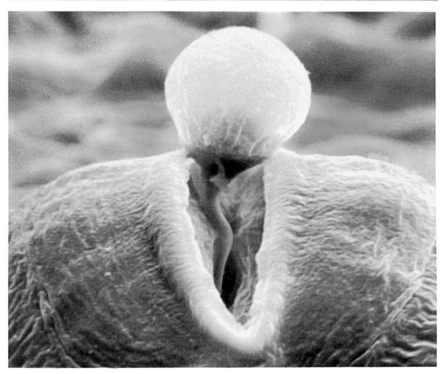

Figure 8.5 A rust spore settled over the aperture of a stoma, with a germ tube penetrating between the two guard cells to infect the internal tissues of the leaf. (Scanning electronmicrograph × 2800, reproduced by kind permission of the Department of Pure and Applied Biology, Imperial College of Science and Technology, London)

Before returning the plants to the greenhouse strip off all infected foliage and burn it, then thoroughly spray them with the same liquid fungicide before replacing them in the greenhouse, ensuring that every part of the plant is coated including the soil and pot. Spray until every plant is dripping with liquid from every surface. Spraying is best carried out early on a summer morning so that the greenhouse can be left open all day to allow the foliage to dry out thereby reducing the risk of botrytis.

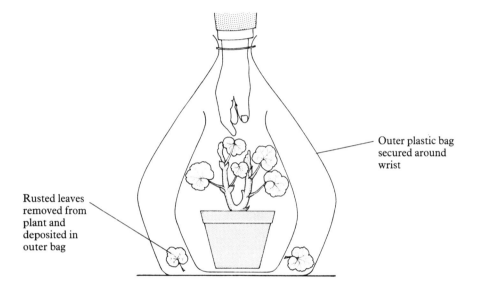

Outer plastic bag secured around wrist

Rusted leaves removed from plant and deposited in outer bag

Figure 8.6 The correct way to strip rusted leaves from an infected plant

Repeat the spraying at five-day intervals for three applications after which a dry powdering with the fungicide once a month should give total control. Liquid spraying is used to cover completely every surface of the plant, but when dusting the powder should never be aimed directly at the plant but projected overhead towards the apex of the greenhouse. It will then be carried by the air currents to the vulnerable surfaces on the plant in exactly the same way as are the rust spores, and any spore alighting upon a leaf surface will find it already coated with fungicide.

'*The Mystery of Pelargonium Rust*' was the title of an article I wrote for *Gardeners Chronicle* in 1972 which included much of the above information. I am grateful to the publishers for permission to reproduce parts of it in this chapter, amended and updated to include the results of extensive investigation and re-assessment over the years.

Aerial Roots

If a Miniature or Dwarf Geranium is grown on and potted into a large pot —

say 5 or 6in (13 or 15cm) — and kept under close conditions in a humid atmosphere without thinning or pruning it can become very dense and bushy. It sometimes happens that growths appear at several of the nodes towards the base of the stem, similar in appearance to galls with a prickly surface. If left, the 'prickles' will develop and extend downwards towards the soil. These are so-called aerial roots, caused by growing in overcrowded damp conditions, rather unsightly but quite harmless and not detrimental to the health of the plant in any way.

Figure 8.7 Aerial roots sometimes develop above soil level in damp conditions

Treatment consists of thinning out by removing all the central growth to permit free air movement and light penetration. The thinnings can be used as cutting material, and any pieces with aerial roots attached can be potted up immediately, burying the roots about 1½in (4cm) below the soil; it will be found that these cuttings will mature much sooner than normal cuttings being partially rooted already. After taking the centre out of the plant look for any inward-growing shoots and remove these also to prevent future congestion, then dust thoroughly against botrytis.

Bacterial Fasciation (Galls)

Aerial roots must not be confused with bacterial fasciation which is caused by the pathogen *Corynebacterium fascians* first described in 1936 by Drs M.S. Lacey and P.E. Tilford. It appears as a cluster of short, swollen or fleshy stems, almost white in colour and distorted, at or just below soil level. An examination of the plant will usually reveal several more galls attached to the roots, and these may develop until they appear above the soil in grotesque growths or clusters.

The plants are usually unaffected although normal growth may be retarded a little, and apart from the unsightly appearance the growths do not appear to have any damaging effect. None the less it is advisable to break off any growths as soon as they are discovered and burn them. The pathogen is soil-borne, so infected soil must not be re-used, and it is inadvisable to use infected plants for propagation. Remember that cuttings taken from an infected plant can contaminate the entire contents of a propagating bed.

9 Heating methods

Miniature and Dwarf Geraniums present few difficulties during the winter months for they will tolerate many forms of heating in almost every kind of environment and come to little harm, so long as a few basic rules are followed. A temperature of about 35–40°F (2–4°C) will be sufficient to ensure their survival although they will tolerate slightly lower temperatures for short periods if kept fairly dry. I have had plants survive one night when the temperature fell to 29°F (-2°C) in the greenhouse but normally they are killed by frost.

Frosted Geraniums (large or small) are immediately noticeable because the foliage becomes semi-transparent or translucent. If the damage is limited to the foliage, there is a possibility of saving the plant by rapid action, but if the stems also are frozen very little can be done. Thawing must be very gradual so place the plant in a cool shady place, in a temperature of 35°F (2°C) or so for a day. On the second day raise the temperature to 40°F (4°C) and hold it at that for a further three days. Examine carefully and remove all leaves showing signs of falling or rotting and return to the shade. If the tips of the shoots begin to go black cut them off just above the next clean node and dust the cuts with a fungicide. If after two weeks the plant is showing no signs of recovery, or if at any time before then the main stems begin to rot, you will have to cut right back to clean wood (treating the cuts as before). Do not water until new growth is apparent — and then only sparingly. If you have had to cut the plant right down almost to soil level it will not need water for several weeks or even months.

It is usually obvious within a fortnight whether a plant is going to recover, but where it has been cut right back it is always worth keeping it until the spring to see if new shoots will eventually arise from the base, but any application of water before the appearance of the new foliage will most certainly kill it.

Zonal and Regal Pelargoniums, and that includes Miniature and Dwarf Geraniums, have no natural dormant period and so can be flowered throughout the year if a temperature of 50°F (10°C) can be maintained and the quality of light is adequate. Best winter results are obtained from plants grown under greenhouse conditions where the glass is clean and free from algae. Supplementary lighting is not normally necessary except in those areas where the hours of winter daylight are very limited, in most parts of the

British Isles natural light is sufficient.

Plants will not do well if kept indoors in poor light for long periods, so if you require potted Geraniums to decorate the house exchange them at intervals of 7 to 10 days with a fresh supply from the greenhouse benches. Plants require light, heat and water if they are to develop properly; a shortage of any of these basic elements will affect the plant, but results can be equally catastrophic if they are not balanced. For instance, if heat and water are correct but light is poor the plant will strain towards the light and produce etiolated growth (commonly termed 'leggy'). Rhubarb growers use this inbalance deliberately to produce 'forced rhubarb' — the edible stems which are normally 9–10in (23–25cm) in length are stretched to more than twice their natural development by excluding all light.

The various methods of heating are examined in the following paragraphs and the final choice will largely depend upon the financial outlay the gardener is prepared to entertain, coupled with the amount of time and physical effort he is willing to expend upon maintaining the best environment for his plants. Many Miniature and Dwarf Geraniums are grown in apartments and houses warmed by a variety of central heating systems, and the even temperatures obtained are ideal for the plants so long as certain requirements are observed.

Houses, Apartments, Sun-rooms, etc.

Since the introduction to Britain of North Sea Gas in the 1960s, gas central heating has become more widespread, and many houses are now fitted with open gas fires. The old 'town gas' produced from coal is now a thing of the past as is its unpleasant and lethal odour. The new natural gas burns cleaner, has a less repulsive smell (in the opinion of some people), and in itself is not harmful to humans if inhaled in small quantities.

However, it is far from ideal when Geraniums (and many other plants) are grown for the fumes produced will kill the plants at fairly low concentrations (it is worth remembering that they will also kill humans if the concentration is high enough). A properly fitted gas fire will be connected to an efficient flue to conduct most of the fumes to the outside atmosphere thus reducing the concentration indoors to acceptable levels for the human occupants — but still too high for the good of the plants. The only real answer is ventilation — and lots of it.

If your heating is by an open gas fire, don't try to grow Geraniums indoors. Gas-fired central heating systems where the gas is used to heat circulating water at a central boiler and where the gas fumes cannot come into contact with the plants are perfectly satisfactory. For the same reasons it is foolish to attempt to grow Geraniums in a kitchen if you cook by a gas appliance or use a gas water heater, or in any situation where a portable gas appliance is in use, for bottled propane and methane has exactly the same effect upon plants as the North Sea product. It must also be remembered that the tiny particles of fat suspended in the atmosphere of a kitchen during frying can also be detrimental to plants.

For all Geraniums electricity is probably the form of heating nearest to perfection one is likely to encounter. It is clean, completely odourless, produces no fumes, and, if properly installed, perfectly safe. It does tend to be rather dry but this minor fault can be easily overcome by the occasional spraying of the foliage with clean water or standing the pot in a tray of damp gravel. Unfortunately, electricity is anything but cheap (in spite of what the advertisements would have us think) and as I write there is little to choose between the cost of heating by electricity or paraffin, but the former is more convenient and you don't have to pay for it in advance unless you are on a metered supply.

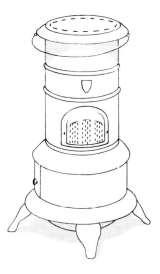

Figure 9.1 Guaranteed to kill all Geraniums and many other plants

Paraffin (kerosene) burned indoors in small portable stoves is one of the most dangerous forms of heating for Geraniums, and the fatality rate can be much higher with this system than with almost any other owing to the quantity of sulphur and carbon monoxide produced during the combustion processes. Paraffin also produces large quantities of water when burned, and in an enclosed room can result in the walls running with condensation within an hour or so of igniting. There is no problem where an oil-fired central heating system is used to heat circulating water and the fumes generated never come into the house, but if paraffin is actually burned in a room the Geraniums will suffer unless adequate attention is given to the ventilation, and the ventilation required is usually such as to reduce the temperature inside the room to a level where it becomes intolerable to both plants and humans.

The old type of oil stove with a circular wick mounted above a gallon or half-gallon (4.5 or 2.25 litres) tank enclosed in a vertical black cylinder with a little mica window through which one could see the yellow flame (which usually smoked ferociously), with a grille on the top for heating a kettle or pan, has long ago been superseded by more modern and efficient models. A blue flame has replaced the old smokey yellow, the unit is far more stable and less likely to be upset, and many now have devices fitted to extinguish the flame should the appliance fall over. None the less, the basic faults remain — sulphur, carbon monoxide and water are still produced in quantities unacceptable to Geraniums. It is true that by using only the best quality paraffin these by-products will be reduced considerably, but they will still be there in sufficient strength to affect the plants.

Open coal fires (or coke fires) present no problems as such, for all the gases produced during combustion are drawn up the chimney and a constant supply or draught of fresh air flows into the room to replace them. Without draughts the fire could not burn; however, rapid fluctuations in temperature can result from allowing the fire to die out during the night, or even through leaving a door open unintentionally, and a plant standing in a chilling draught will soon begin to show signs of distress.

It is quite common for Miniature and Dwarf Geraniums (and indeed many other plants) to be grown on a window ledge and this can present a few minor problems, for although maximum light is essential for flower development, in this position they are often subjected to severe chilling draughts, especially close to the glass and separated from the warmth of the room by the curtain. Even with modern double glazing the temperature close to the glass will be several degrees lower than that on the other side of the curtain. The obvious answer is to bring the plants into the room but if this is done they must not be sited too close to the source of heat, and during the night it is best to place them on a table in the centre of the room if this is possible. *Don't* put them on the floor where draughts are strongest.

A crowded room filled with people smoking and breathing can rapidly produce conditions hostile to plants. Tobacco smoke, whether cigarette, pipe or cigar, is not in itself harmful to Geraniums, in fact it can be slightly beneficial, for nicotine is a plant food and also kills aphids. As previously mentioned, until the mid-1980s it was widely used commercially for the control of aphids but has since been banned because it was said to cause cancer among operatives if incorrectly handled. I well remember being escorted around the Shrewsbury Parks Department's greenhouses by that great plantsman, Percy Thrower, accompanied by his foreman who was smoking a disgusting old pipe. At one point Percy drew the foreman's attention to a greenfly on the leaf of an Ivyleaf Geranium — the man took a deep pull on his pipe before blowing a lungful of smoke directly at the plant, and assured us that this was his normal way of dealing with such pests. Not only did the greenfly die instantly, Percy and I had to make a rapid exit from the greenhouse choking and gasping for breath.

Every possible opportunity should be taken to provide the plants with the full benefits to be gained from natural ventilation, and this can be simply achieved by standing them outside in the open air for a couple of hours each day, depending upon the outside temperature. By choosing a time in the early afternoon it will be found that in sheltered positions the temperature rarely falls below 35°F (2°C) even in mid-winter, but it goes without saying that the plants must not be put out on those few days when freezing conditions prevail.

Some flat and apartment dwellers have no balcony, but there is usually a windowsill which can be used for standing-out the plants, but great care must be taken for plants can easily be dislodged by a high wind, and quite apart from the minor consideration of killing or maiming a passing pedestrian below, the plant may be damaged beyond recovery and in any case will suffer a severe shock.

Greenhouses

The same basic principles apply to Miniature and Dwarf Geraniums grown in a greenhouse as to those grown indoors, but fewer problems will be encountered since they will be growing in an environment specially designed for plants, and are not being forced to exist in and adapt to conditions created primarily for humans.

So far as I am aware the old type of coal gas ('town gas') was never used in greenhouses, either amateur or professional, but some gardeners do now use the portable gas appliances which burn either liquid propane or methane. Whether used in the house or greenhouse they still have the same basic fault — fumes which are lethal to Geraniums (and many other plants).

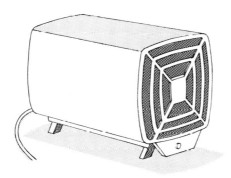

Figure 9.2 Electric fan heater for a greenhouse

There is no doubt that electricity scores on all points except cost, since it is (or can be) completely automatic, clean, and as near to 100 per cent efficient as it is possible to achieve. The most popular method of electric heating is through the use of a fan heater by which cold air is drawn across a heating element to warm it, then discharged into the greenhouse atmosphere. Fan heaters specially constructed for greenhouse use are invariably far superior to the normal domestic kind and, although basic in design, are more robust and able to withstand the damp atmosphere often encountered. I purchased a 'Humex' greenhouse heater over 20 years ago and it has been in regular use ever since — in winter for heating, in summer for extra ventilation. For maximum economy the greenhouse should be free from gaps or cracks in the glass so that it is reasonably air-tight and the captive air is constantly re-circulated through the fan. Air leaks can be very costly in current consumed, apart from interfering with the air flow.

103

This system has the added advantage of eliminating pockets of stagnant air so botrytis can be almost disregarded. Many fan heaters have built-in thermostats, but it is my opinion that accurate thermostatic control can be achieved only by the use of an independent thermostat located well away from the source of the heat and, if possible, so connected as to operate on the heating circuit only, leaving the fan running permanently. The extra cost involved in the continual operation of the fan against intermittent stops and starts is so slight that it can be disregarded, but the advantages of continual air circulation are manifold.

Electric heating by means of metal tubes of varying lengths and about 2in (5cm) in diameter containing a strip heating element is quite good, but not so efficient as fan heating and considerably more expensive to run and install. Furthermore, since it relies upon convection for distributing the heat generated there is comparatively little air movement, and a much higher temperature will have to be maintained if botrytis is to be avoided. Such tubular heaters must always be sited at ground level, for any plant at a lower level than the tube will derive no benefit from it whatsoever.

The system which uses an electric domestic immersion heater to heat the water in a tank or cylinder placed at one end of the greenhouse, from which pipes radiate to the far corners, seems to me to be more trouble than it is worth. The cost of the initial installation is likely to be very much more than the price of a good fan heater, current consumed (assuming that both are thermostatically controlled) will be almost identical, and the fan is far simpler to operate and maintain — and far more efficient. It has the added advantage of taking up less space in the greenhouse, and during the summer months it can be stored under a bench or in a nearby shed until required again.

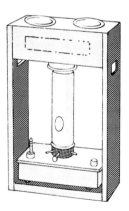

Figure 9.3 Greenhouse paraffin heater

Paraffin used to be the cheapest and therefore the most commonly used form of heating for the amateur's greenhouse. Today there is little difference between electricity, liquid gas (as used in portable heaters) and paraffin. If you must use paraffin every precaution should be taken for improperly used it can be the cause of many failures; there is no doubt that Geraniums strongly object to paraffin fumes and show this initially in the effect upon the foliage if subjected to them for prolonged periods. Many types of paraffin heaters are available but you will be best advised to purchase one of those specially designed for greenhouse use rather than try to make do with an ordinary domestic stove, and if you can find one, get a heater which is equipped with a chimney to carry the fumes and waste gases away to the outside atmosphere. These are now not too easy to come by, but are obtainable from a few of the better ironmongers, or are sometimes advertised in the Gardening Press.

Careful attention to ventilation is essential when using paraffin, and I would suggest that the greenhouse should be thrown wide open for at least half an hour each morning and evening, even in winter, in order to provide the absolute maximum change of air. The risk of damage to the plants will be increased by the burning of poor quality oil, since most cheaper oils have a higher sulphur content. Too much emphasis cannot be laid upon the need to use only high-grade paraffin and to keep the equipment perfectly clean and the wick evenly trimmed; a wick with a high spot or one which is not properly fitted will smoke and quickly fill the greenhouse with sulphurous gases. It is important to purchase a heater with a reservoir of sufficient capacity to ensure steady burning for at least 12 hours, 24 if possible, and to be able to place the appliance in a draught-free situation. Draughts and gusts of wind, however slight, may cause flaring which not only creates a dangerous fire risk but the smoke generated by the faulty burning will increase the pollution of the atmosphere inside the greenhouse.

Heating a greenhouse by the use of hot water flowing through cast iron pipes was the favourite system during Queen Victoria's reign, and can still occasionally be seen in the conservatories and greenhouses attached to a few of the 'stately homes' in Britain. The cost of installing and maintaining such a system these days is horrific, but where already in existence it provides almost perfect conditions for Geraniums, particularly when they are grown on slatted benches to encourage maximum air movement. In Victorian times these systems were always fired by solid fuel and the boiler was usually built into one of the end walls of the greenhouse with the smoke stack rising outside. Circulation of the water was by convection, and the piping was laid with a steady rise to ensure a continual flow — hot water rising away from the boiler, cooling water falling back to be reheated; the outflow pipe being at the top of the boiler, the return into the bottom.

Although providing ideal conditions for the plants there were several disadvantages from the human angle, not least of which was the permanent chore of loading the fuel into the fire-box and removing the spent ashes and clinker. It was usually necessary to check the fuel level during the night or early hours of the morning, especially in the winter months, for a sudden change in wind velocity or direction could result in the fuel burning through too rapidly, or an unexpected calm might allow the fire to die out from lack of draught. In the larger houses where several gardeners were employed this presented only a minor problem, for it usually became the duty of the youngest to deal with this night-time inspection and stoking, a job which was quickly passed on to a new arrival at the earliest opportunity.

My nursery in Gloucestershire was equipped with such a system when I purchased it in the early 1960s, and during the first winter there it was necessary for me to inspect and re-fuel the boilers every night at 10pm, 2am and 6am since we employed no living-in staff. This meant stoking over a ton of coal every night, usually in bitter cold weather, often in pouring rain or snow with the wind whistling around the ears, for all the boilers were outside the greenhouses with only a corrugated iron lean-to over them for protection. Just one winter of this was sufficient for me; the following spring the entire nursery was converted to oil and I was able to enjoy a full night's sleep again.

Similarly, as labour became more expensive and the daily (and nightly) chores fell to the owner's own efforts, more thought was given to reduce or possibly eliminate some of the manual side of gardening, and one of the first items to receive attention from the owner-stoker would most certainly have been the interruption of his repose. At first these efforts were largely unsuccessful as far as the amateur was concerned, resulting in the dismantling of a great number of small greenhouses in private gardens as they fell out of favour with their owners. Commercial boilers could be converted to burn oil or gas, even automatic stokers were invented which could fuel a boiler with coke or coal for 24 hours without attention, but the cost of such conversions was well beyond the reach of most amateurs, and in the early days considerable expertise was required to operate them efficiently.

In recent years, however, numerous advances have been made towards complete automation of small greenhouses, with the result that sales have multiplied, prices have reduced to acceptable levels, and we now have more gardeners with heated greenhouse accommodation than ever before in the history of gardening in Britain.

Polythene Liners

I have never favoured the lining of greenhouses with polythene whether in sheet form or the bubbly type since so much condensation is produced, but there is no doubt that heating costs can be reduced by its use. To overcome the condensation problem some writers recommend restricting the polythene liner to the vertical walls of the greenhouse, leaving the roof unlined. This will certainly prevent the formation of water droplets in a position where they are able to fall upon the plants, but since about 95 per cent of heat loss is through the roof I suggest you save yourself the time and expense and content yourself with the plain glass, unless you are intending lining the roof of your greenhouse as well as the walls.

Covering the greenhouse with polythene thrown over the outside is an excellent way of reducing heat loss, if there are no projections to damage the polythene, and if it can be properly secured against wind damage, but in my experience wind will tear it to shreds very quickly unless the entire unit is protected by strong netting which is very firmly secured at the base — and netting strong enough to resist a winter gale will cost a lot more than you will spend on heating an uncovered greenhouse.

106

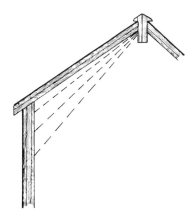

Figure 9.4 Adjust the angle of the polythene until the drips run down

So we return to the internal polythene liner. Condensation forms all over the surface of polythene in tiny droplets which gradually amalgamate with their neighbours and enlarge until the weight of the water in each drop, combined with gravity, causes it either to fall off or run down according to the angle of the lining. Where the lining is vertical, as on the sides and ends of the greenhouse, the water will travel straight down and run off at the bottom, and by adjusting the edge of the polythene sheet it can be collected into a convenient receptacle. Were the lining to be stretched horizontally the droplets would not attempt to run down but would simply fall where they formed, giving an even distribution of water over the entire area. Between these two extremes we have the normal slope of the amateur's greenhouse roof, which can vary considerably according to the specifications of the various manufacturers, and it is therefore necessary to provide a general guide which can be applied in principle to all makes and angles.

Use only new clear polythene, and if possible buy it in sheets large enough to enable you to line the greenhouse without joining anywhere on the sloping areas. Attach the lining firmly along the length of the ridge bar, supporting it on a piece of 2 x 1in (5 x 2.5cm) timber running down the entire length of the house. Stretch the polythene out to the eaves and attach to the wall by another piece of timber also running the entire length of the house. Treat both eaves in the same manner, and the job is almost completed. The polythene must always be kept under slight tension or drips will occur at any point where it sags; and if it is found that the condensation falls onto the plants instead of running off to the eaves, the outer timber strips should be lowered down the walls a little until the desired effect is achieved.

Whenever a polythene lining has been fitted to a greenhouse great care must be taken when entering or leaving for a slammed door or similar disturbance will bring down a cascade of condensation from the lining and help to provide ideal conditions for the spread of botrytis, apart from the inconvenience caused to any person inside at the time. It is not possible to

107

eliminate condensation entirely when using polythene unless a constant heat of around 70°F (21°C) can be maintained, but it must be kept to the minimum by adequate ventilation — even in winter. Those commercial growers who use polythene 'tunnels' for growing salad crops and similar, always try to site the tunnels on sloping land so that natural ventilation is achieved by opening the two ends for a period every day; but most amateur greenhouses are on level sites so even if the ends can be opened very little air movement will occur except in windy conditions which will result in even more problems.

An electric fan heater is really the only satisfactory answer, but it is essential to use only a heater designed specially for greenhouse use because the relative humidity under polythene is so high that there is a grave risk of electrocution if normal domestic heaters are used. *Never* use a paraffin heater under a polythene lining or the condensation will run down the lining in rivers.

Many greenhouses are fitted with roof ventilators, often the only means of ventilation except for leaving the doors open, and these can present a problem when lining with polythene. Where an efficient extractor fan is fitted there will be no difficulty for the ventilators can remain sealed throughout the winter, but if it is necessary to operate the ventilators (and ventilation is essential for the well-being of the plants), proceed as follows: after lining the greenhouse as detailed in the last paragraph, tack the polythene around the edge of the ventilator frame using large-headed drawing pins, then cut out the polythene using the ventilator frame as a guide. The ventilator can now be opened in the usual way, and if you wish, the cut-out portion of polythene can be pinned to the actual ventilator to give additional insulation.

The insulation of wooden greenhouses can be fairly simply undertaken by most handymen using the foregoing methods, but metal erections require a slightly different approach. Many manufacturers supply attachments at a small extra cost to enable their products to be lined with polythene, and several garden centres offer gadgets such as rubber suckers which do the same job. It is often possible to find holes already existing in the roof- and eaves-members to enable a timber batten to be attached, and if this is so the same method can be applied as for a wooden house. If no such holes can be found it is a simple matter to drill aluminium without damaging or weakening the structure, but if the greenhouse is made of galvanised iron it will be difficult to drill and the resulting damage to the galvanic skin will encourage oxidisation and probably render any guarantee inoperative. Sticking polythene directly onto the glass with adhesive tape is quite useless; it provides no heat insulation at all and only results in unnecessary light restriction.

Polythene gradually becomes more opaque as it ages and it is important to remove it in the spring or the quality of the light in the greenhouse will be impaired, and for the same reason it should not be re-used. The ultra-violet resistant polythenes (usually a pale yellow material) are not suitable for greenhouse lining where Geraniums are being grown because they limit the light penetration; they are intended for use in commercial polythene tunnels for crops where the quality of light is less critical.

The grade of polythene to be used for lining is of little importance from the growing angle, but the heavier weights are rather unwieldy and difficult to manipulate, whilst the very thin qualities are easily damaged and will often split when a drawing pin is used. To some extent this can be overcome by placing a piece of cardboard about 1in (25mm) in diameter against the polythene then pinning through the centre of it, thereby spreading the area of pressure, but a grade of 250 to 300 is easy to manage, will take pinning with little risk of splitting, and is often cheapest in the end.

I am sorry to have to say that those 'greenhouses' consisting of a weak aluminium frame covered with a polythene sheet are, in my opinion, quite unsuitable for housing Geraniums through a normal British winter. All too often one sees these structures in tatters after the first gale, polythene shredded and the frame buckled beyond repair. Regarded as an oversize cloche to be used for raising spring-sown cabbage plants, they are probably ideal but almost certain death to any of the Pelargonium family if used as winter protection.

Bottled Gas

The use of bottled gas has become more widespread in recent years and there are now several types of appliance sold for use in greenhouses. The portable domestic heaters I have tried all caused severe damage to the foliage, noticeable within a few days, and although the Geraniums were immediately transferred to more congenial surroundings it was all of six months before they recovered, and an azalea in the same room was killed outright.

Figure 9.5 The 'Thermogem' bottled gas greenhouse heater by Aeromatic-Barter Ltd of London

109

Because of these experiences I have been reluctant to experiment with those propane and methane gas heaters specially designed for greenhouse use without first obtaining reassurance from the manufacturers as to their safety when used with Geraniums. None of the manufacturers was prepared to give such an assurance, in fact in general I have found them quite unco-operative when queries have been raised — with one exception. This was Aeromatic-Barter Ltd of London N18 who went to a great deal of trouble to assure me of the complete safety of their product which is fitted with a system of filters to ensure that no harmful bi-products are discharged into the atmosphere of the greenhouse. According to their calculations, a saving of over 50 per cent in heating costs can be achieved (against electricity), and an additional benefit is the CO_2 enrichment which results from the use of their heating unit.

Regretfully I have been unable to install their heaters in my own greenhouse because it is located some 300ft (91m) away from the nearest hard road, and the liquid gas company refuse to supply to the site. But for those in a more favourable position it could well be worth investigating, especially where the larger greenhouse is involved.

However, there are other types of liquid gas appliances on the market, some of which are definitely detrimental if used when growing Geraniums. In one case the manufacturer himself advises that 'adequate ventilation is essential at all times' if a build-up of injurious fumes is to be prevented — in plain English this means that you must never close the ventilators or you will lose your plants, and that can be costly in winter.

10 Alphabetical list of varieties

This list is included to assist the grower to identify his plants. Where known, the raiser's name and date of raising appears in brackets following the name of the plant. Correct identification must include the habit of the plant as well as the colour and shape of the foliage coupled with the description of the flower.

As previously discussed, plants do not always fall neatly into man-made categories but as a rough guide the following scale has been adopted throughout the list to provide some kind of guide for the reader's assistance: Miniature 5in (12.7cm); Dwarf 8in (20.3cm); Semi-dwarf 10in (25.4cm); and Micro-miniatures 3in (7.6cm). Measurements are taken from the top of the pot (or soil if planted in a garden) to the highest growing tip excluding flowers. Based upon a normal year's growth in average conditions in central England.

Readers will appreciate that I have not grown every plant listed, so in some cases descriptions have been taken from nurserymen's catalogues, and others from the invaluable Check List published by the Australian Geranium Society as the International Registration Authority.

I have avoided the use of the colour references as detailed in the Horticultural Colour Charts because they are too precise and make no allowance for colour variations brought about by climatic vagaries, soil and environmental differences, colour changes which can develop from the use of unbalanced fertilisers, seasonal changes, and the difference between plants grown out of doors and those under protected cultivation.

For those unfamiliar with the terms used, 'Rosebud'-type describes a plant carrying tight double florets similar to tiny rosebuds, e.g. 'Garnet Rosebud'; 'Stellar'-type foliage is deeply cut and roughly star-shaped, the single flowers normally have two erect narrow upper petals and three broader wedge-shaped lower petals, flowers can be either double or single, e.g. 'Formosum'; flowers described as 'primitive' have five narrow, well-separated petals usually evenly spaced, e.g. 'Bird Dancer'.

A

Ada Sutterby (*Sutterby 1972*) Rose-pink double flowers. Dwarf 'Rosebud'-type with mid-green foliage.
Adagio Large single flowers of pale pink. Dwarf variety with mid-green foliage.

Adele *(Parrett 1968)* Phlox-pink double flowers. Dark green leaf with darker zone. Miniature.

Aerosol *(Gillam pre-1980)* Canadian miniature variety. Soft mauve single flowers with purple 'bird's egg' speckles on the narrow petals. Mid-green foliage with slight zone.

Aerosol Improved *(Gillam 1986)* Improved form of above.

Ailsa *(Parrett 1972)* Free flowering semi-double white miniature with mid-green zoned foliage.

Akela *(Parrett 1974)* Miniature. Single Fuchsia-purple flower with white eye.

Alban *(Stringer 1966)* Semi-double orange flowered miniature with mid-green foliage.

Alban Nana *(Delesalle 1887)* Dwarf variety with large single white flowers.

Alba Princess *(Money 1970)* Single white flowered miniature, light green leaf with no zone.

Albert Sheppard *(Peat 1971)* Fancyleaved dwarf variety. Bright cherry-red double flowers, golden foliage with broad wavy chestnut zone.

Alcyone *(from USA pre-1966)* Miniature. Free flowering plum-red double flowers with dark foliage. Not to be confused with the English variety of the same name.

Alcyone *(English raiser unknown)* Large single flowers of medium pink with mid-green foliage. Dwarf.

Alde *(Stringer pre-1964)* Free flowering miniature, single, salmon-pink with white eye. Dark green leaf with distinct zone. Sometimes wrongly attributed to Hill who first listed it.

Aldebaran *(Arndt 1953)* Dwarf variety with single bright salmon-pink flowers and small black leaves.

Alexia *(Parrett 1972)* Large single flowers of mandarin-red with white base to upper petals. Mid-green zoned foliage. Miniature.

Algenon *(Parrett 1964)* One of Parrett's best miniatures. Double flowers. Top petals carmine with white base, lower Tyrian rose. Mid-green foliage with faint zone. (Raiser's spelling, not 'Algernon'.)

Alice *(Holborow pre-1966)* Miniature. Double flowers of soft apricot-pink with white centre. 'Leonore' x 'Small Fortune'.

Alisoa *(Parrett 1964)* Dwarf variety with large flowers of scarlet with white eye. Mid-green foliage with black zone. This could be a mis-spelling of 'Alison' — the description is identical and Parrett's catalogues are notorious for spelling errors.

Alison *(Parrett 1964)* Description as 'Alisoa' (above).

Allison *(Holborow pre-1973)* Australian miniature variety with double flowers of bright orange-red carried on long stems, well above the light-green foliage which is faintly zoned.

Alma *(Parrett 1966)* Fancyleaved miniature. Single azalea-pink flowers, pale green foliage maturing to golden with bronze zone. Miniature form of 'Golden Harry Hieover'.

Altair *(Stringer pre-1965)* Between rose-red and salmon-red double flowers with white reverse to petals. Dark green leaf without zone. Miniature variety.

Amber *(Miller 1972)* Miniature variety. Single flowers, orange with white eye. Released after Holmes Miller's death by his wife Dorothea.

Ambrose *(Stringer 1966)* Full double rosettes of creamy-white flushed pale pink. Mid-green foliage with distinct zoning. Dwarf variety.

Amelia *(Parrett 1966)* Single rhodamine-pink flowers with white base to upper petals. Foliage mid-green with darker zone. Miniature variety.

Amelia *(Morf 1969)* The Australian Amelia. A miniature with double lilac-rose flowers and dark green foliage.

Andrea *(Parrett 1968)* Miniature variety with single orange flowers and white eye. Mid-green zoned foliage.

Andromeda *(Stringer 1966)* Large single creamy-white flowers, petals flushed and edged pale pink. Miniature variety.

Angela *(origin unknown pre-1968)* Single salmon-scarlet miniature with white eye.

Angela Read *(Read pre-1970)* Dwarf orange-scarlet single. Similar to 'Anglia' but with no white eye.

Anglia *(Taylor/Read 1949)* Single orange-scarlet dwarf variety with white eye. Mid-green foliage. Weak grower, parentage includes 'Salmon Kovalevski'.

Anna *(Wells pre-1967)* Dwarf variety. Single mauve-pink with white eye. Large flat blooms with overlapping petals. Mid-green foliage with faint zone.

Annabelle *(Parrett 1967)* Single lilac-pink dwarf variety, slightly paler than 'Amelia' and without the white eye. Mid-green zoned foliage.

Anna Heide *(Heide, USA 1966)* Double white semi-dwarf flowers which seldom show signs of pinking. Pale green leaf, no zone.

Anne Cherylette *(Both pre-1962)* Australian miniature. Double lavender-pink flowers, small dark green leaves.

Anne-Marie *(Parrett 1966)* Miniature variety. Large single white flowers, veined porcelain-rose and blotched azalea-pink. Foliage is mid-green without zone.

Annette *(Both pre-1962)* Australian miniature. Small salmon-pink flowers, dark foliage.

Annette Both *(Both pre-1962)* Australian miniature. Single pale lilac flowers with narrow petals and dark foliage.

Antares *(Stringer 1965)* One of Stringer's earliest miniatures. Light salmon-pink single flowers.

Antoinette *(Parrett 1967)* Single amaranth-rose miniature. Mid-green foliage, no zone. (Spelling varied in Parrett's catalogues, sometimes 'Antoinett'.)

Apache Squaw *(Wells 1965)* Large salmon-red single flowered miniature. Dark green well zoned foliage.

Apricot Dwarf variety with single flowers of medium apricot, dark green leaves and black zone. A dwarf 'Stellar' variety similar to 'Bird Dancer' but much larger flowerheads.

Arcturus *(from USA about 1960)* Semi-dwarf variety. Bright scarlet semi-double flowers and mid-green foliage. Excellent for bedding outdoors but perhaps too vigorous for indoor use. Not to be confused with Stringer's miniature of the same name.

Arcturus *(Stringer 1966)* Semi-double flowers of creamy-white flushed pale pink. Miniature variety, not to be confused with the dwarf of the same name from the USA (above).

Aries *(Stringer 1965)* Single orange-red miniature variety with near-black foliage, black zone. Seedling of 'Alde'.

Arizona *(Stringer 1972)* Dwarf variety with medium purple double flowers and mid-green foliage.

Artemis *(Arndt, USA 1949)* Dwarf variety with double flowers of rose-pink shaded white. Mid-green leaf with purple-brown zone, sometimes reddish edges to foliage.

Athene Large single flowers of mauve-pink with serrated edge to petals, veined and blotched. Mid-green foliage. Dwarf.

Autumn Sunset *(Parrett 1964)* Fancyleaved miniature. Single red flowers, slow growing and compact. Golden tricolour foliage.

Avalon Double flowers of brilliant white on a dwarf plant with mid-green foliage.

B

Baby Bird's Egg *(Wells about 1965)* The flowers on this miniature variety are mainly white with pink speckles. It is slow growing and not easy to propagate.

Baby Brocade *(Miller 1974)* Large double red flower with distinct white eye. Released by Boone in Canada probably from stock or seed acquired from Dorothea Miller of California after her husband's death.

Baby Clare *(pre-1982)* Bright orange-red single flowers with white eye. Mid-green foliage. Miniature.

Baby Helen *(pre-1982)* Miniature. Single flowers are a strong shade of pink with white eye. Mid-green foliage.

Baby James *(pre-1982)* Miniature. Neyron-rose single flowers with white eye and mid-green foliage. It is possible that this variety and the previous two came from the same raiser.

Badley Dwarf variety with large single salmon-pink flowers.

Ballerina *(Peat 1969)* Free flowering dwarf variety with orange-red double flowers and light green foliage.

Bandit *(Stringer 1970)* Large single cerise flowers with white eye and mid-green foliage. Miniature.

Bantam *(Miller 1960)* Between a dwarf and a miniature. Double flowers of strong apricot or perhaps nearer to salmon. Free flowering with large clusters of flowers and mid-green foliage.

Banwell *(Peat 1976)* Miniature variety with bright red single flowers and dark green foliage.

Barham *(Bidwell 1972)* Bright orange-red double flowers, mid-green foliage. Miniature.

Bashful *(Rober 1938)* Miniature variety with single lavender flowers and mid-green foliage. One of Rober's 'Snow White and the Seven Dwarfs' group.

Bath Beauty *(Bennett 1972)* A dwarf seedling of 'Monica Bennett'. Single salmon flower, dark green leaf with darker zone. Stronger grower than parent, almost falls into the semi-dwarf class.

Baylham Miniature variety with single white flowers, petals faintly edged purple.

Beachball *(Stringer)* One of Stringer's earlier dwarfs. The only description we have is 'Large flowers, single pink'.

Beacon Hill *(Gillam 1982)* Canadian miniature variety. Carmine single flowers with distinct white centre. Foliage is dark green with almost no zone.

Bede *(Stringer 1966)* Salmon-pink single with small white eye, all petals veined and blotched deeper colour. Mid-green foliage with strong zone. Miniature.

Belinda Adams *(Parrett 1970)* Large double flowers, mainly white but striped and flushed dawn-pink. Mid-green foliage. Miniature.

Belstead *(Bidwell 1972)* Pale lilac single flowers with white base to upper petals. Dark green foliage with faint zone. Miniature seedling from 'Deacon Lilac Mist'.

Belstead *(Hill)* Large single flowers of pure scarlet, mid-green foliage. Miniature.

Benedict *(Stringer 1966)* Medium size single flower, pure orange with small white eye and mid-green foliage. Miniature.

Ben Nevis *(Payne pre-1986)* Dwarf variety with white double flowers. Buds have a slight green tinge which disappears as the floret opens. Mid-green foliage.

Berenice *(Stringer 1965)* Compact semi-double, white with delicate pink tinge. Miniature.

Beryl Read *(Read)* Dwarf variety with single mauve-pink flowers and mid-green foliage.

Beta Dwarf fancyleaf variety. Pale pink single flowers, golden-green foliage with pale green zone.

Betsy Trotwood *(Bagust 1966)* Fairly large single flowers of satin-pink with white base to upper petals. Zoned mid-green foliage. Dwarf.

Bettina *(Parrett pre-1966)* Double flowers of Dutch vermilion, mid-green foliage without zone. Dwarf.

Betty Pfitzel Dwarf plant with dark green foliage and near-black zone. The single flowers are a shade of light purple.

Betty Read *(Read 1966)* Single flowers of coral-pink, dark green foliage. Dwarf.

Bill Starmes *(Parrett 1972)* Fancyleaved miniature. The single flowers are mandarin-red blushed white, leaves are grey-green with silvery edge. Slow-growing variety.

Billy Read *(Read)* Double flowers of carmine-red suffused magenta. Mid-green foliage. Dwarf.

Bingo *(Miller pre-1970)* Double flowers of bright scarlet with white centres. Dark green foliage. Miniature. Sometimes incorrectly listed as being of Canadian origin.

Bird Dancer *(Bird)* Dwarf 'Stellar' variety with very pale pink single flowers and dark green 'Stellar' foliage.

Black Dwarf Dark red semi-double flowers on a semi-dwarf plant. Excellent for bedding but normally too vigorous for indoor use.

Black Knight Similar to 'Black Dwarf' and probably from the same raiser, but flowers are single, orange-scarlet.

Blakesdorf *(Blakedown pre-1967)* 'Red Black Vesuvius' x 'Friesdorf'. Single orange-red primitive-type flower similar to 'Friesdorf'. Greyish bloom to the sage-green leaves with distinct black zone. Slightly more compact than 'Friesdorf'. Dwarf.

Blanchland Cerise *(Clyne)* Large single cerise flowers, dark green foliage. Large miniature, almost a dwarf.

Blanchland Dazzler *(Clyn)* Miniature variety with soft red single flowers and dark green foliage.

Blyth *(Hill 1964)* Apricot-pink flowers, petals shading to white at edges. Slightly bronzed foliage. Miniature.

Blyth *(Hill about 1964)* Single flowers of pale pink overlaid salmon, with distinct white eye. There is some confusion over the above two varieties but I have listed both.

Bob Cratchett *(Bagust 1966)* Deep crimson single flowers with large white eye. Colour deepens slightly as the flower matures. Mid-green foliage. Dwarf.

Boudoir *(Peat 1971)* Dwarf fancyleaf variety. Flowers are double, mid-pink, foliage is a pale shade of gold with irregular bronze zone.

Bramford *(Bidwell 1970)* Dwarf seedling of 'Claudius'. Large single flowers of soft red. Dark green foliage with narrow darker zone.

Brenda *(from Canada pre-1970)* Clusters of deep rose double flowerheads on a compact miniature plant with distinctly zoned foliage.

Brenda Holborow *(Holborow 1963)* Formerly listed as 'Brenda'. Single deep salmon flowers, rounded petals with paler edges. Small dark green leaves with darker zone. Australian miniature.

Brenda Hyatt *(Parrett 1975)* Double flowers of mauve-pink with white centres. Mid-green foliage. Dwarf variety.

Brenda Laws *(Morden about 1972)* Double flowers of pure scarlet. Compact dwarf variety.

Brett *(Hill 1962)* Large single flowers of velvety-red with white eye. Miniature.

Bric Brac *(Wells pre-1970)* Compact dwarf variety with single flowers of medium red with white eye. Mid-green foliage.

Bridal Veil *(Parmenter 1984)* Miniature fancyleaved variety with white single flowers. The golden foliage has faint zoning.

Bridesmaid *(Stringer 1972)* Dwarf fancyleaved variety, thought by many to be Stringer's greatest achievement. The double flowers are a light peach-pink, and the golden-green foliage has a velvety sheen and clear zone.

Brightwell *(Bidwell)* Deep pink double flowers, mid-green foliage.

Bristol Dandy *(Peat 1974)* Very large double flowers of orange-scarlet with small white eye. The golden foliage has a broad copper zone fading towards the centre of the leaves. Fancyleaved dwarf variety.

Broadway (*Pierrt 1977*) Canadian miniature. Single flowers of strong neon-red.

Brookside Primrose (*Hopkins pre-1985*) Miniature fancyleaved variety. Pale pink double flowers, golden foliage.

Brownie (*Arndt pre-1950*) Large single scarlet flowers. Mid-green foliage with purple-black zone. Miniature, seldom exceeds 4in (10cm).

Bucklesham (*Bidwell 1974*) Dwarf variety with large single flowers of orange-pink with distinct white eye.

Bumblebee (*Rover 1949*) Semi-dwarf variety with large single flowers of dark red and dark green foliage. Sometimes listed as light red — I have not grown it, it could be either.

Burstall (*Bidwell pre-1986*) Deep red, double-flowered miniature with mid-green foliage.

Butley (*Hill 1964*) Large single flowers of soft salmon-pink, paler at edges of petals. Foliage is medium green with dark zone. Miniature.

Butterfly (*Miller 1972*) A sport of 'Perky'. Clear bright red single flowers with white eye, pale butterfly mark on the dark green foliage. Fancyleaved miniature released after Holmes Miller's death by his wife Dorothea.

C

Caligula (*Stringer pre-1964*) Miniature with double flowers of rose-red on dark foliage. Sometimes erroneously spelt 'Caligua'.

Camely (*Peat 1970*) Fancyleaved dwarf with rose-pink double flowers. Golden foliage with broad wavy zone.

Cameo (*May 1965*) Semi-double flowers of rich carmine-rose with white throat. Mid-green foliage. Dwarf.

Camilla Deep fuchsine-pink single flowers with small white eye carried on long stems above the mid-green foliage. Dwarf.

Candlewick (*Stringer 1968*) Apricot-pink double flowers on a golden-leaved plant with a soft velvety, almost furry sheen to the lightly zoned foliage. Dwarf.

Candy (*Salmon 1968*) Miniature variety with double picotee flowers, white edge and flushed neyron-rose. Dark green foliage with black zone.

Capel (*Bidwell 1971*) Dwarf variety with double flowers of deep red. Dark green foliage with faint zone.

Capella (*Stringer 1966*) Miniature. Single light orange flower, mid-green foliage. (Arndt raised a 'Capella' in the USA in the 1950s. It is described as a dwarf with double pale salmon flowers and dark zoned foliage; as far as I know it is no longer in cultivation.)

Capricorn (*Stringer 1966*) Double flowers of pink and white. Foliage is mid- to dark green. Miniature.

Cariboo Gold (*Gillam 1980*) Dwarf fancyleaved 'Stellar' variety from Canada. Single scarlet flowers, golden foliage with wide chocolate zone. Sometimes spelt 'Caribou Gold' ('Medallion' x 'Stellar Red Devil').

Carla (*Parrett pre-1972*) Single poppy-red flowers with white base to petals. Mid-green zoned foliage. The habit is between miniature and dwarf.

Carlton Velma (*Arndt 1948*) Dwarf fancyleaved variety from the USA. Single light salmon flowers, bright green foliage with golden yellow border to leaves and brown zone splashed with mulberry, scarlet and crimson.

Carmelette (*Both pre-1962*) Australian miniature having single white flowers with red edges to petals.

Carol Cooper Dwarf variety with double flowers of bright salmon-pink.

116

Carolyn *(Parrett pre-1964)* Miniature variety with large single flowers of dawn-pink. Dark green foliage with faint zone. Sometimes incorrectly spelt 'Caroline'.
Carmette *(Both pre-1962)* Slow-growing Australian miniature variety. Single flowers, outer edge deep rose shading to soft apricot-pink. Petals recurved at edges. Mid-green, faintly zoned foliage.
Casilda *(Stringer 1969)* Large single salmon flowers with white eye. Mid-green zoned foliage. Dwarf.
Cassio *(Stringer 1967)* Slow-growing miniature, seldom making more than 4–5in (10–12.5cm). Semi-double medium pink flowers, mid-green foliage.
Cecilie *(Butters pre-1974)* Compact miniature with tangerine-red double flowers, white reverse to petals. Leaves small, mid-green with faint zone.
Celia *(Parrett pre-1965)* Dwarf variety with single pale mauve-pink flowers almost white, with pearly-white eye. Dark green foliage.
Charlotte Read *(Read pre-1977)* Blood-red single flowers with white splashes on upper petals and dark green foliage. Dwarf.
Charm *(Parrett 1962)* The single flower is basically white with scarlet edges to petals which are blushed and speckled carmine-rose. Miniature.
Charmaine *(Parrett pre-1965)* Miniature variety with mid-green foliage. The large single flowers are orange-red when newly opened, maturing to deeper orange-red with large white eye.
Charming *(possibly Parrett about 1964)* Similar to 'Charm' but with considerably more red towards the edge of each petal and slightly larger single flower.
Chattisham *(Bidwell pre-1966)* Neat and compact miniature having pale green foliage with wide copper zone. The small single flowers are carried well above the foliage on long stems. When newly opened they are pale pink, flushed deeper pink towards the edges of the petals and veined magenta. As they mature most of the pink fades and the flowers then appear to be white with a very light pink flush, stronger towards the centre, and with magenta veins radiating outwards. The general effect is that of a central eye or halo.
Cheddar *(Peat 1980)* Fancyleaved dwarf with golden foliage, wavy bronze zone, and single salmon flowers.
Chelsworth *(Bidwell 1974)* Double flowers of orange-salmon on mid-green zoned foliage. Miniature.
Cherie *(Parrett pre-1965)* Single cherry-red flowers with white base to upper petals. Mid-green foliage without zone. Dwarf.
Cherrie Wells *(Wells about 1965)* Miniature variety with phlox-pink single flowers and mid-green foliage.
Cherry *(Key pre-1980)* Scarlet and white single bi-colour. Miniature.
Cherub *(Miller 1962)* Slow-growing miniature from the USA with large single white flowers, slightly flushed salmon with distinct pink eye. Dark green foliage. Seldom exceeds 5in (12.5cm).
Chi-Chi *(Stringer 1968)* Single peach-pink flowers with distinct white eye and deeper veining on petals. Mid-green foliage with black zone. Miniature.
Chico *(Campbell 1965)* Slow-growing, rare micro-miniature. Small single flowers of medium salmon. Dark green foliage with black zone. Leaves seldom exceed ¼in (5mm) in diameter. Difficult to propagate.
Chieko *(Parrett 1970)* The double flowers are a mixture of crimson and purple. Miniature variety with dark green foliage.
Chiltern Beacon *(Money pre-1979)* Double flowers of poppy-red with deep green foliage. Miniature.
Chiltern Maid *(Money pre-1970)* Double flowers of rosy-mauve with deep green leaves and black zone. Miniature.
Chime *(Miller 1970)* Miniature variety from the USA. Large double flowers of

coral-rose with white eye. Dark green foliage.

Christine Read *(Read 1960)* Large golden-orange flowers, mid-green leaves. Dwarf seedling of 'Beatrice Little'.

Cindy Mid-green foliage with wide zone fading towards edge of leaf. The double flowers are carried in large ball-shaped heads consisting of a variety of pink shades, some florets with white undertones. Similar in appearance to 'Deacon Romance' of which it may be a seedling. Compact habit between dwarf and miniature.

Cindy Miniature variety. Single soft red flowers with small white eye, mid-green foliage.

Cindy Lou *(Richards pre-1970)* Miniature sport of 'Anne Cherylette'. Double flowers of lavender-pink.

Clara Read *(Read pre-1960)* Single flowers, orange-red on white base. Dwarf.

Clare McFarland *(Holborow pre-1964)* Single powder-pink flowers with silvery sheen and white eye, white reverse to petals. Pea-green foliage without zone. Australian dwarf sometimes listed as 'Clare' in England.

Clarissa *(Parrett pre-1967)* Single turkey-red flowers with white base to upper petals. Dark green foliage. Habit between miniature and dwarf.

Claude Read *(Read 1960)* Single scarlet flowers with white centres. Dark green compact foliage. Dwarf.

Claudette *(Parrett pre-1964)* Large single white flowers flushed and veined camellia-rose. Dark green leaves with near-black zone. Slow-growing miniature variety, seldom exceeds 5in (12.5cm).

Claudius *(Burrows pre-1955)* Large single almost white flowers faintly tinged mauve-pink. Dark green foliage with deeper zone. Habit falls between miniature and dwarf.

Claydon *(Bidwell pre-1970)* Dwarf seedling of 'Denebola'. Lavender-pink double flowers, dark green foliage with darker zone.

Coddenham *(Bidwell 1975)* Dwarf seedling of 'Clara Read'. Bright orange-red double flowers on long stems. Mid-green zoned foliage.

Colour Sergeant *(Gillam 1980)* Canadian miniature. Full-bodied rich red single flowers with small white eye. Mid-green foliage with darker zoning.

Comet *(Stringer 1968)* Miniature form of 'Orangesonne'. Double orange flowers on mid-green foliage. Very self-branching.

Concorde *(Stringer 1968)* Flower is a loose double with pink and white petals joined haphazardly at the base in a casual and attractive manner. Pale green foliage, dwarf, rather sprawling habit.

Contrast Fancyleaved dwarf with small scarlet single flowers. Leaves are yellow with green overlay, zoned scarlet, crimson and copper. Similar leaf-colouring to 'Mrs Henry Cox' but more dentate. Origin unknown but listed by Miller in the USA in 1950.

Copdock *(Bidwell 1969)* Salmon-pink double flowers, mid-green foliage with broad zone. Miniature.

Coquette *(Bagust 1965)* Compact miniature with brilliant scarlet large single flowers and mid-green zoned foliage.

Coral Doll *(Flora Vista pre-1976)* Small single coral-pink flowers, tiny dark green leaves with black zone. Miniature from the USA.

Coral Frills *(Miller 1970)* P. acetosum x 'Minx'. Primitive single flowers of coral-pink with long thin petals carried on slender stems. Similar to 'Frills' but deeper colour. Leaves are mid-green, fleshy and shiny showing the species parentage. Dwarf.

Coretta Dwarf variety with single red flower and dark green foliage. Origin unknown but before 1976.

Cottontail *(Morf pre-1971)* Australian miniature. Double white flowers, dark green foliage with near-black zone.

118

Creamery *(Peat 1977)* Creamy-white double flowers, buds have a definite yellow tinge. Foliage is mid-green. Dwarf.

Crimson Pickaninny *(Bagust 1966)* Miniature sport from Parrett's 'Pickaninny'. Slow-growing variety with bright crimson single flowers. Dark green foliage with deeper zone.

Crimson Vesuvius *(pre-1966)* Origin unknown but first listed by Hazeldene in 1966. Crimson single flowers, otherwise identical to 'Red Black Vesuvius'. Miniature.

Crowfield *(Bidwell pre-1973)* Lilac-pink double flowers, dark green foliage with deeper zone.

Cupid *(Parrett pre-1964)* Double flowers. Carmine upper petals, rose-pink lower. Leaves dark green with black zone. Habit between miniature and dwarf.

Cynthia *(Parrett 1968)* Large single white flowers, centres flushed mauve-pink. Mid-green foliage. Miniature.

Cyril Read *(Read pre-1978)* Single salmon-pink flowers, colour deepening at outer edge of petals. Dwarf.

D

Dainty Lassie *(Flora Vista 1977)* Dwarf fancyleaved variety. Single red flowers. Leaves have irregular green centres with dark brown blotches in a roughly zonal formation, and cream edges. Leaf colouring varies considerably from leaf to leaf. (Originally distributed as 'Dainty Lady'.)

Dame Anna Neagle *(Roberts pre-1985)* Dwarf variety with double flowers of pale powder-pink.

Dancer *(Miller 1957)* Large single flowers of salmon-pink, lighter at edges. Dark green leaves with black zone. Fast-growing dwarf. Tends to flower profusely between rests.

David Duval *(Both pre-1962)* Australian miniature with single orange flowers and dark green foliage.

David John *(Payne pre-1968)* Dwarf. Flowers are double, white developing a pink flush as they mature. Mid-green foliage.

Davina *(Parrett 1970)* Large very full double flowers of salmon-pink. Mid-green foliage. Miniature.

Dawn *(Parrett pre-1966)* Large single flowers of turkey-red with large white eye, flushed Tyrian-rose. Dark green foliage. Miniature.

Daydream *(Stringer)* Dwarf fancyleaved variety. Double flowers of rosy-crimson, pea-green to gold leaves, zoned.

Deacon Varieties *(Stringer 1969)* The 'Deacon' hybrids are often listed as dwarf or semi-dwarf but this can be misleading because the size of the plant is governed to some extent by the size of the pot in which it is planted. I have grown 'Deacon Bonanza' over 3ft (90cm) in diameter in an 18in (46cm) pot (see Plate 19) yet if grown in a 4in (10cm) pot they will make a tidy plant some 8in (20cm) in height. Derived from a cross between a miniature and an ivyleaf, they have a compact, sturdy habit with no tendency to sprawl. Self-branching, they will carry several ball-shaped flowerheads at the same time. Many new ones are being raised every year developed from the Stringer originals which are listed as follows.

First Release 1970 (introduced by Wyck Hill Geraniums) Bonanza, Coral Reef, Fireball, Lilac Mist, Mandarin, Romance

Second Release 1973 (introduced by Wyck Hill Geraniums) Arlon, Barbecue, Flamingo, Minuet, Sunburst, Trousseau.

Later Releases (introduced by a variety of nurseries) Birthday, Clarion, Constancy, Finale, Gala, Jubilant, Moonlight, Peacock, Picotee, Summertime, Suntan, Regalia.

119

This constitutes the complete list of 'Deacon' varieties raised by Reverend Stanley Stringer at Occold and Debenham, Suffolk.

Deben (*Hill about 1963*) Miniature variety with delicate light pink single flowers.

Delicate Double flowers of white flushed pale salmon. Mid-green foliage. Dwarf.

Deeak (*Parrett pre-1972*) Miniature variety with large single flowers of rich porcelain-rose. Dark green foliage with black zone.

Della (*Stringer*) Pale rosy-purple double flowers and mid-green foliage. Miniature.

Delphin (*Crane about 1960*) Semi-dwarf seedling of 'Perky' raised in the USA. Large single pink flowers, dark green leaves with black zone.

Delta (*Taylor 1976*) Miniature seedling of 'Chi-Chi'. Double flowers of lavender and neon-pink, narrow petals with some veining. Dark green foliage with heavy narrow zone.

Denebola (*Stringer 1966*) Violet-pink semi-double with white centre to flowers and mid-green foliage. A miniature version of the Irene variety 'Party Dress'.

De Witts (*pre-1962*) Very dark green foliage with single salmon flowers. Very strong grower, can make all of 10in (25cm) under ideal conditions.

Di (*Hill*) Deep mauve-pink double flowers. Miniature.

Diane (*Parrett pre-1964*) Miniature variety with double flowers of soft salmon-pink shading deeper to base of petals. Dark green, lightly zoned foliage.

Dick's White White double flowers with faint greenish tinge, tight flowerhead, and bright green foliage. Similar to 'Fantasie' but not so compact and the flowerhead is tighter. Origin unknown but I first saw it in 1959 at Blakedown, Worcestershire. Dwarf.

Didi (*Key pre-1975*) Single salmon flowers, dark green foliage with deeper zone. Miniature.

Diddi-Di (*Shellard pre-1985*) Miniature variety with double flowers of deep pink, ball shaped flowerheads and deep green foliage with deeper zone.

Dinky (*Stringer pre-1979*) Double flowering miniature of bright cerise-red. Mid-green foliage, free flowering plant.

Display (*Miller 1948*) Semi-dwarf fancyleaved variety from the USA. Small single scarlet flowers. Slow-growing plant with large flat leaves of pale creamy-green splashed with irregular green areas overlaying ragged narrow chestnut zone.

Distinction (*Pre-1870*) Although usually grown as a dwarf or semi-dwarf plant, under some conditions it can make up to 12in (30cm) in height. Small single cherry-red flowers, rich green leaves with toothed and crinkled edges and well defined black pencilled zone near edge.

Doc (*Rober 1938*) USA dwarf. Large brilliant scarlet single flowers. Dark green foliage with black zone. One of Rober's original group of 'Snow White and the Seven Dwarfs'.

Doc (*Arndt 1949*) Deep red semi-double flowers. Small pale green leaves with no zone, margins scalloped and ruffled. Slow-growing miniature, seldom exceeds 4in (10cm). The name had been previously used by Rober in 1938.

Dolly Read (*Read about 1950*) Single flowers of white with pink centre and white eye. Dark green foliage. Dwarf.

Dolphin (*Stringer 1971*) Single flowers of soft red shading to pale vermilion with white eye. Clear green foliage. Miniature.

Dopey (*Rober 1938*) Single rose-red flowers with distinct white eye. Dark green foliage. One of Rober's original group 'Snow White and the Seven Dwarfs'.

Dopey (*Arndt 1949*) Single miniature with bright cerise-pink flowers and small dark green leaves overcast purple and slightly scalloped. Arndt probably had no knowledge that the name had been used by Rober some ten years earlier.

Dorette (*Both pre-1962*) Australian miniature with single flowers of bright pinkish-red and small white eye.

Double Grace Wells (*Wells about 1965*) Tight, many-petalled double flowerheads of rose-pink. Mid-green foliage. Miniature.

Dove (*Hill pre-1964*) Single bright-white flowers with mid-green foliage. Miniature.

Dovedale (*Shellard 1982*) Dwarf variety with semi-double white flowers, golden foliage with lighter centres.

Dr Miroslav Tyrs (*pre 1960*) Semi-dwarf from Czechoslovakia. Clear red double flowers with small petals and neat flowerheads carried well above the pale green foliage. Often listed as 'Dr Tyrs' or 'Dr. M. Tyrs'.

Duku (*Parrett pre-1972*) Improved miniature form of 'Norma'. Reddish salmon single flowers, mid-green foliage.

Dulcie (*Parrett pre-1973*) Large single scarlet miniature with white eye, blushed Tyrian-rose. Mid-green foliage.

Dunkler Schoene (*Both pre-1962*) One of the few 'Stellar'-type dwarfs. Flowers are single pink with the two top petals narrower than the lower three. Leaves are very dark green, deeply cut in the usual 'Stellar' pattern. Australian variety, rare in Britain.

Dusky Red (*Holborow pre-1968*) Australian miniature variety with large single flowers of dull dusky red on a short compact plant.

Dutch Vermilion (*pre-1960*) Single orange-scarlet flowers, mid-green foliage. Miniature.

Dwarf Mandarine (*Bodey pre-1972*) Another of the rare 'Stellar'-type miniatures from Australia. Warm salmon-red single flowers with reddish hue to the dark green foliage which is deeply cut in the usual 'Stellar' manner.

Dwarf Miriam Basey (*Read about 1950*) This is the raiser's spelling but it is often listed as 'Dwarf Miriam Baisey'. Single flowers, white overlaid with red, lighter in lower petals. Deep green foliage. Slow-growing miniature variety, identical to 'Maureen'.

E

Earl King (*1968*) Compact dwarf with mid-green zoned foliage. Large semi-double flowers of cerise-red.

Eclipse (*Stringer pre-1967*) Dark red to crimson double flowers, dark green foliage, black zone. Habit between dwarf and miniature.

Eden Gem (*Parrett pre-1969*) Double flowers of crimson and neyron-rose. Leaves mid- to dark green with faint zoning. Miniature.

Edith Steane (*pre-1982*) Vermilion double flowers leaning towards poppy-red. Dark green foliage with black zone. Dwarf.

Edwin Clarke (*Portas pre-1979*) Large miniature or small dwarf. Single flowers of brilliant red, dark green foliage with deeper zone.

Egmont (*Dugust 1969*) Large flowered miniature, single flowers, bright scarlet with paler centre. Mid-green foliage.

Elaine (*Parrett pre-1964*) Single flowers of rich camellia-rose with trowel shaped petals. Yellowy-green foliage with slight zone. Dwarf.

Elaine Knight (*Tilley pre-1980*) Semi-double flowers of mauve-purple. Miniature.

Elf (*Arndt 1949*) Miniature from the USA. Single flowers of velvety dark scarlet with rounded petals. Mid-green foliage with scalloped margins, no zone. Slow growing, seldom grows taller than 4in (10cm).

Elf (*Miller 1952*) Miniature fancyleaved variety from California. Small single flowers of bright scarlet. Leaves are small, dark grey-green with wide yellow border zoned with irregular splashes of scarlet. Slow growing. Acknowledged to be one of Holmes Miller's greatest introductions. Sometimes incorrectly listed as 'Elfin'.

Elizabeth Thompson *(Peat pre-1967)* Large single flowers of cerise-red, dark green foliage. Miniature.

Ella *(Parrett pre-1975)* Miniature variety. Single flowers of phlox-pink with white eye. Leaves dull green.

Elmer Garfield *(Garfield pre-1969)* Short-jointed dwarf plant with single flowers of magenta-purple and mid-green foliage. Mr Garfield was a Canadian who took up residence in England where he devoted most of his time to his collection of Geraniums.

Elna *(Parrett about 1965)* Pure white single flowers on a miniature plant with mid-green foliage.

Elsie Portas *(Portas pre-1980)* Dwarf fancyleaved variety with double flowers of pure scarlet. Foliage is yellow-green to gold with light bronze zone.

Embassy *(Stringer 1972)* Large single flowers of orange-vermilion with small white eye. Mid-green foliage, zoned. Habit between dwarf and miniature.

Embers *(pre-1969)* Single flowers of salmon-orange with separated petals and mid-green foliage. Habit between dwarf and miniature.

Emma Hössler *(Hössle 1910)* Semi-dwarf with small light rose-pink double flowers and light green leaves darkening towards the edges. Bushy habit. Also listed as 'Frau Emma Hössler', 'Frau Emma Hössle', etc. It seems possible that the latter is the originator's name.

Emma Jane Read *(Read about 1975)* Double flowers of deep mauve-pink. Dark green foliage. Dwarf.

Empress of China *(Gillam 1980)* Miniature fancyleaved variety with single vermilion flowers. Foliage is mainly white with central 'butterfly' of light green overlaid with rich rose zone. ('Medallion' x 'Gwen'). Canadian.

Ena *(Parrett 1968)* Single white flowers with a circle of pink around the eye giving a halo effect similar to 'Mauretania'. Dark green zoned foliage. Miniature.

Endora *(pre-1967)* Single flowers of soft cherry-red. Mid-green leaves with paler zone. Habit between miniature and dwarf.

Enid Read *(Read 1960)* Single flowers of dark coral-red with mid-green foliage. Dwarf seedling of 'Beatrice Little'.

Epsilon *(Arndt about 1950)* Single flower, soft pink shading to white towards centre with deeper pink ring. Foliage is pale green. Similar semi-dwarf habit to 'Emma Hössler' but more compact.

Epsilon Two *(Taylor 1979)* Miniature seedling of 'Cupid'. Single flowers of coral suffused flame towards centre with darker veining. Unusual petal shape and formation. Dark green leaves, heavy zone.

Erica *(Morf pre-1969)* Miniature Australian variety with rose-pink double flowers and very dark green leaves with black zone.

Erwarton *(Bidwell pre-1972)* Bright red double flowered miniature with bright green foliage. Multi-branching growth. Often erroneously listed as 'Edwarton', 'Erwalton' and 'Ewarton'.

Escapade *(Hartsook about 1960)* Californian dwarf, 'Best Seedling' award at the International Geranium Society's 1965 Show. Double flowers, colour between light coral and apricot occasionally with some white. Dark green foliage with slight zone.

Essie Myers *(Holborow pre-1969)* Australian miniature. Double flowers of a soft cream with pink and mauve glow or shading, centres flushed jasper-red. Dark green foliage with lacy zone.

Etna *(pre-1965)* Single cherry-red flowers, dark green foliage with black zone. Miniature.

Evelyn *(Parrett pre-1976)* Single rose-pink flowers with white flush. Miniature.

Excelsior *(Stringer 1969)* Large blood-red single flowers with distinct white eye. Mid-green foliage. Dwarf.

122

F

Fairy *(Arndt 1949)* Miniature from the USA. Single salmon-pink flowers. Small mid-green leaves with near-black zone.

Fairyland *(Miller 1951)* Californian fancyleaved miniature. Small single light-scarlet flowers. Small grey-green leaves, wide ivory border zoned with irregular splashes of rose-red. Slow growing and difficult to propagate. Seldom grows more than 4in (10cm); best in 3in (8cm) pot.

Fairy Princess Large single flowers of pale apricot-pink. Dark green foliage. Miniature.

Fairy Storey *(Storey 1971)* Fancyleaved miniature variety. Single scarlet flower. Yellow leaves with pink, red and green overlays. One of Don Storey's earlier releases and still among his best.

Fairy Tales *(from USA pre-1965)* Single white ruffled flowers with pale lavender centres. Mid-green zoned foliage. Slow-growing dwarf.

Falkenham *(Bidwell 1978)* Large single flowers of orange-cerise. Miniature.

Falkland Hero *(Shellard 1982)* Dwarf fancyleaved variety with single red flowers. Leaves are pale yellow with green centre and red zone overlaying both colours. Colouring similar to 'Mrs Henry Cox' but more delicate and the leaf is more dentate.

Fanciette *(Both pre-1962)* Dwarf fancyleaf from Australia. Single white flowers shading to red edge. Originator's spelling, not 'Fancyette'.

Fancy Free *(Campbell 1963)* Dwarf fancyleaved variety. Single, primitive-type salmon flowers. Leaves creamy-yellow with green butterfly marking in centre overlaid pink and red. Probably has 'Prostrate Boar' among its parentage.

Fantasie Brilliant white, free flowering double, possibly an improved strain of 'Dick's White'. Pea-green foliage with no zone. Much favoured as a seed parent. Sometimes wrongly listed as 'Fantasia'. Dwarf.

Feneela *(Parrett pre-1966)* Double flowers of geranium-lake red with porcelain-rose at base of petals. Foliage mid-green, zoned. Dwarf. Raiser's spelling, not 'Fenella'.

Festal *(Stringer pre-1979)* Double flowers of orange-salmon. Golden foliage. Large miniature or small dwarf. Parentage apparently includes some 'Deacon' blood.

Filigree *(Miller 1953)* Dwarf fancyleaf from California. Deep salmon single flowers, silvery-green leaves, bordered creamy-white and delicately zoned with pink and chestnut overlays.

Finito *(Read pre-1978)* Dwarf. Double flowers of candy-pink, mid-green foliage.

Firecracker *(Miller 1970)* P. acetosum hybrid. Small double red flowers, profuse bloomer. Dark green shiny leaves, scalloped as parent. Miniature from California.

Firefly Double flowers of medium red with dark green foliage. Compact miniature. There is also a 'Firefly' in the USA with double crimson flowers introduced about 1962.

Fire Glow *(Parrett pre-1964)* Miniature. Bright red single flowers, dark green zoned foliage.

Firelight *(Parrett about 1965)* Bright scarlet double flowers and very dark green foliage with black zone. Seldom exceeds 5in (12.5cm).

Flakey *(Pierrt 1979)* Canadian miniature ivyleaf raised by Mrs. Pat Pierrt ('Mrs Pat'). Double pale mauve flowers, almost white. The waxy green leaves are flaked and streaked with white. Sport of 'Gay Baby' sometimes listed as 'Variegated Gay Baby'. Similar to 'Wood's Surprise' but the latter has deeper mauve flowers.

Flash *(Parrett pre-1964)* Single bright scarlet flowers with white base to upper petals, lightly flushed purple and orange sheen all over. Mid-green foliage. Miniature.

Fleming Mead *(Wells pre-1971)* Dwarf variety with light red double flowers and mid-green foliage. Wells lived in a road named Fleming Mead in Mitcham, Surrey, England.

123

Fleurette *(Case about 1955)* One of the earlier dwarf varieties used almost universally as a seed parent, but an excellent plant in its own right. Double flowers of coral to salmon-pink, flushing slightly with age. Deep green foliage, zoned. Sometimes erroneously listed as 'Fleuretta'.

Flirt *(Miller 1961)* Double flowers with creamy-white base to petals, heavily flecked and streaked salmon-pink. Mid-green foliage. Fast-growing dwarf. Flower markings may vary from plant to plant.

Flowton *(Bidwell 1970)* Dwarf seedling of 'Denebola'. Double flowers of soft red with dark green leaves.

Formosum *(May pre-1970)* Raised by Clara and Harry May of Long Beach, California from seed collected from an Australian import. Double 'Stellar'-type flowers of salmon-red on the usual 'Stellar' foliage. Easy to grow, semi-dwarf in Britain but can develop into a 24in (61cm) bush in California and similar climates.

Foxbury White *(pre-1969)* Origin unknown but first listed by Anthony Ayton in 1969. Single white, lightly flushed pink with mid-green foliage. Small dwarf, compact habit rather similar to 'Vesuvius'.

Foxfire *(Roth pre-1980)* Single pale orchid flower, white base to upper petals and dark green foliage. Fast growing, large miniature or small dwarf.

Foxhall *(Bidwell pre-1973)* Single salmon-pink flowers with narrow petals and dark foliage. Dwarf.

Francis Parrett *(Parrett 1965)* Bright lavender double flowers carried in tight clusters above mid-green foliage. Originator's spelling, not 'Frances Parrett'. Miniature.

Francis Read *(Read pre-1970)* Dwarf variety with rich deep pink double flowers and mid-green foliage. Raiser's spelling, not 'Frances Read'.

Francis Westwood *(Peat 1969)* Miniature. Double flowers of cerise-pink on a compact bushy plant.

Frank Headley *(Headley 1957)* Semi-dwarf fancyleaved variety. Single primitive flowers of dawn-pink. Leaves mid-green with deep irregular creamy-white border and occasional chestnut zoning.

Freak of Nature *(Gray about 1880)* Small red single flowers. Leaves have crenulated edge of green with large creamy-white blotch in centre. Stems almost transparent white with faint pink and green vertical stripes. Not easy to propagate but a very interesting dwarf variety to grow.

Freston *(Bidwell 1973)* Single orange-pink flowers, mid-green foliage with darker zone. Dwarf.

Freya *(Parrett pre-1973)* Single scarlet flowers with lighter centre. Dark green zoned foliage. Miniature.

Friary Wood *(Peat pre-1967)* Large loose double flowers of fuchsine-pink with slight white eye. Large golden-green leaves with finely serrated edges, the ragged chestnut zone on young foliage gradually fades as the leaf ages. Dwarf.

Friesdorf *(Löbner 1927)* Single medium red flowers with crimson overtones and narrow primitive-type petals. Leaves are dark green with black zone. Tends to spindly growth if not controlled. Semi-dwarf. In 1967 Hazeldene raised a more compact strain which was marketed as 'Friesdorff'.

Frills *(Miller 1966)* Californian dwarf variety derived from P. acetosum. Loose double flowers of soft coral-salmon with many narrow petals giving a shaggy appearance. Dark green leaves on slender stems, shiny and fleshy as its parent.

Frolic *(Miller 1959)* Californian dwarf variety. Large double flowers of salmon-pink with buff and apricot tones, often paler at edges of petals. Dark green foliage with deeper zone.

Frosty *(Stringer pre-1977)* Single white flowers, mid-green foliage. Miniature.

Fynn *(Hill pre-1964)* Single flowers of dazzling orange-red. Dwarf.

124

G

Garnet Rosebud *(Miller 1970)* Tiny plant from California with dark red 'Rosebud'-type flowers and mid-green foliage. Slow growing, seldom exceeds 4in (10cm). Almost in the micro-miniature class.

Gay Baby The first miniature ivyleaf variety, raised in Australia, my introduction into England in 1965 via the F.R.E. Coates nursery of Melbourne. Tiny shield-shaped leaves and small pale mauve flowers.

Gay Baby Supreme *(pre-1986)* Sport of 'Gay Baby' with much larger pale lilac flowers and stronger growth. Dwarf ivyleaf variety.

Gemma *(Stringer 1984)* Fancyleaved miniature variety. The single flowers are white based, flecked and speckled red. Golden-green foliage with bronze zone.

Geoff May Large single flowers of porcelain-rose with large white eye. Dark foliage with deeper zone. Dwarf.

Geraldine *(Parrett pre-1966)* Miniature. Large single vermilion flower with white eye. Mid-green foliage.

Gerald Wells *(Parrett pre-1966)* Single fuchsine-pink flowers with white base to upper petals. Mid-green foliage. Miniature.

Gill *(Parrett pre-1966)* Cactus-type flowers with quilled petals of deep cherry-red. Dark green zoned foliage. Miniature.

Gipsy Gem *(Wilson 1961)* Double flowers of cherry-red with ruffled petals. Dark green scalloped foliage. Raised in the USA where it is spelt 'Gypsy Gem'. Semi-dwarf.

Gladys Robinson's Hill *(Southport Parks Dept 1968)* Single camellia-rose flowers with serrated petals and mid-green foliage. Dwarf sport of 'Mrs. E.G. Hill'.

Gladys Stevens *(Parrett)* Miniature variety with double flowers of Persian-rose and dark green zoned foliage.

Glenis *(Parrett pre-1965)* Large single flowers of pure vermilion. Mid-green foliage with darker zone. Dwarf.

Goblin *(Kerrigan)* Miniature from the USA. Double scarlet flowers, dark green foliage. Rapid grower and easy to propagate. (Holmes Miller also raised a 'Goblin' which is similar but a deeper red.)

Golden Butterfly Fancyleaved dwarf sport of 'Robert Fish'. Single red flowers, pea-green foliage with a yellow butterfly mark in the centre of each leaf.

Golden Chalice *(Stringer 1985)* Small olive-green cupped leaves with dark zone and brilliant yellow towards edge, often showing a frilly red border. Semi-primitive single flowers, powder-pink, streaked and spotted scarlet. A collector's gem but rare. Min.

Golden Crest *(Stringer pre-1970)* Not a true dwarf or miniature but so slow growing that it can reasonably be included as a semi-dwarf variety. Single rose-pink flowers with slightly separated petals, rather sparse and frail. The foliage is a glorious golden-yellow, slightly frilled and very dense. Short-jointed, self-branching habit, will take several years to reach 10in (25cm) under British conditions.

Golden Ears *(Gillam 1982)* Miniature 'Stellar' variety with pale green leaves and brown blotch. Single vermilion flowers on a small and compact plant. Of Canadian origin, named after the peaks of Mount Blanshard east of Vancouver.

Golden Fleece *(Stringer)* Fancyleaved miniature variety. Double flowers of soft porcelain-rose. Frilled gold-green leaves with bronze zone.

Golden Gate Fancyleaved miniature with single salmon-orange flowers and golden foliage with chestnut zone.

Golden Harry Hieover *(Cannell pre-1878)* Fancyleaved semi-dwarf. Strong-growing golden-leaved variety with bronze zone and single red flowers. Good bedding plant but rather too vigorous for inside use.

Golden Mist *(Stringer)* Dwarf fancyleaf. Pink double flowers, golden-yellow foliage.

Golden Orfe Coral-pink single flowers, yellow foliage with copper zone. Dwarf fancyleaved variety.

Golden Oriole Bright pale green leaves with copper zone. Single light salmon flowers almost continually in bloom. Semi-dwarf.

Golden Petit Pierre *(May)* Miniature sport of 'Petit Pierre' raised by Harry May in California. Single rose-pink flowers on golden foliage.

Golden Prince *(Parrett pre-1966)* Medium size single flowers in a deep shade of orange. Mid-green foliage with no zoning. Dwarf.

Golden Princess *(Parrett pre-1966)* Large single flowers of azalea-pink deepening towards the base of the upper petals. Mid-green leaf. Miniature form of 'Golden Lion'.

Golden Roc *(Parrett)* Single vermilion flowers, yellow leaf with golden zone. Miniature.

Golden Tears *(Stringer 1984)* Miniature ivyleaf variety. Pale lilac double flowers (almost white) with small golden-green leaves.

Golden Treasury *(Stringer 1971)* Very attractive fancyleaved miniature, not easy to grow or propagate. Green and gold foliage with red single flowers.

Gold Leaf *(Stringer)* Dwarf fancyleaved variety with bright red semi-double flowers and golden foliage.

Grace Read *(Read)* Blush-white single flowers with salmon ring and mid-green foliage. Miniature.

Grace Wells *(Wells pre-1966)* Miniature with large single flowers of fuchsine-pink veined darker, white base to upper petals. Dark green foliage with black zone.

Granny Hewitt Small double flowers of brilliant scarlet and pale green foliage. Very short dense-growing miniature, free flowering and easy to propagate. Said to have been discovered growing in the garden of an old lady in Gloucestershire after whom it is named, but the county seems to vary to match the origin of the relator.

Greengold Kleine Liebling *(Miller 1964)* Miniature fancyleaved sport of 'Kleine Liebling' (syn. 'Little Darling', 'Petit Pierre'). Small single pale crimson flowers with white centres. Yellow-green foliage with irregular cream blotch in centre of leaves. Sometimes listed as 'Greengold Petit Pierre'.

Grenadier Dwarf variety with single flowers of bright crimson, dark green leaves, almost black.

Grey Sprite *(Miller 1969)* Miniature fancyleaved sport of 'Sprite'. Dark grey-green leaves with narrow ivory border often tinged with pink. Single coral flowers.

Grozser Garten Originator's name, not 'Grossersorten' or any other variation. Dwarf plant with single pink flowers and mid-green foliage.

Grozser Garten Weiss White sport of 'Grozser Garten', identical except for colour of flower. Dwarf.

Grumpy *(Robert 1938)* Single cerise flowers, mid-green foliage. One of Rober's group of 'Snow White and the Seven Dwarfs'.

Gwen *(Parrett)* Fancyleaved miniature, one of the first to be raised and marketed in Britain. Very short and close-growing therefore subject to botrytis infection unless kept clean and open. Single red flower. The foliage is white, overlaid green and red, often with pink edges. The area of zoning varies from leaf to leaf but is produced by the red pigment. Difficult to propagate in Britain except during July and early August. Grows on average less than 1in (25mm) a year and the plant seldom makes more than 3in (7.5cm).

Gwen Moody *(Peat pre-1968)* Dwarf variety with bright mauve single flowers and dark green foliage.

126

H

Happy *(Rober 1938)* One of Rober's 'Snow White and the Seven Dwarfs' group. Double flowers of dark poppy-red. Mid-green foliage.

Hazel Dwarf. Single cherry-red flowers, dark green foliage. The flowers are borne on long stems and stand well clear of the leaves.

Heidi Double-flowered miniature, white flaked carmine with deep pink edges.

Henhurst Gleam *(Parrett pre-1965)* Crimson double flowers blushed purple. Foliage is pale green with faint zone. Dwarf.

Henley Large double flowers of pale violet-pink. Miniature.

High Tor *(Portas)* Fancyleaved semi-dwarf variety. Double flowers of strong appleblossom-pink. Pea-green leaves with copper zone.

Hintlesham Salmon-pink single flowers, mid-green foliage. Miniature.

Hitcham Miniature variety with double flowers of bright orange.

Honeywood Matthew *(Thorpe pre-1982)* Single flowers of Dutch-vermilion with large white eye and mid-green foliage. Dwarf.

Honneas Fluorescent dark red single flowers. Miniature.

Hope Valley *(Portas)* Dwarf fancyleaved variety. Double flowers of rose-pink, yellow-green leaves with pale zone.

Horace Read *(Read)* Dwarf variety with single flowers of strong pink with white eye.

Hurdy-Gurdy *(Storey)* Double crimson flowers, leaves are green and cream with a thin red zone. Fancyleaf variety with habit between miniature and dwarf.

I

Ian Read *(Read pre-1966)* Deep red double flowers, mid-green foliage. Miniature.

Ice Cap *(Stringer)* Miniature variety with single white flowers and mid-green foliage.

Imp *(Miller 1951)* Surprisingly large flowers for such a small plant, single medium salmon. Foliage almost black. Very slow-growing miniature.

Improved Nicor Star *(Brawner pre-1985)* Dwarf variety raised by Faye Brawner of Oregon, USA. Single white flower with red 'star' in the centre and narrow red edge. Dark green foliage.

Ipswich Town Dwarf variety with cerise-pink double flowers.

Isaac Read *(Read 1968)* Dwarf seedling of 'Elizabeth Cartwright'. Single flowers of deep brick-red overlaying orange. Mid-green foliage.

Isolda Attractive semi-double miniature with flowers of a deep shade of pink. Mid-green foliage with dark zone.

J

Jack Read *(Read)* Large fiery scarlet single flower with white base to top petals and mid-green foliage. Dwarf.

Jane Biggin *(Portas 1976)* Dwarf fancyleaved variety with double flowers of strawberry-pink. The large leaves are bright golden-yellow with distinct chestnut zone on young foliage which fades as the leaves mature.

Jane Shoulder *(Greeves 1980)* Light red, single flowered miniature with dark green foliage.

Janet Kerrigan *(Kerrigan)* Full double flowers of pale salmon-pink, mid-green zoned foliage. Dwarf to miniature habit.

Jaunty *(Miller 1961)* Large double flowers of geranium-lake with white base to some petals and blushed carmine. Mid-green foliage. Miniature.

127

Jay Palest powder-pink single flower with slightly deeper veining. Dwarf.

Jayne *(Parrett 1966)* Dawn-pink double flowers deepening towards centre. Dark green foliage with black zone. Miniature.

Jayne Eyre *(Stringer 1968)* Deeper shade of lavender than 'Francis Parrett' and the leaf is zoned, otherwise the plant is very similar. Often wrongly listed as 'Jane Eyre'. Dwarf.

Jean Beatty White double flowers. Free flowering compact dwarf.

Jenifer *(Parrett pre-1965)* Large single rose-pink flowers, dark green foliage with deeper zone. Miniature.

Jenifer Read *(Read 1966)* Single flowers of pale camellia-rose with white eye. Dwarf seedling of 'Mauretania'.

Jill Portas *(Portas)* Tangerine single flowers, golden foliage with bronze zone. Dwarf fancyleaved variety.

Joan *(pre-1965)* Australian dwarf variety. Rose-pink single flowers, dark green foliage.

Joan Hayward *(Parrett pre-1966)* Soft salmon single flowers, flushed azalea-pink. Dark green foliage with black zone. Miniature.

Joan Shearman *(Parrett pre-1966)* Soft peach-red single flowers, dark green foliage with black zone. Miniature.

Joyful Geranium-lake single flower with large white eye, lightly blushed Tyrian-rose. Dark green foliage. Miniature.

Judy *(from Australia pre-1965)* Coral-pink single flowers, similar to but slightly larger than 'Joan'. Mid-green foliage. Dwarf.

Judy Read *(Read 1967)* Single flowers of bright reddish-pink with mid-green foliage. Slow-growing dwarf variety.

Jupiter Medium size single flowers of rose-red. Dark green foliage. Easy to propagate. Miniature.

Just William *(Hopkins pre-1986)* Bright red double flowers, yellowy-green foliage. Miniature.

K

Kaleidescope *(Bagust 1970)* Miniature fancyleaf. Single red flowers, leaves have a yellow base with green centre and pink tinges.

Karanette *(about 1962)* Australian miniature with soft carmine-pink single flowers. Dark green foliage with deeper zone.

Karen *(Peat about 1985)* Dwarf fancyleaved variety with single orange-salmon flowers. Foliage is pea-green to yellow with broad chestnut zone fading towards edge of leaf and distinct copper medallion in centre.

Katherine Young Single flowers of dull scarlet with small white eye. Dark green foliage. Miniature.

Kathryn *(Parrett 1968)* Single geranium-lake flowers, dark green foliage. Miniature.

Keepsake *(Miller 1962)* Californian fast-growing dwarf variety. Double flowers of deep purple-rose with white centres in large clusters. Dark green foliage.

Ken Salmon *(Salmon 1981)* Double vermilion flowers, deep green foliage. Dwarf.

Kerensa *(Parrett 1968)* Semi-double flowers of cherry-red edged white. Mid-green leaf. Miniature.

Kershy *(1978)* Very large single flowers of deep pink with white eye. Miniature.

Kippen *(1962)* Dwarf plant with salmon-pink double flowers. Free flowering, mid-green foliage.

Kirton Compact miniature with soft red double flowers.

Kitten *(May 1965)* Californian miniature with single brilliant scarlet flowers. Mid-green foliage with darker zone.

Kleine Liebling Dwarf variety raised in Germany about 1920. Small single flowers of rhodamine-pink carried in abundance on slender erect stems. Small mid-green leaves with some zoning. Synonymous with 'Little Darling' and 'Petit Pierre'.
Kosset *(Bagust 1982)* Double-flowered miniature with large pale pink to white flowerheads. Mid-green zoned foliage.
Krista *(probably Parrett)* Ball-shaped double flowers of mandarin-red with dark green foliage and black zone. Dwarf.
Kyra Double white flowers with pale pink base to all petals. Mid-green zoned foliage. Dwarf.

L

Lady Kybo *(Thorp 1967)* Raised by Reg Thorp of Brackley, Northants. Large single flowers of apricot-pink overlaid carmine. Dwarf.
Lady Lexington Miniature ivyleaf variety. Lavender-pink double flowers on cream-and-green foliage. Often sports flowers of pink and white on the same plant.
Lagoon *(Stringer)* Pale mauve double flowers, mid-green foliage. Some 'Deacon' in its ancestry. Dwarf.
Lark *(Hill)* Orange-red double flowers, bright green foliage. Miniature.
Lavender-Pink Bird's Egg Canadian miniature with semi-double flowers, basically white but lightly speckled red. Mid-green foliage.
Layham Dwarf variety with bright pink large double flowers.
L'Elegante *(Cannell 1868)* Dwarf ivyleaf variety. Very pale mauve flowers (almost white) with purple veining. Green-and-white variegated leaves which will develop shades of pink and purple if the plant is grown hard.
Len Chandler Single crimson flowers with distinct white centre and mid-green foliage. Miniature.
L'Enfer Of French origin, identical to 'Mephistopheles' which see. Dwarf.
Leo *(Stringer 1965)* Very large single flowers of bright orange with no trace of red unless over-fed with potash. The plant is vigorous but compact with pale green foliage almost unzoned. Miniature.
Leslie Salmon *(Salmon)* Compact dwarf with a green-gold leaf with faint zone. The single scarlet flowers have a tiny white eye and a deeper red cast at the petal edges.
Levington Salmon-pink double flowers. Miniature.
Lilian *(Parrett pre-1966)* Large white single flowers with bright orange stamens and medium green leaf. Dwarf.
Lisa *(Dorrell)* Fancyleaved miniature variety. Single pale pink flowers, golden-yellow leaf with deep bronze zone.
Little Darling Synonymous with 'Petit Pierre', and 'Kleine Liebling' which see.
Little Margaret *(Storey 1971)* Miniature fancyleaved variety. Single red flowers. Leaves are white based, with green splash and pink-and-mahogany shading.
Lively Lady *(Stringer 1968)* Single orange-scarlet flowers with small white eye. Pale pea-green foliage without zone, compact dwarf bushy habit.
Loretta *(probably Parrett)* Single flowers of turkey-red with large white eye and blushed magenta. Mid-green foliage. Dwarf.
Lorna Deep crimson tight double flowers held well clear of the mid-green foliage on long slender stems. Dwarf. Probably one of Parrett's raising but it does not appear in any of the lists I have.
Lorraine White based single with cerise overlay. Dwarf. Could be from Parrett.
Loxton *(Peat 1980)* Large orange single flowers. Yellow-green leaves with wavy bronze zone. Dwarf.
Lucilla Rose-red single flowers blushed purple. Mid-green foliage. Miniature.

Lucinda *(Parrett pre 1966)* Large single flower of signal-red with tiny white eye. Zoned mid-green foliage. Miniature.

Lucy Single flowers of cherry-red. Miniature.

Lynne *(Parrett pre-1966)* Small single flowers of signal-red with tiny white eye. Dark green leaf with black zone. Miniature.

Lyric *(Miller pre-1960)* Californian miniature. Lavender-pink double with white centre. Large flowers and flowerheads freely produced. Dark green foliage, compact habit, fast grower. 'Margery Stimpson' is identical in England but in western USA the colour is paler.

M

Madame Butterfly *(Reg Thorp 1958)* Semi-dwarf fancyleaf variety with cerise double flowers. Foliage is cream and deep green with butterfly mark on most leaves. Only just gets into the semi-dwarf class, under ideal conditions in warm climates can grow up to 18in (46cm) but makes little more than 9in (23cm) in Britain.

Madame Fournier *(Lemoine 1895)* Very old variety, one of the first miniatures recorded. Small single scarlet flowers, very dark foliage. Possibly a parent of 'Red Black Vesuvius', certainly very similar. Dwarf to miniature.

Madame Salleron *(Lemoine 1840–50)* Sometimes listed erroneously as 'Madame Salleroi'. Six inch (15cm) diameter domes of mid-green leaves with silvery edges. The leaves are almost circular and lemon-scented. Does not flower. An excellent edging plant. 'Little Trot' is similar but has a slightly larger and darker leaf, more upright habit and single red flowers.

Madge Hill Single bi-colour flowers of white and crimson. Miniature.

Magda *(Stringer 1984)* Large double flowers of pale pink with red splashes and stripes and much speckling. Mid-green foliage. Dwarf.

Maid of Honour Single salmon-pink flowers shading paler towards edge of petals and suffused white. Mid-green foliage. Miniature.

Manta *(Stringer)* Bright orange single flowers with white eye. Miniature. Sometimes wrongly listed as 'Mantar'.

Mantilla *(Stringer 1969)* Large flowered crisp orange single with large white eye. Mid-green foliage with slight zoning. Miniature.

Margery Stimpson *(Stimpson about 1967)* In Britain identical to Holmes Miller's 'Lyric' which pre-dates it by at least seven years, but in California and Oregon the flower is paler. Miniature.

Marion *(Parrett pre-1966)* Large azalea-pink flowers, dark green foliage with near-black zone. Raiser's spelling, not 'Marian'. Miniature.

Marmalade Californian dwarf variety I introduced from Road Runner Ranch in 1968. Orange-red double flowers on long stems, mid-green foliage.

Marnia Mauve-pink single flowers with white eye. Miniature.

Martin Parrett *(Parrett 1970)* Miniature variety with deep rose-pink double flowers and mid-green foliage.

Mary Ellen Tanner Pure white double flowers, mid-green foliage. Miniature.

Mary Read *(Read 1966)* Pure white single flowers, mid-green foliage. Dwarf.

Mary Screen Miniature variety with red semi-double flowers.

Mary Steven Large single lavender-mauve flowers with serrated petals. Mid-green foliage with darker zone. Dwarf.

Maureen *(Parrett pre-1966)* Miniature variety with large single flowers of white overlaid red, lighter in lower petals. Deep green foliage. Identical to 'Dwarf Miriam Basey'.

Meditation *(Miller 1963)* Purple-rose single with tiny white eye. Dark green, bushy foliage. Dwarf.

Medley *(Miller 1961)* Double white miniature. Buds first open with a distinct greenish-yellow tinge which changes to pale pink as they develop. Petals are often veined red on reverse. Dark green foliage.

Melanie *(Parrett pre-1966)* Dawn-pink double flowers with deeper blush. Dark green leaf with black zone. Miniature.

Melissa *(Parrett pre-1966)* Single flowers begin life as pure white gradually changing to pale pink. Dark green zoned foliage. Miniature.

Memento Double flowers of light apricot-salmon. Dark green leaves distinctly zoned. Miniature.

Mephistopheles *(Lemoine 1893)* Miniature with red single flowers and almost black leaves. Often confused with 'Red Black Vesuvius' which is almost identical.

Merry-Go-Round Dwarf fancyleaved variety thought to have been raised by Don Storey. Leaves are basically creamy-yellow with a large green butterfly mark in centre, overlaid with deep pink narrow zone. The pink is distinct on the young foliage but fades as the leaf matures. Single red flower.

Meteor Narrow-petalled bright scarlet single flowers, dark green foliage. Miniature.

Michelle Dwarf fancyleaved variety with single flowers of medium pink. The foliage is golden-yellow with bronze zone.

Mimi *(Peat pre-1985)* Miniature fancyleaf. Loose double flowers of deep powder-pink, pale green foliage with faint zone.

Minsmere *(1965)* Tiny plant, seldom exceeding 4in (10cm) with small mid-green leaves and brilliant scarlet star-like flowers.

Minuet *(Peat 1969)* Dwarf fancyleaved variety. Pale yellow-green foliage with bronze medallion-type splash in centre of each leaf. Claret-mauve double flowers.

Minx *(Miller 1955)* Blend of red and crimson double flowers. Colour can vary between red and near-purple in different parts of the flower and at different seasons. Dark green foliage. Miniature.

Miranda *(Parrett pre-1965)* Large single flowers of signal-red. Mid-green foliage. Dwarf.

Mischief *(Miller 1951)* Semi-dwarf variety from California. Cactus-type double flowers with narrow rolled and twisted petals in orange-scarlet. Dark foliage. Strong grower, only just gets into the semi-dwarf class.

Miss Burdett-Coutts *(Grieve 1869)* Fancyleaved semi-dwarf with single vermilion flowers. The leaves are creamy-white with splashes of green at centre overlaid with a distinct red zone.

Miss Muffett *(Stringer 1984)* Bright lavender-pink double flowers, dark green foliage faintly zoned. Miniature.

Miss Potter *(Bagust 1966)* Large single flowers of deep satiny-red. Dark green foliage with darker zone. Miniature.

Miss Prim *(Stringer 1969)* Masses of medium sized single white flowers with bright red stamens and pink veining. The crisp semi-primitive flowers are startling against the mid-green foliage. Miniature.

Miss Wackles *(Stringer 1970)* Large deep red double flowers with well zoned mid-green foliage. Dwarf.

Misty Pure white single flowers carried in abundance on long stems above the mid-green foliage. Miniature.

Mitzi Single flowers of pale pink. Miniature.

Moonbeam Slightly cupped single flowers of pale orange with salmon tints. Dark green foliage with deeper zone. Dwarf.

Monica Bennett *(Bennett pre-1966)* Flowers very similar to 'Grace Wells' in colour and size but there is a slight difference in the leaf-shape and the zoning is more pronounced. 'Grace Wells' is more compact. Dwarf.

131

Monsal Dale *(Portas)* Dwarf fancyleaf variety with double flowers of strawberry-pink. The leaves are golden-yellow with a copper zone.

More Mischief *(Miller 1959)* The humour of Holmes Miller is revealed in his choice of names. This semi-dwarf cactus-flowered variety is similar to 'Mischief' but the flowers are double, pale salmon with deeper veining.

Morning Cloud *(Stringer 1970)* Large ragged double flowers of pale lilac with pea-green foliage. Miniature.

Morning Sunrise *(Parrett pre-1966)* Miniature fancyleaved variety with small single orange-red flowers. Small-leaved plant, the foliage is mid-green splashed with pale green blotches. Slow growing but easy to propagate.

Morval *(Portas 1976)* Dwarf fancyleaf. Double flowers of soft blush-pink. Golden-yellow leaves with chestnut zone. Named after the Cornish village.

Morwyn *(Parrett 1968)* Double flowers of phlox-pink with dark green foliage. Miniature.

Mountie *(Flora Vista 1977)* Compact dwarf Canadian introduction with large single scarlet flowers. Dark green foliage with near-black zone.

Moya *(Parrett pre-1966)* Single flowers of mandarin-red with upper petals blushed vermilion. Dark green zoned foliage. Miniature.

Mr Everaarts Semi-dwarf of Dutch origin. Double flowers of rose-pink with white centres. Free flowering with large flowers and flowerheads. Vigorous bushy habit, larger than most dwarf varieties and excellent for outside bedding. Sometimes listed as 'Mrs Everaarts'.

Mr Pecksniff *(Bagust 1967)* Medium size single flowers of mauve-pink with white base to upper petals. Mid-green foliage with deeper zone. Miniature.

Mr Pickwick *(Bagust 1964)* Large flowered single flowers of deep salmon with orange and red overtones. Dark foliage with darker zone. Dwarf.

Mrs Pat *(Gillam 1984)* Sister seedling of 'Golden Ears' but with salmon single flowers. ('Mrs Pat' is the affectionate name by which Mrs Pat Pierrt is known in British Columbia.)

Myra *(Stringer 1965)* Large single shell-pink flowers. Short compact plant with mid-green foliage. Miniature. Sometimes listed as 'Mira' but 'Myra' is the raiser's spelling.

N

Nadine *(Parrett about 1965)* Large dawn-pink double flowers on a strong growing plant. Pale green foliage with golden zone. Dwarf.

Nancy Grey Also often listed as 'Nancy Gray'. Camellia-rose single flowers with white base to petals. Miniature.

Neene Deep cerise single flowers. Dwarf.

Nell Gigg Magenta-red double flowers. Miniature.

Nerina Attractive semi-double flowers in a shade of shocking-pink. Mid-green zoned foliage. Miniature.

Nero *(Burrows 1955)* Very small plant seldom exceeding 4in (10cm). Flowers are large, single, Dutch-vermilion. Dark green foliage with black zone, centre of leaf often flushed red.

Nicola *(Parrett about 1962)* Large single flowers of bright rose-pink. Dark green foliage with black zone. Miniature.

Night & Day Very large pale pink single flowers shading almost to white at edge of petals. Dark green foliage with faint zoning. Dwarf.

Nodrog Single white flowers with slight pink blush on mature petals. Mid-green foliage. Miniature.

Noon *(Stringer)* Double bright red flowers, mid-green foliage. Miniature.

Norma *(Parrett 1966)* Large single flowers of strong salmon-pink. Very dark green foliage with black zone. Miniature.

North Star *(Merry Gardens 1962)* Sport of 'Polaris' from the USA. Large single white flowers with attractive pink veining and mid-green foliage. Dwarf.

Nuala *(Parrett 1968)* Mid-purple double flowers with white base to upper petals. Mid-green foliage. Dwarf.

Nugget *(Miller 1955)* Miniature fancyleaved variety from California. Small single pale salmon flowers seldom produced. This variety is grown chiefly for its beautiful foliage — olive-green centre and bright yellow edge to each leaf with an irregular chestnut zone. Small bushy plant, difficult to grow and propagate. Similar in habit to 'Gwen' but not such a range of colour in the foliage.

O

Occold Embers *(Stringer pre-1984)* Dwarf fancyleaved variety with double flowers of salmon-pink. The foliage is golden-yellow with bronze zone.

Occold Icecap *(Stringer pre-1985)* Dwarf variety with double white flowers.

Occold Lagoon *(Stringer pre-1985)* Double flowers of pale pink with rose-pink edge. Dark green, heavily zoned foliage. Some 'Deacon' in its parentage. Dwarf.

Occold Orange Tip *(Stringer pre-1984)* Double white flowers, each petal tipped with orange. Miniature.

Occold River *(Stringer)* Double orange flowers, mid-green foliage. Miniature.

Occold Ruby *(Stringer)* Deep red single flowers, golden foliage. Dwarf.

Occold Shield *(Stringer pre-1984)* Orange-red semi-double flowers, pale green leaves with large bronze 'shield' in centre. Fancyleaved dwarf.

Occold Surprise *(Stringer pre-1985)* Bright salmon-red double flowers. Miniature.

Occold Tangerine *(Stringer)* Large single flowers, orange with white eye. Dwarf.

Occold Volcano *(Stringer pre-1984)* Poppy-red double flowers carried on long stems above the pale green foliage. Dwarf.

Offton Dwarf variety with single cerise flowers.

Old Peggotty *(Bagust 1966)* Large deep velvety-red flowers on strong straight stems. Mid-green foliage. Dwarf.

Onnalee *(Parrett pre-1967)* Medium size single flowers of deep pink with white base to upper petals. Mid-green foliage with some zoning. Dwarf.

Opal *(Parrett pre-1965)* Large white single flowers edged with pink. Bright orange stamens and dark green leaves with faint zone. Miniature.

Opalescent *(Parrett pre-1966)* Single flowers of poppy-red with large white eye. Mid-green foliage. Miniature.

Orangeade *(Bidwell)* Bright orange double flowers, mid-green foliage with darker zone. Dwarf.

Orange Galore *(pre-1962)* Dwarf variety from the USA. Single pure orange flowers with mid-green foliage. Habit is between dwarf and semi-dwarf with a tendency to straggle, but very good outdoor variety.

Orange Glow Mandarin-orange double flowers on a dwarf plant.

Orange Gnome *(Parrett about 1964)* Pure orange single flowers. Short stocky plant with dark green foliage. Miniature.

Orange Imp *(Schmidt 1964)* Fast-growing bushy dwarf from California. Intense bright orange double flowers. One of the few dwarf Zonals raised by Bill Schmidt who tended to specialise in Regals.

Orange River Orange double flowers, mid-green leaves with no zone. Dwarf.

Orion *(Stringer 1965)* Very double orange-red variety. Short, compact habit seldom growing taller than 5in (12.5cm). Foliage deep green with slight zoning. Miniature.

Orwell *(Hill)* Single cherry-red flowers with white eye. Miniature.

Otley Pink single flowers with white base to upper petals. Miniature.

P

PAC Minipel Karminot *(Elsner)* Carmine-red single flowers, dark green foliage with darker zone. Dwarf. PAC is the registered prefix of Wilhelm Elsner of the GDR.

PAC Minipel Orange *(Elsner)* Orange single flowers, dark green foliage with darker zone. Dwarf. PAC is the registered prefix of Wilhelm Elsner of the GDR.

PAC Minipel Rosa *(Elsner)* Rose-pink single flowers, dark green zoned foliage. Dwarf. PAC is the registered prefix of Wilhelm Elsner of the GDR.

PAC Minipel Scharlach *(Elsner)* Brilliant scarlet single flowers, dark green foliage with darker zone. Dwarf. PAC is the registered prefix of Wilhelm Elsner of the GDR.

Paddie *(Parrett about 1965)* Single flower of Dutch vermilion. Dark green foliage with broad black zone. Miniature.

Papoose *(Flora Vista 1977)* Compact Canadian miniature with purple-red single flowers, flushed scarlet in upper petals.

Patricia Read *(Read)* Poppy-red single flowers, suffused orange. Miniature.

Patsy 'Q' *(Portas 1976)* Fancyleaved semi-dwarf variety with large salmon-pink single flowers. The golden-yellow leaves have a bright chestnut zone.

Patty Single satin-pink flowers, dark green foliage with darker zone. Miniature.

Paula *(Parrett about 1962)* Rose-pink single flowers, dark green foliage with black zone. Miniature.

Pauline *(Parrett about 1960)* Medium size semi-double flowers of carmine-rose with white or pale pink reverse to all petals. Dark green foliage with darker zone. Miniature.

Pavilion *(Gillam 1980)* Canadian miniature variety. Single purple flowers flushed vermilion, dark green foliage with narrow black zone.

Peace Large single salmon-pink flowers and large flowerheads. Foliage almost black. Miniature.

Peace Palace Single flowers of cerise-pink with white base to upper petals. Mid-green foliage with darker zone. Dwarf, tends to straggle unless trimmed regularly.

Pearly Queen Double-flowered miniature, basically pale pink flecked deeper pink.

Pegasus *(Stringer 1966)* Compact double flowers of rose-pink with shades of white. Dense mid-green foliage with very faint zone. Miniature.

PELFI Lila Cascade *(Fischer)* Dwarf ivyleaf variety. Single pale lilac flowers, dark green leaves with paler markings in centre. PELFI is the registered prefix of Pelargonien Fischer of the GFR.

Percival Dwarf variety with white double flowers with little tendency to pink. Mid-green foliage.

Perky *(Miller 1952)* Californian miniature variety. Clear bright red single flowers with distinct white eye. Olive-green leaves with no zone. Slow grower.

Persian Ruler *(Stringer)* Miniature variety with double flowers of royal purple.

Pete *(Parrett about 1965)* Large single azalea-pink flowers which deepen with age, and small white eye. Dark green foliage with near-black zone. Miniature.

Peter Read *(Read 1967)* Brilliant scarlet double flowers on a vigorous plant. Mid-green foliage. Dwarf.

Petite Blanche Full double variety, flowers are pure white under some conditions but more often carry a distinct pink blush. Fast growing and a popular seed parent. Dwarf.

134

Petit Pierre Synonymous with 'Little Darling', and 'Kleine Liebling' which see.

Petrushka Bright scarlet double flowers with occasional streaks of white. Mid-green zoned foliage. Miniature.

Phloxette *(pre-1963)* Australian miniature. Medium size single white flowers with a faint pink eye which is more obvious during hot weather.

Phyllis Read *(Read 1967)* Large pastel-pink single flowers with distinct white eye. Mid-green foliage. Miniature seedling of 'Phyllis'.

Pickaninny *(Parrett 1965)* Single flowers of porcelain-rose with fancy white eye. Dark green leaves with black zone. Miniature. Originator's spelling.

Pigmy Dwarf variety with double flowers of brilliant scarlet and mid-green foliage.

Pink Bird's Egg A Canadian miniature introduction. Semi-double flowers of pale pink blotched and spotted rose-pink. Mid-green foliage.

Pink Black Vesuvius The pink sport of 'Red Black Vesuvius'. Identical in form and habit to its parent, only the flower colour is different. An excess of nitrogen will alter its miniature habit, and too much potash will change the colour of the flower to red. A correctly balanced feed is most important for this variety.

Pink Brooks Barnes As 'Red Brooks Barnes' but with pink double flowers. Dwarf.

Pink Fondant *(Stringer 1969)* Soft fondant-pink languid double flowers with mid-green distinctly zoned foliage.

Pink Golden Harry Hieover As 'Golden Harry Hieover' but with pink flowers. Dwarf.

Pink Grace Wells *(Wells about 1964)* The pink sport of 'Grace Wells', identical except for the flower colour. Miniature.

Pink Grozser Garten Dwarf variety with dark green leaves, near-black zone. Single salmon-pink narrow-petalled flowers carried in profusion.

Pink Ice Double flowers, mainly frosty-pink but with some white splashes. Dark green foliage. Miniature.

Pink Profusion *(Stringer)* Double-flowered pink miniature with mid-green foliage.

Pink Snow *(Stringer)* White double flowers with pink edge to the petals. Miniature.

Pin Mill *(Bidwell)* Oyster-cream double flowers, mid-green foliage. Miniature.

Pixie *(Miller 1947)* Light salmon single flowers with dark green foliage. Dwarf variety from California.

Pixie *(Parrett about 1960)* Large single rose-pink flowers and dark green foliage. Dwarf.

Playford Deep velvety-red single flowers. Miniature.

Playmate *(Miller pre-1970)* Californian miniature identical to 'Urchin' except that the flower is basically pink fading to cream at the tip of the petals and shading to near-crimson in the centre.

Polaris *(Gamble 1967)* Medium size single flower, basically white flushed pink to edge of petals. Mid-green foliage. Dwarf.

Poppet *(Stringer)* Dwarf fancyleaved variety. Single medium pink flowers, golden-yellow foliage.

Pride *(Eisley 1950)* Very large cup-shaped single flowers of salmon-pink. Dark green foliage. Strong grower, habit between dwarf and semi-dwarf.

Prince Valiant Large single flowers of brilliant crimson carried in large clusters. Dark green foliage. Dwarf.

Priscilla *(Parrett about 1965)* Single white flowers veined and blushed pale pink. Mid-green leaves with faint zone. Dwarf.

Prudence *(Stringer)* Peach-red single flowers which do not shatter easily. Mid-green foliage. Miniature.

Psyche *(Parrett about 1965)* Single flowers, scarlet blushed vermilion with small white eye and trowel-shaped petals. Dark green leaves with faint zone. Miniature.

Purple Gem *(Parrett pre-1966)* Large single flowers of Tyrian-purple with dark green

135

foliage. Miniature.

Purple Light (*Parrett about 1966*) Would seem to be a re-naming of the above; Parrett's description for each is identical.

Pygmalion (*Peat 1969*) Dwarf fancyleaved variety. Yellow-green foliage with narrow wavy copper zone and scarlet double flowers.

R

Rachel (*Parrett pre-1965*) Geranium-lake single flowers, dark green foliage with faint zone. Dwarf.

Red Admiral (*Stringer 1967*) Miniature fancyleaved variety. Deep red double flowers carried in large clusters above the unusual foliage. Leaves are several shades of green with distinct 'butterfly' mark in centre.

Red Black Vesuvius One of the earliest miniatures recorded. The medium size single flower is bright scarlet and the foliage almost black although it will occasionally sport a green leaf or a patch of green on a black leaf. Slow growing.

Red Brooks Barnes (*Ross pre-1965*) A USA origination, same colouring and flower-form as 'Red Black Vesuvius' but faster growing and more vigorous. Dwarf.

Red Comet Medium size scarlet single flowers with white eye. Mid-green foliage with narrow black zone. Fairly fast-growing miniature.

Red Fox Bright red single flowers. Miniature.

Red Glow (*Parrett about 1966*) Single geranium-lake flowers, dark green foliage. Miniature.

Red Grace Wells (*Wells about 1965*) Miniature seedling of 'Grace Wells'. Large flat single flowers of dull scarlet with small white eye. Mid-green foliage with darker zone.

Red Mini Cascade (*Fischer*) Dwarf ivyleaf variety. Single scarlet flowers with narrow petals and mid-green foliage. Rather poor in my opinion; its very floriferous habit is best viewed from a distance.

Redondo (*Lumsden pre-1965*) Large double red flowers with dark green foliage and darker zone. Originated by Mrs. James Lumsden of Redondo Beach, California. Semi-dwarf.

Redondo Introduced by Gamble in 1967, probably of German origin. Salmon-red double flowers, small dark green leaves. Miniature.

Red Pearl (*Bagust 1980*) Bright scarlet single flowers with white eye and lettuce-green frilly foliage. Miniature.

Red Ridinghood (*pre-1966*) Australian semi-dwarf variety with single bright scarlet flowers produced in abundance. Pale green foliage. Best grown as an outdoor plant; it tends to etiolate under glass. Note: there is a USA 'Red Ridinghood' with double scarlet flowers.

Red Spider (*Miller 1951*) Californian semi-double cactus-flowered variety. Single flowers of intense scarlet with narrow twisted and quilled petals. Very dark green foliage, tall growing and only just gets into the semi-dwarf class.

Red Streak (*Ross 1966*) Miniature from the USA. Cactus-flowered variety with narrow twisted and quilled petals, white with red streaks. Zoned mid-green foliage. Miniature.

Renata Medium red single flowers, colour deepens towards edge of petals and there is some deeper veining. Mid-green foliage. Dwarf.

Richard Key (*Peat 1966*) Dwarf fancyleaf variety. Delicate mauve double flowers. Golden leaf with chestnut zone.

Rigel (*Stringer about 1966*) Very double scarlet flowers. Deep green foliage with slight zone. Dense, compact miniature habit.

Rober's Dwarf Red (*Rober pre-1960*) Only just gets into the semi-dwarf class. Very vigorous, dark red double flowers with dark green foliage. Excellent outdoor variety from the USA.

Rober's Lavender *(Rober pre-1960)* Large flowered lavender single with slightly cupped petals. Dark green foliage with black zone. Dwarf variety from the USA.

Robin Hood Similar to 'Rober's Dwarf Red' but flower is bright cherry-red and the plant has a more compact habit. Dwarf. The USA 'Robin Hood' is nearer to vermilion.

Robinson Crusoe *(Peat 1969)* Dwarf fancyleaved variety with large cherry-red single flowers and golden-yellow foliage with chestnut zone.

Rock Dove *(Reg Thorp 1968)* Large lavender-pink single flowers, mid-green foliage. Dwarf.

Rocket *(Miller 1957)* Deep velvety-red double flowers usually overlaid with smokey tones. Dark green foliage. Californian dwarf.

Roderick Dhu Dwarf fancyleaf. Single salmon flowers. Foliage is a pale green overlaid red and copper.

Rosaleen *(Parrett pre-1965)* Medium size single white flowers, lower petals blushed pale pink when floret first opens and this later extends to all petals. Miniature.

Rosalie *(Parrett about 1965)* Large single flowers of rich rose-pink. Dark green leaves with black zone. Miniature.

Rose Mini Cascade *(Fischer)* Dwarf ivyleaf variety. Identical to 'Red Mini Cascade' except for the colour of the flower which is a dull pink.

Rose Tip *(Stringer)* Double flowers of white with rosy tips to petals. Miniature.

Rosetta *(Stringer)* Golden-leaved dwarf variety with single red flowers.

Rosette White single flowers flushed rose-pink. Mid-green foliage with faint zone. Dwarf.

Rosette *(Stringer)* Golden-leaved dwarf variety with single scarlet flowers.

Rosina *(Parrett about 1962)* Large flowered single variety, strong rose-pink with some darker veining. Mid-green foliage with deeper zone. Dwarf.

Rosina Read *(Read)* Appleblossom-pink merging to cream. Single. Pale green zoned foliage. Dwarf. Sometimes listed as 'Rosine Read'.

Rosinda Large single dull red flowers. Mid-green foliage with deeper zone. Slow-growing miniature, seldom exceeds 5in (12.5cm).

Rosita *(May 1965)* When Harry May raised 'Rosita' in California in 1965 it was the only dwarf or miniature 'Rosebud' variety in cultivation. The double scarlet flowers consist of clusters of tight rosebud-like pips, and the foliage is mid-green with slight zoning. Dwarf.

Rosy Dawn *(1968)* Miniature from the USA with dull orange double flowers and dark green foliage. A high-potash feed will change the flower to bright scarlet.

Royal Carpet *(Stringer)* Tight double rosettes of rich plum-purple with dark green foliage. Miniature.

Royal Flush *(Stringer)* Dwarf plant with double flowers of royal-purple.

Royal Norfolk *(Stringer)* Double flowers of reddish-purple. Dark green zoned foliage. Dwarf.

Royal Sovereign *(Peat 1969)* Fancyleaved variety with dwarf, rather spreading habit. The semi-double flowers are neon-magenta with a hint of scarlet towards the centre and pale reverse to all petals. The pale green leaves have golden frilled edges and a broad copper zone with a distinct medallion in the centre which fades towards the edge.

Ruby *(Parrett 1968)* Claret-red single flowers with white base to petals. Dark green foliage with near-black zone. Miniature.

Ruffles *(Miller 1952)* Californian dwarf variety. Soft salmon semi-double flowers with ruffled petals. Slow-growing, spreading habit, dark green foliage.

Rufus Introduced from Belgium in 1974, probably from Schockert of Arlon. Enormous heads of single scarlet flowers, vigorous upright habit. Dark green zoned foliage. Could be synonymous with 'Stradt Bern'. Dwarf.

Rushmere *(Bidwell)* Deep salmon double flowers. Dark green zoned foliage. Dwarf.

Rusty *(May 1962)* Dwarf fancyleaved variety from California. Pale green-yellow foliage with broad coppery zone. The double flowers are a deep cherry-red.

S

Salmon Beauty Bright salmon-red double flowers, mid-green foliage. Miniature.

Salmon Black Vesuvius *(early 1900s)* Miniature sport of 'Red Black Vesuvius'. Identical to parent except that flowers are bright salmon-pink.

Salmon Comet Free blooming salmon single flowers with rather narrow petals. Dark green foliage with near-black zone. Miniature.

Salmon Grozser Garten Identical to 'Grozser Garten' but flowers are salmon. Dwarf.

Salmon Splendour *(Parrett pre-1965)* Medium size single flowers of azalea-pink. Foliage is almost black. Miniature.

Sandra *(Parrett pre-1965)* Large single vermilion flowers lightly blushed crimson. Dark green foliage with black zone.

Sara Single flowers of long narrow violet-pink petals. Dark green foliage with distinct zone. Spindly habit, rather like a pink form of 'Friesdorf'. Dwarf.

Sasha Coral-pink single flowers on a miniature plant.

Satin Lady *(Wells about 1962)* Large pale pink single flowers. The foliage is dark green with a near-black zone and a serrated edge to the leaves. Miniature.

Saturn *(pre-1964)* Bright scarlet double flowers on a compact bushy plant. Dark green foliage with black zone. Miniature.

Saxifragioides *(1888)* Although often listed as a miniature ivyleaf, it is in fact a Pelargonium species which was discovered, un-named, in the Royal Horticultural Society garden at Chiswick. Small near-white petals with purple pencil-lines from the base. The three- or five-lobed dark green leaves are thick and fleshy.

Sea Mist *(Stringer 1970)* Pure white single flowers, mid-green foliage. Miniature.

Sea Spray *(Stringer 1967)* Large loose double flowers of pure white carried in abundance above the lettuce-green foliage. Miniature.

Serena *(Parrett pre-1965)* Large geranium-lake single flowers blushed magenta. Dark green foliage. Miniature.

Scarlet O'Hara Single vermilion flowers with pink blush. Very dark green foliage with black zone. Dwarf.

Scarlet Pimpernel *(Peat pre-1967)* Dwarf fancyleaved variety with large double strawberry-red flowers. Golden-yellow foliage with chestnut zoning.

Sharon *(Parrett about 1966)* Cream double flowers blushed pink. Mid-green zoned foliage. Miniature.

Sheena *(Parrett 1968)* Mandarin-red single flowers with upper petals slightly deeper shade at base. Dark green zoned foliage. Miniature.

Sheila *(Parrett 1968)* Lilac-pink single flowers with white base to upper petals and dark green zoned foliage. Dwarf.

Sheila Thorp *(Portas)* Deep salmon double flowers, dark green zoned foliage. Dwarf.

Shelley *(Bidwell)* Single flowers of pale pink with red splashes and stripes in irregular patterns from petal to petal and from plant to plant. Mid-green foliage. Sometimes listed as 'Shelly'.

Sheraton Double flowers in a deep shade of salmon-pink with dark green foliage. Dwarf.

Shirley Anne *(Payne pre-1986)* Deep rose-pink double flowers on a dwarf plant.

Shotley Vivid scarlet single flowers, the plant is miniature.

Silas Marner *(Bagust 1967)* Medium size single flowers in a shade of dull red, slightly paler towards the centre with some veining. Dark foliage with faint zone. This variety often produces six petals to a flower and sometimes seven, but there is no overlapping and it could never be described as semi-double. Dwarf.

Silver Kewense Originally raised at Kew Gardens, hence its name. A painfully slow-growing silver-leaf variety which can eventually attain about 8in (20cm). Flowers are primitive single, crimson. Dwarf.

Silver Perky *(Miller 1972)* A sport of 'Perky'. Same flowers but the mid-green leaves have a creamy-white variegation. Raised by Holmes Miller in California and released by his widow. Miniature.

Simon Read *(Read 1950)* Dwarf seedling of 'Paul Crampel'. Single flowers of vivid velvety-red. Strong grower with mid-green zoned foliage.

Sirius Small single flower, salmon-pink with white eye. Free flowering. Deep green foliage. Miniature.

Sleepy *(Rober 1938)* One of Rober's group 'Snow White and the Seven Dwarfs' from the USA. Large single flowers of light salmon-pink with mid-green foliage.

Sleigh Bells *(Stringer 1970)* Intense white double rosettes, mid-green foliage. Miniature.

Sleurings Robin Brick-red double flowers, frilly dark green zoned foliage. Miniature.

Small Fortune *(Miller 1958)* Californian miniature variety. Double white flowers edged and flecked with pink. Small olive-green leaves.

Smarty *(Miller pre-1969)* Large coral-pink double flowers, mid-green foliage.

Sneezy *(Rober 1939)* Very large scarlet single flowers with distinct white eye and dark green foliage. Although the habit is quite compact the plant tends to run up under glass and is best used for bedding outdoors. USA semi-dwarf. One of Rober's group 'Snow White and the Seven Dwarfs'.

Snowy Baby *(Case)* Pure white double flowers, mid-green foliage. American dwarf, rather similar to 'Fantasie' but the leaves are a darker green.

Snowflake Pure white single flowers and mid-green foliage. Miniature.

Snow White *(Rober 1938)* Semi-dwarf from the USA. Large pure white single flowers which only 'pink' under very hard growing conditions. Free blooming and easy to propagate. One of the largest in Rober's group 'Snow White and the Seven Dwarfs'.

Somersham Single flowers of deep cerise. Miniature.

Sonata *(Miller 1963)* Californian dwarf variety. Double flowers of creamy-white, lightly flushed lavender-pink with darker centre. Colour deepens as the flower matures. Very good indoors but will often rot outside in a damp season.

Sorcery *(Miller 1960)* Californian dwarf. Small single scarlet flowers freely produced on a low spreading plant. Olive-green foliage with a heavy black blotch.

Sparkle *(Miller 1955)* Californian semi-dwarf variety with large scarlet semi-double flowers and very dark green foliage. Fast grower.

Sparkler Masses of small white single flowers with separated petals and mid-green foliage. Miniature.

Spray Paint *(Gillam 1980)* 'Baby Bird's Egg' x 'Meditation'. Single flowers, upper petals almost white, lower pale pink heavily spotted deeper pink except for white eye. Canadian miniature.

Sprite *(Miller 1949)* Californian fancyleaved miniature. Small, dark greyish-green leaves with ivory-white border, often flushed coral. Single coral-pink flowers.

Starry Eyed *(Pierrt 1977)* Canadian dwarf variety. Salmon-pink single flowers deepening towards centre and with lighter eye. Dark green foliage with black zone.

Stella Read *(Read 1968)* Appleblossom-pink double flowers, mid-green foliage.

139

Dwarf seedling of 'Emperor Nicholas'.

Stephen Read *(Read pre-1966)* Large single salmon-pink flowers, deeper shade than 'Patty' which it otherwise resembles. Miniature.

Stewart Read *(Read)* Large single geranium-lake flowers, flushed magenta. Dark green foliage. Dwarf.

St Helen's Favourite *(Hill pre-1965)* Single deep salmon flowers. Mid-green zoned foliage. Miniature.

Stradt Bern Strong upright-growing semi-dwarf variety with brilliant scarlet single flowers in large trusses. Dark green foliage with almost black zone. Excellent for bedding outdoors but tends to run up in the greenhouse.

Stutton *(Bidwell)* White single flowers shaded pink. Dark green foliage. Miniature.

Suffolk Gold *(Stringer)* Miniature fancyleaved variety with single scarlet flowers and yellowy-gold foliage.

Sugar Baby The second miniature ivyleaf variety to come to England. More vigorous than 'Gay Baby' and with a bright pink flower. Often erroneously listed as 'Pink Gay Baby'.

Sunbeam *(Stringer)* Glowing salmon-rose double flowers, shiny dark green foliage with near-black ragged zone. 'The Boar' is probably one of its ancestors. Dwarf.

Sun Rocket *(Stringer 1970)* Semi-dwarf variety with brilliant orange-scarlet flowers with paler reverse to petals. Large flowerheads and large lettuce-green floppy leaves.

Sunspot Petit Pierre *(Miller)* Another sport of 'Petit Pierre' raised by Holmes Miller of California. Identical to its parent but each light green leaf has a pale butterfly mark in the centre. Miniature.

Sunstar *(Stringer 1967)* Crisp pure orange double, very short stocky habit with dense pale to mid-green foliage of unusual shape. Miniature replica of the Swiss Zonal variety 'Orangesonne', exact in every detail. Miniature.

Supernova Orchid-mauve double flowers with cerise edge to petals. Miniature.

Susan Dwarf variety with single flowers of bright scarlet with white eye.

Susan Payne *(Payne pre-1986)* The pale-pink double flowers mature to deeper pink as the flowerhead ages. Dark green foliage. Dwarf.

Susan Read *(Read 1960)* Salmon single flowers. Mid-green foliage. Dwarf seedling of 'Salmon Kovalevski'.

Susie 'Q' *(Portas 1976)* Semi-dwarf fancyleaved variety with soft pink double flowers. Golden-yellow foliage with light bronze zoning.

Sweetheart *(Stringer)* Double scarlet flowers, mid-green foliage. Miniature.

Sweet Sue *(Parrett pre-1965)* Single mandarin-red flower with large white eye and mid-green foliage. Miniature.

Sylvia Marie Dwarf variety with salmon-orange double flowers.

T

Tammy *(May 1962)* Californian miniature. Medium size semi-double flowers of bright scarlet. Pale green foliage with faint zone. Fast growing for a miniature and easy to propagate.

Tangelo *(May 1965)* Cactus-flowered dwarf from California with large orange-red flowers and mid-green foliage.

Tangerine Single salmon flowers with orange tints and tones. Dark green foliage. Miniature.

Tanya *(Stringer)* Near-white single cup-shaped flowers shading to palest pink. Mid-green foliage with faint zone. Miniature.

Tapestry *(Stringer)* Miniature fancyleaved variety with single deep salmon flowers. Leaves are basically light yellow with green centres, overlaid with irregular zoning of red, showing deep bronze where it overlays the green. Occasionally the red pigment dominates. Brighter colouring than 'Mrs Henry Cox' and leaf is more indented.

Tattoo *(Gillam 1980)* Miniature Canadian form of 'Staplegrove Fancy'. Single flowers, basically white with deep red edges and speckling. Petals are slightly crinkled.

Taurus *(Stringer 1965)* Salmon single flowers with long narrow, almost primitive petals. Mid-green foliage with distinct black blotch in centre of each leaf. Low spreading habit. Miniature seedling of 'The Boar' or 'Prostrate Boar'.

Telstar *(Stringer 1972)* Double flowers of deep rose-red shading to crimson with white flecks on most petals. Mid-green foliage. Miniature.

Tempter *(Miller 1959)* Californian dwarf variety with single purple-crimson flowers. Dark green foliage with darker zone.

Terence Read *(Read pre-1966)* Medium size single crimson flower with small white eye. Mid-green zoned foliage. Miniature.

Teresa *(Parrett 1965)* Single flowers, rose-pink with lower petals slightly lighter shade. Dark green zoned foliage. Miniature.

The Prince *(Parrett pre-1965)* Deep red single flowers, blushed purple at base of petals. Dark green foliage. Miniature.

Thomas Gerald Single pink flower with white eye. Pale green to gold foliage. Very free flowering.

Tiberius Medium size single cherry-red flowers on a short, slow-growing plant. Dark foliage with a slight zone. Miniature.

Tiffany *(Miller 1972)* Double flowers of garnet-red on a compact plant. Californian miniature raised by Holmes Miller and released by his widow Dorothea.

Tilly *(Parrett pre-1968)* Salmon-pink single flowers with bottle-green distinctly zoned foliage. Strong-growing miniature variety.

Tim Primitive single flowers of pure scarlet on a miniature plant.

Timothy Clifford *(Burrows 1955)* Deep salmon double flowers. Short compact miniature with dark green foliage.

Timsbury *(Peat 1970)* Dwarf fancyleaved variety with bright pink single flowers. Golden-yellow foliage with wavy chestnut zone.

Tina Small double flowers of fuchsine-pink. Tiny compact plant, seldom exceeding 4in (10cm). Miniature.

Tineke Deep mauve single flowers, dark green foliage. Miniature.

Tinkerbelle *(pre-1964)* Origin unknown but thought to be one of Holmes Miller's raising. Very large pure-white single flowers which are resistant to shattering. Mid-green leaf with faint zone. Dwarf.

Tiny Tim *(pre-1964)* Tiny single flowers of strong pink on small dark foliage. Slow growing, seldom exceeds 4in (10cm). Miniature. There is another 'Tiny Tim' which appears occasionally on lists, identical to above except that it has red flowers — could be a sport.

Tom Portas *(Portas pre-1982)* Strong pink double flowers, dark green leaves with darker zone. Dwarf.

Tom Tit Tiny single flowers of salmon pink with deeper toning. One of the smallest-flowered varieties but the plant tends to grow rather spindly. Dwarf.

Tony *(Parrett pre-1968)* Orange-red single with narrow petals. Grey-green zoned foliage. Very small and slow growing, almost a micro-miniature.

Torch *(Miller 1970)* Californian dwarf with large single bright orange flowers, deeper colour towards the edge of petals. Mid-green foliage, no zone.

Trajan *(Burrows 1955)* Large single signal-red flowers with small white eye, upper petals tend to fade at top edge. Dark green foliage with black zone. Miniature.

Tricia Medium size single vermilion flowers with large white eye. Mid-green foliage with faint zone. Thought to be one of Frank Parrett's seedlings. Miniature.

141

Trimley Dwarf variety with cerise-pink double flowers.

Trinket *(pre-1964)* Thought to have been raised by Holmes Miller in California but not confirmed. Rare variety with large heads of salmon-apricot double flowers and dark green foliage. Needs careful cultivation. Miniature.

Trixie *(Parrett pre-1966)* Single vermilion flowers with large white eye. Mid-green foliage. Miniature.

Trudie *(Parrett pre-1968)* Primitive single flowers of amaranth-rose. Olive-green foliage with black zone. Miniature.

Tuddenham *(Bidwell)* Miniature variety with double flowers of magenta-red with orange tones. Mid-green foliage with deeper zone.

Tunia's Tango *(pre-1966)* An Australian dwarf variety very rare in England. Tango-pink single flowers with dark green foliage.

Turkish Delight *(Gillam 1984)* Compact Canadian dwarf fancyleaved variety. Lettuce-green leaves with ivory butterfly marking and rose-red zone. White stems often pink tinted. Flowers are single vermilion.

Tutone Semi-dwarf from the USA. Similar to 'Emma Hossler' but deeper two-tone pink, mid-green foliage.

Tweedle-Dee *(Miller 1954)* Californian semi-dwarf. Single flowers with narrow salmon petals and mid-green foliage. Excellent for outdoor use, but tends to run up under glass.

Tweedle-Dum *(Miller 1954)* Same habit and foliage as 'Tweedle-dee' but the flowers are a deeper shade of salmon. Californian semi-dwarf.

Twinkle *(Miller 1954)* Fast-growing Californian dwarf variety with bushy spreading habit. Coral-pink double flowers held close to the dark green foliage.

Tuesday's Child Dwarf fancyleaved variety with dawn-pink single flowers. The foliage is yellow-green with a bronze zone.

U

Urchin *(Miller 1970)* Ragged single flowers of deep red. The foliage is small, 'five-fingered' and mid- to dark green. The habit is very compact, bushy and dome-shaped. Miniature. Raised by Holmes Miller in California but the mature plant looks just like a young hedgehog — could Miller have known that the old English name for the hedgehog is 'Urchin'?

Ursula Key *(Peat 1969)* Dwarf fancyleaved variety. Double flowers in a rare shade of coral-salmon. Foliage is golden-yellow with chestnut zone.

V

Valentina *(Parrett pre-1968)* Pinkish-mauve double flowers with white upper petals. Mid-green foliage. Dwarf.

Variegated Kleine Liebling *(Miller 1956)* Miniature fancyleaved variety from California. Silver-leaved with small crinkled foliage of mid-green marked with white or cream. Sport from 'Kleine Liebling' with identical flowers, but slower growing than its parent. Synonymous with 'Variegated Petit Pierre'.

Variegated Petit Pierre Synonymous with 'Variegated Kleine Liebling' above.

Vasco Da Gama *(Bagust 1966)* World's first dwarf 'Irene' variety. 'Irene' x 'Emma Hössler'. The glowing red flower of 'Irene' with the dwarf habit and mid-green foliage of 'Emma Hössler'.

Vega *(Stringer 1966)* Micro-miniature which seldom grows larger than 3in (7.5cm) high with leaves less than 3/8in (1cm) in diameter. The single flower, large for the size of plant, is a strong orange with large white eye. Pale green frilly foliage. Slow growing and needs very careful attention.

Venus *(Arndt about 1950)* From the USA. Pale pink double flowers with dark green foliage. Dwarf.

Vermilion Grace Wells *(Wells about 1966)* Miniature seedling of 'Grace Wells'. Large flat single flowers of pure vermilion with small white eye. Mid-green foliage with darker zone.

Vina *(Shellard pre-1984)* Coral-pink double flowers shading to orange-pink in centre. Lettuce-green leaves with wide margins of deeper green. Dwarf.

Vinolia Possibly raised by Parrett but not confirmed. Deep mauve-pink single flowers with small white eye. Flowers are large and carried in clusters on long stems. Mid-green foliage with deeper zoning. Miniature.

Virgo *(Stringer 1965)* Large single white flowers which tend to 'pink' if grown under hard conditions. Mid-green foliage. Miniature.

Viva Dwarf variety with velvety-red single flowers.

Vi Wilson White single flower with ring of pink between the centre and edge of petals. Miniature.

W

Wallis Friesdorf Same habit and foliage as 'Friesdorf' but with a double red flower. Sometimes listed as 'Double Friesdorf'. Dwarf.

Washbrook Miniature variety with brilliant orange double flowers.

Waveney *(Hill pre-1964)* Orange-scarlet single flowers, dark green foliage with well defined zone. Miniature.

Wedding Royale *(Smith pre-1984)* 'Rosebud'-type dwarf variety with tight double flowers of carmine-rose and mid-green foliage with dark green zone.

Wedmore *(Peat 1975)* Large double red flowers carried on long stems well above the foliage. Leaves are pale green with dark chestnut medallion in centre. Miniature.

Wellsdorf *(Wells 1968)* Primitive single flowers similar in form to 'Friesdorf' of which it is a seedling, but the colour is mauve. Dark green foliage with near-black zone (as parent) and same tall erect habit unless regularly stopped. Semi-dwarf.

Wendy *(Parrett)* Medium size single flowers of salmon-pink suffused white. Dark green foliage. Miniature.

Wendy Read *(Read)* Dwarf variety with deep rose-pink double flowers and dark green zoned foliage.

Wensum *(Hill)* Deep salmon double flowers, flushed pale pink. Miniature.

Wherstead *(Bidwell)* Pink single flower with white eye. Bright green foliage. Miniature.

Whitecap *(Miller 1952)* Californian dwarf variety with medium size white single flowers carried in large clusters. Compact plant with dark green leaves. Needs less sunshine than most and must be slightly shaded in high summer.

White Eggshell Large flat single white flowers with petals streaked and speckled red. Mid-green foliage. Miniature.

White Gem *(Parrett pre-1960)* Medium size single white flowers which seldom 'pink'. Short bushy habit with light green crinkly foliage. Miniature.

White Roc *(Parrett pre-1965)* Large flowered double which remains pure white under most conditions. Dark green foliage with deeper zone. Miniature.

Wine Red *(Stringer)* Rich ruby-red double flowers, mid-green foliage. Miniature.

Winnie Read *(Read)* Dwarf variety with double flowers of appleblossom-pink and dark green zoned foliage.

143

Witnesham (*Bidwell*) Double flowers of bright orange-salmon with mid-green foliage, faintly zoned on young leaves. Miniature.

Wood's Cyclamen (*Wood pre-1972*) Identical plant to 'Wood's White' and probably a sport from it but flower is single cyclamen-pink. Poor grower with tendency to legginess. Dwarf.

Wood's White (*Wood pre-1972*) Semi-primitive single white. As the plant ages the petals become narrower and the flowerheads more sparse. Mid-green foliage. Said to be a good seed-parent. Dwarf.

Wycombe Lodge (*Peat pre-1967*) Dwarf fancyleaved variety with double flowers of rosy-magenta. The golden-yellow leaves have a pronounced chestnut zone.

Wycombe Maid (*Money*) Double flowers of light pink flushed salmon. Dark green foliage. Miniature.

Y

Yellow Hammer (*Stringer 1971*) Miniature fancyleaved variety with single red flowers. The leaves are yellow based with a mid-green splash and deep green zone.

York Minster Believed to be raised by Don Storey but not confirmed. Dwarf fancyleaved variety with cream-based foliage splashed with green from centre with a delicate deep pink zone. Similar to 'Filigree' but the pink zone is usually more pronounced.

Z

Zip (*Hartsook pre-1965*) Tiny plant which seldom exceeds 4in (10cm). Dark leaves and bronze zone. Profusion of small orange-scarlet single flowers. Miniature. Frances Hartsook lived for some years in Mexico before moving back to her native California — I am not certain in which country this variety was raised.

144

Miniature Regals

Otherwise known as 'Angel Pelargoniums' or 'Angel Geraniums' in the USA. These are the Cinderellas of the Miniature group for they have been largely overlooked by the hybridists to date. Langley-Smith produced a few varieties about 1914 by crossing *P. crispum* with 'The Shah', and extended his range between the wars using 'Prince of Orange', 'Crispum Minor', 'Crispum Variegatum', etc. However all the cultivars raised so far bear similar single flowers in varying shades of purple, mauve and white, some slightly larger than others, some with overlapping petals, others more separated. The growth habit varies slightly from variety to variety but they all tend to be rather upright with similar foliage and, fully grown, average about 8in (20cm) in height. Regular stopping will improve the shape and bushiness of the plant but must delay flowering. They are rather prone to attack by whitefly and should be sprayed regularly with a systemic insecticide as a control.

Most specialist nurseries carry a few varieties and the following list includes most of those in current commercial production:

Betty Hulsman
Captain Starlight (Gillam)
Catford Belle (Langley-Smith 1935)
Chinese Coral
Earliana
Gosbeck
Hemingstone
Julie
Kerlander (Langley-Smith 1940)
Little Love
Mairi
Madame Layal
Manx Maid
Moon Maiden

Mrs Dumbrill (Langley-Smith 1940)
Mrs. G.H. Smith
Rietje Van Der Lee
Rita Scheen
Rose Bengal (Langley-Smith 1940)
Sancho Panza
Seeleys Pansy
Shirley Ash
Solferino
Spring Park
Tip Top Duet (Taylor 1977)
Valanza
Velvet Duet (Taylor 1980)
Wayward Angel (Taylor 1977)

Hardiness zone maps

Britain

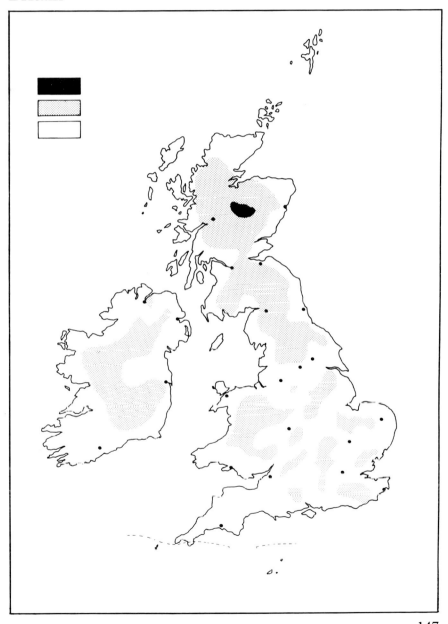

Europe

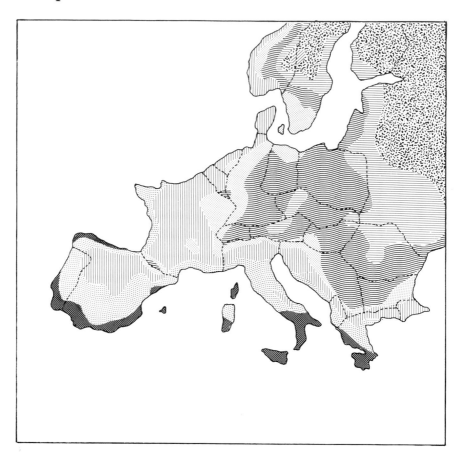

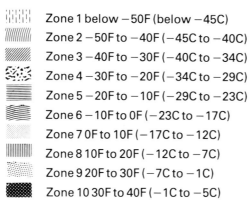

Zone 1 below −50F (below −45C)
Zone 2 −50F to −40F (−45C to −40C)
Zone 3 −40F to −30F (−40C to −34C)
Zone 4 −30F to −20F (−34C to −29C)
Zone 5 −20F to −10F (−29C to −23C)
Zone 6 −10F to 0F (−23C to −17C)
Zone 7 0F to 10F (−17C to −12C)
Zone 8 10F to 20F (−12C to −7C)
Zone 9 20F to 30F (−7C to −1C)
Zone 10 30F to 40F (−1C to −5C)

North America

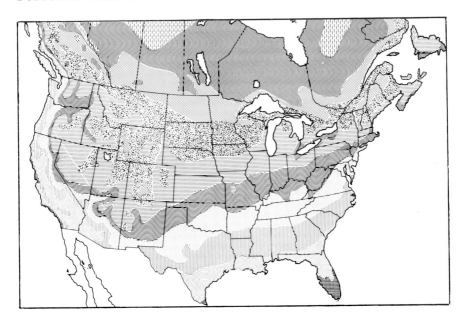

List of suppliers of Miniature and Dwarf Geraniums

United Kingdom

Arcadia Nurseries
Brasscastle Lane, Nunthorpe,
Middlesbrough, Cleveland
(0642–310782)

Beckwood Geraniums
New Inn Road, Beckley,
Oxford
(Stanton St John 780)

Beech Hill Nursery
Swanland, North Ferriby,
East Yorkshire
(0482–633670)

R.C Bidwell
13 Sidegate Avenue,
Ipswich, Suffolk
(0473–712964)

Clapton Court Gardens
Crewkerne, Somerset
(0460–73220)

Cypress Nursery
Powke Lane, Blackheath,
Birmingham

Denmead Geranium Nurseries
Hambledon Road, Denmead,
Portsmouth, Hants.
(0705–240081)

Exbridge Nurseries
Exbridge
Dulverton, Somerset
(Dulverton 23503)

Greybridge Geraniums
Fibrex Nurseries
Evesham, Worcestershire

Grimston Park Nurseries
Tadcaster,
North Yorkshire
(0937–832188)

Jennifer Fraser
Highfield Vineyards,
Longdrag Hill (A373),
Tiverton, Devon
(0884–256362)
Telephone first and you may be able to link your visit with a tour of the vineyards and a wine-tasting

Kent Street Nurseries
Sedlescombe,
East Sussex
(0424–751134)

Mariawood Geraniums
Hulver, Beccles,
Suffolk
(0502–76647)

F.W. Mepham
The Geranium Nursery, Chapel Lane,
West Wittering,
West Sussex
(0243–513065)

Oakleigh Nurseries
Monkwood,
Alresford, Hants.
(096277–3344)

F. Parmenter
619 Rayleigh Road,
Eastwood, Essex
(Southend 525915)
Telephone first, Mr Parmenter is semi-retired

Redvale Nurseries
St Tudy,
Bodmin, Cornwall

Thorp's Nurseries
257 Finchhampstead Road,
Wokingham, Berks.
(0734–781181)

The Vernon Geranium Nursery
Cuddington Way,
Cheam,
Sutton, Surrey

West Country Geraniums
Viney Nursery,
Staunton Lane,
Whitchurch,
Bristol, Avon
(0272–832762)

Westdale Nurseries
Holt Road,
Bradford-upon-Avon, Wilts.
(02216–3258)

A.D. & N. Wheeler
Pye Court, Willoughby,
Rugby, Warwicks.

Paul Williams
71 Mill Street
Ottery St Mary, Devon
EX11 1AB
(Ottery St Mary 2987)
Please telephone first.

Canada

Strata Landscaping
Site 2, Box 22,
Port Moody,
Vancouver V6H 3C8

P & J Greenhouses
20265 82nd Avenue,
Langley, B.C.
V3A 6Y3
No mail order

Chestnut Greenhouses
17974 40th Avenue,
Surrey, B.C.
V3S 4N8
No mail order

USA

Faye Brawner
2330 Wilbur Road,
Roseburg,
Oregon 97470
Mail order only

Cook's Geranium Nursery
712 North Grand,
Lyon's,
Kansas 67554

Davidson-Wilson Greenhouses
Crawfordville,
In. 47933

Merry Gardens
1 Simonton Road,
Camden,
Maine 04843

New Leaf Nursery
2456 Foothill Drive,
Vista,
California 92083
Tel. (619) 726–9269
Nursery visits by appointment only

Shady Hill Gardens
821 Walnut,
Batavia,
Illinois 60510

The Geranium House
1331 Tunnel Road,
Santa Barbara,
California 93105
No mail order

Young's Mesa Nursery
2755 Fowler Lane,
Arroyo Grande,
California 93420

Australia

Cloyne Geraniums & Craft
Rose Valley Road,
Bunyan, via Cooma,
N.S.W. 2630

Copihue Nursery Pty Ltd
23b Macpherson Street,
Warriewood,
N.S.W. 2102
Wholesale only

Donovan's Nursery
65 Eastwood Road,
Leppington,
N.S.W. 2171
Wholesale only

La Jolla Nursery
Newbury Park Estate,
Narromine Road,
Dubbo,
N.S.W. 2830

Mini Gem Place
3 Glenview Crescent,
Hunter's Hill,
N.S.W. 2110
Visits by appointment only

Mr & Mrs J. Fessey
28 Park Road,
Bulli,
N.S.W. 2516

Schulz Nursery Pty Ltd
218 Annangrove Road,
Annangrove,
N.S.W. 2156
Wholesale only

The College Nursery
5 Raym Road,
Kenthurst,
N.S.W. 2156
Wholesale only

Geranium Cottage Nursery
3 Cotswold Road,
Dural,
N.S.W. 2158
Wholesale only

Georyl Pelargonium Nursery
63 Graydens Road,
Tyabb,
Victoria 3913

The Geranium Cottage Nursery Regd.
123 Fisken Road,
Mt Helen, via Ballarat,
Victoria 3350
No mail order. Open Sat, Sun, Mon only

Street's Geranium Garden
84 Dinwoodie Road,
Thornlands,
Queensland 4163

Warren Park Nurseries
Corner Boundary & Harkaway Roads,
Narre Warren East,
Victoria 3804
Wholesale only

New Zealand

St Martin's Nursery
13a St Martin's Road,
Christchurch 2

South Africa

Amberglo Gardens (Pty) Ltd
PO Box 219,
Merrivale 3291

Banyan Cottage Nursery
PO Box 17,
Alexandria 6185

Bouquet Garni Nursery
PO Box 15873,
Lynn East 0039

Braaks Indoor Plants
PO Box 6
Pretoria 0001
Wholesale only

Elgin Lodge Nursery
PO Box 379,
Kempton Park 1620

Gift Acres Nursery
PO Box 11448,
Brooklyn 0011

Petersfield Nurseries
PO Box 101,
Kroondal 0350

Sittig Nursery
PO Box 48,
Hartbeesport 0216

Tarlton Nursery
PO Box 72,
Tarlton 1749

A.J. van Wyk
Dykeweg 40,
Penhill 7100

List of Geranium (Pelargonium) Societies

The addresses given are usually those of individual officers who may be replaced from time to time. They are correct at time of publication.

United Kingdom

British & European Geranium Society,
1 Roslyn Road, Hathersage,
Sheffield 30.

British Pelargonium & Geranium Society,
Joint Membership Secretaries
7 Stour Valley Close
Upstreet, Canterbury
Kent CT3 4DB

USA

International Geranium Society
4610 Druid Street,
Los Angeles,
California 90032

South Africa

South African Pelargonium & Geranium Society,
PO Box 55342,
Northlands,
Johannesburg 2116

Netherlands

Nederlandse Pelargonium en Geranium Vereniging,
Hollands End 89,
1244 NP Ankeveen

Canada

Canadian Geranium & Pelargonium Society,
4040 West 38th Avenue,
Vancouver, B.C.
V6N 2Y9

Australia

The Australian Geranium Society is the International Registration Authority for *Pelargonium* and is in the course of publishing a Check List and Register of Cultivar Names, copies of which may be obtained from the Society. Applications for the registration of names, or further details, may be obtained from:

The Australian Geranium Society,
The Science Centre, 6th Floor,
35–43 Clarence Street,
Sydney, N.S.W. 2000

Index

Acidity 65
Aerating 11, 17
Aerial roots 96, 97
Aeromatic-Barter Ltd 109,110
Aerosols 77
African Ground Nuts 15
Agar, nutrient 43, 44
Air heating cables 47
Air pocket(s) 16, 23, 73
Air space(s) 16
Air thermostats 46
Algae 22, 69, 70, 99
Aluminium 108, 109
Analysis 65
Anchoring roots 25, 71
Animal manure (s) 16, 65
Animals, domestic 14, 77, 79
Ant powders 76
Anthers 51, 52, 53
Ants 76, 77, 80
Apartments 100
Aphids 45, 75, 76, 77, 102
Appliances, gas 100, 103
Arrangements, flower 9
Ash 14, 17
Atmosphere, dry 60
Atmosphere, humid 46, 47, 97
Australian Geranium Society (AGS) 5

Bacteria 82, 83
Bacterial blight 82, 83
Bacterial fasciation 97
Bacterial stem rot 82
Baekeland, Dr. 19
Bags, plastic 11, 13, 88, 96
Baiting 78
Bakelite 19
Balcony troughs 8
Balls of soil 15, 28, 29, 30, 31, 68, 69, 72, 73,
Bark 61, 62
Baskets, hanging 63
Bedding plants 8, 34, 64, 73
Bee power 52
Beer 77
Bees 45, 50, 54, 55, 76
Beetles, carnivorous 76
'Betsy Trotwood' 71
Bill Wells 50
Birds 78
Black leg 29, 39, 83
Blight 64, 82, 83
Bloated roots 42, 43

Blood dried 64
'Boar, The' 87
'Boars, King of the' 87
Bodies, foreign 12
Bone dry 73
Bonemeal 64
Border plants 8, 34, 64
Boron 64
Botrytis 34, 35, 39, 45, 67, 75, 84, 96, 97, 104, 107
Botrytis cinerea 84
Bottled gas 109
Bottom watering 67, 68
'Boudoir' 50
Bouquets 9
Breakages 19
Breathe, breathing 21
Brick dust 11
'Bridesmaid' 50
British Pelargonium & Geranium Society 5, 30, 86
Brittle roots 42, 43
Brushes, camel hair 55
Buds, budding 61, 62
Butterflies 78

Cables, air heating 47
Cables, overheating 48, 49
Cables, soil heating 47, 48
Cal-Val 56
Calcium 64, 65
Camel hair brushes 55
Campbell, Miss Mary 87
Capillary action 68, 70
Carbohydrates 65
Carbonmonoxide 101, 102
Carnivorous beetles 76
Catalogues 7
Caterpillars 76, 77, 78, 80
Cats 14, 79
Central heating, gas-fired 100
Central heating, oil-fired 101
Certificate of health 81, 86
Chalk, ground 13
Characteristics 35, 56, 59, 61, 62
Checks 24
Chelsea Flower Show 21, 62
Chemical feeds 64
Chemical ingredients 30
Chemical retardant 51
Chemical sterilisation 14
Chemicals 15
'Chico' 6

157

Children 77
Chlorophyll 35
Chocolate, milk 78
Claims, exaggerated 7
Clay 11, 14, 19, 21, 30
Clay content 14
Clay pots 22, 27, 29, 30
Cleanliness 35
Coal fires 17, 102
Coding 57
Coke fires 102
Cold tea 65
Colour(s) 16, 19, 66
Com-Pel 65
Compost 11, 15, 16, 17, 21, 22, 24, 26, 27,
    28, 29, 30, 31, 40, 44, 66, 68, 73, 83
Compost, Fison's Levington 41, 56
Compost, J. Arthur Bowers' 41, 56
Compost, John Innes 8, 11, 13, 14, 16, 40,
    42, 56, 63
Compost, University of California 11, 15,
    16, 41
Compost, lightweight 12
Compost, loam-based 13
Compost, mushroom 15
Compost, open 15
Compost, soil-less 8, 12, 40, 41, 56
Condensation 60, 106, 107, 108
Conditions of sale 7
Congestion 36
Conservatories 9
Copper 64
Corynebacterium fascians 97
Cotton-reel mallet 20
Cotyledons 24
Cow manure 11
Crawling insects 14
Crinkle virus 82
Crocking 24, 28, 29
'Crocodile' 82
Cross, John 23
Culture indexing 83
Cuttings 16, 26, 33, 34, 35, 36, 38, 39, 40,
    42, 43, 45, 46, 48, 56, 57, 59, 61, 67, 68
Cuttings, fleshy 16
Cuttings, internodal 36
Cuttings, leaf-axil 35
Cuttings, nodal 36
Cuttings, tray rooted 44
Cuttings, wilting 40

DDT 45, 76
Damping-off 24
Darkness 56
'Deacon Bonanza' 21
Decay 36
Dehydrate 60
Derris 78
Diffuser 46

Dilution 66
Disease(s) 35, 59, 73, 75, 81
Dogs 14
Domestic animals 77
Domestic heaters 109
Dormancy 99
Drainage 12, 14, 16, 21, 30
Draught 102, 105
Drench 75
Dried blood 64
Drought 16
Drying-out 12, 46, 47
Dust(s) 45, 99
Dusting 24, 78

Earthworms 14, 15, 17, 30, 80
Earwigs 30
Eggs 14, 78
Eggs, caterpillar 78
Electricity 48, 100, 101, 103, 104, 110
Elements 16, 64
Embryo 56
English Oak 85
Environment 27, 30, 39, 41, 84, 99, 100, 103
Etoilated 8, 100
Evaporation 67
Exaggerated claims 7
Examination, visual 16
Exhibiting 21, 54
Extractor fan 108

Fabric 69, 70
'Fairy Storey' 34, 71
Fancy leaves 30
Fan, extractor 108
Fasciation, bacterial 97
Feed, liquid 27, 30, 35, 63
Feeding roots 25, 31, 71
Feeding, supplementary 12
Feeds 27, 30, 63, 64, 65, 66
Fertilise 51, 52, 53, 54
Fertiliser, balanced 66
Fertiliser, rose 65
Fertiliser(s) 27, 30, 63, 64, 65, 66
Fertiliser(s), liquid 27, 30, 35, 63
Fibre 14
Fires, coal 17, 102
Fires, coke 17, 102
Fires, oil 101
Fishmeal 64
Fison's Levington compost 41, 56
Five-to-a-pot 44, 83
Flannelette 68, 69
Flaring 105
Fleshy cuttings 16
Fleshy leaves 16
Flies 12, 55, 76, 80, 81
Flies, sciarid 12, 81
Flower arrangements 9

Flowerbeds 8
Flowerpots 17
Flying insects 14
Foliage, scorched 21, 66, 67, 76
Foreign bodies 12
Formulae 66
Frank Parrett 6
Friable loam 15
'Friary Wood' 50
Frogs 80
Frost 99
Fruit fly 81
Fuel, solid 105
Fumes 100, 101, 103, 105, 110
Fumigants 45, 75, 77, 81
Fungicide 31, 36, 84, 88, 96, 99
Fungi(us) 15, 75, 83, 84, 87
Fungus gnats 12, 81
Fungus spores 34
F_1, F_2 hybrids 33, 51

Galls 97, 98
Gardeners' Chronicle 96
Gas appliances 100, 103
Gas fired central heating 100
Gas fires 100
Gas water heater 100
Gas, North Sea 100
Gas, bottled 109
Gas, coal 103
Gas, liquid 104
Gas, methane 100, 103, 110
Gas, natural 100
Gas, propane 100, 103, 110
Gas, town 100, 103
Gas, waste 105
Gel 43
Genes 51
George Russell 8
Geranium Society 5
Geraniums, Lady Washington 5
Germination 51, 55, 56
Gnats, fungus 12, 81
'Golden Chalice' 34, 38
'Golden Flute' 34, 38
'Grace Wells' 50
Graft 60, 61
Grafting 59, 82
Grafting wax 59, 62
Grains 16
'Granny Hewitt' 34, 38
Gravel 70
Greenfly (see also aphid) 75, 76, 102
Greenhouse dry 73
Greenhouses 103, 106, 107, 109
Grist 13
Grit 14, 15, 70
Ground chalk 13

Growing media (see also compost) 11, 44
Growths 98
Grubs 17, 45
'Gwen' 34, 38

Hair root 16, 25, 29, 44
Hanging baskets 63
Hard stem 38
Health certificates 81, 86
Heat, 56
Heated bench 47
Heated panel 46
Heaters, cost 106
Heaters, domestic 109
Heaters, immersion 104
Heaters, paraffin 104
Heaters, portable 104
Heaters, tubular 104
Heating 51, 99
Heating, central 100
Heating, electric 103
Heating, fan 103, 104, 108
High water content 15
Holmes C. Miller 50
Honeydew 75, 76
Hoof and Horn 13, 64
Hormone rooting powders 39, 40
Hostile environment 27, 41
Hoverflies 76
Humex 103
Humus 11
Hybrids F_1, F_2 33, 51
Hydrogen, inorganic 65
Hygiene 84

Immersion heaters 104
Infection 62
Ingredients, chemical 30
Inorganic hydrogen 65
Insecticides, systemic 45, 75, 76, 77
Insects 12, 14, 15, 50, 54, 55, 59, 75, 76
Insects, crawling 14
Insects, flying 14
International Registration Authority 5
Internodal cuttings 36
Invisible root hairs 16, 25
Iron 11, 64
Ivyleaf geraniums (pelargoniums) 5, 21, 36, 73, 82, 84, 102

J. Arthur Bowers' Compost 41, 56
Jeyes Fluid 22, 39, 84
Jiffy-7s 24, 25, 26, 27, 41, 44, 55, 56, 84
John Cross 23
John Innes Composts 8, 11, 13, 14, 15, 16, 40, 42, 56, 63
John Innes Horticultural Institute 11, 13
John Innes Producers 14
Joseph Paxton 9

Kerosene 101
'King of the Boars' 87
'Kleine Liebling' 34
Knives, surgical 37, 55, 59
Knives, unsterilised 39

Lady Washington geraniums 5
Ladybirds 45, 76, 77
Ladybugs (USA) 45, 76
Leaching 15, 64
Leaf axil cuttings 35
Leaf scorch 21, 66, 67, 76
Leaf-curl virus 84
Leaning 8
Legginess 8, 100
Levington compost 41, 56
Light 8, 56, 100, 102
Lightweight compost 12
Limestone 13
Liquid feeds 27, 30, 35, 63
Liquid fertilisers 27, 30, 35, 63,
Liquid Gas 104
Living pictures 9
Loam 11, 13, 14, 15
Loam-based compost 13
Loose-rooting 26
Low voltage wire 47
Lukewarm (or tepid) water 24, 25, 26, 28,
  31
Lush growth 38
Lycopersicum esculentum 6

'Madame Salleron' 8
Maggots 12, 17, 81
Magnesium 64
Mail order 7
Malathion 45, 77
Mallet, cotton-reel 20
Manganese 64
Manure, animal 65
Manure, cow 11
Manure, farmyard 63
Manure, sheep 11
'Maxime Kovalevski' 66
Measurements 6
Methane gas 100, 103, 110
Mice 78, 79, 80
Micro-miniatures 7, 30, 31
Mildew, powdery 65
Milk chocolate 78
Miller, Holmes C. 50
'Minx' 6
Miss Campbell 6, 87
Moisture, content 73
Moisture, meter 73
Moisture, soil 73
Molybdenum 64
Moths, 77, 78
Moulds 34

'Mrs Henry Cox' 66
Multipot trays 26
Mushroom compost 15
Mushroom fly 81

NPK 64
Natural gas 100
Necrotic spots 65
Net virus 84
Netting 27, 78, 106
New varieties 50
Nicotine 75, 102
Nitrates 63
Nitrogen 13, 16, 35, 64, 65, 66, 83
Nodal cuttings 36
Nodes 35, 36, 37, 38, 39, 59, 62, 97, 99
North Sea gas 100
Nucleus 16
Nutrient agar 43, 44
Nutrients 15, 42, 64
Nymphs 75

Oak, English 85
Oedema 84
Oil stove 101
Oil-fired central heating 101
Open compost 15
'Orion' 34, 50
Ovary 51, 52, 53, 54
Over-watering 20, 21, 22, 71, 72
Over-wet medium 16
Overcrowding 34
Overheating 46, 48, 49
Oxford University 86
Oxidisation 108
Oxygen 16, 56

Paraffin 101, 104, 105, 108
Parrett, Frank 6
Partial sterilisation 14
Pathogens 12, 14, 15, 24, 31, 45, 64, 65, 75,
  83, 97, 98
'Paul Crampel' 66
Peat 8, 11, 12, 13, 15, 49, 81, 100
Peat flies 81
Peat plugs 49
Peat, Sam 50, 52
Peg board 26
Pests 75
Pets 78, 80
Phosphoric acid 13
Phosphorus 64, 65
Photosynthesis 62, 65
Pink Pearl 33
Plant growth 30
Plant tissue 30
Plants, bedding 8, 34, 64, 73

Plants, border 8, 34, 64
Plastic 9, 22, 68, 69
Plastic bags 11, 13, 88, 96
Plastic pots 12, 19, 21, 22, 27, 30
Plastic trays 50
Poisons 78
Pollen 50, 52, 53, 54
Pollination, self 51, 52
Pollution 87
Polystyrene 26, 49
Polythene 48, 59, 60, 61, 62, 68, 106, 107, 108, 109
Poor drainage 14
Pot culture 15
Pot plants 16, 27, 63
Potassium 64, 65, 66
Potato 1
Potlets 26, 49
Pots 21, 28
Pots, clay 22, 27, 29, 30
Pots, peat 26, 44, 45, 56
Pots, scrubbing 20
Pots, transport 23
Potting 8, 13, 23, 24, 25, 27, 41, 44, 45, 55, 56
Potting compost 8, 11, 13, 14, 15, 16, 40, 41, 42, 56, 63
Potting, final 13
Potting-on 8, 13, 23, 24, 27, 41, 56
Potting-up 23, 24, 25, 44, 45, 55
Powdering 96
Powdery mildew 65
Predators 76
Probe 73
Propagating 24, 25, 26, 33, 35, 41, 45, 46, 47, 48, 49, 55, 57, 81, 83, 84, 85, 98
Propane gas 100, 103, 110
'Prostrate Boar, The' 87
Prune 34, 97,
Puccinia pelargonii-zonalis 84
Pythium 39, 83, 84

Quality 20
Quarantine 81, 85

Rabbit droppings 11
Rabbit tail 54, 55
Rainwater 66, 67, 72
Rampant growth 16
Raw loam 14
Re-potting 29, 30
'Red Pearl' 33
Regal pelargoniums 5
Registration Authority, International 5
Respiration 21
Retardant, chemical 51
Reverend Stanley Stringer 7, 9, 50, 52

Rhubarb 16, 100
Ripe wood 38
Rodents 78
Root ball 12, 13, 23, 29, 30, 73
Root development 65
Root disturbance 23
Root growth 29
Root hairs 16, 25, 29, 44
Root pruning 31
Root structure 29
Root system 26, 27, 29, 31, 39, 41, 44
Root tip 44
Rooted cuttings 21, 24, 49
Rooting cuttings 13, 26
Rooting medium 37, 39, 45
Rooting powders, hormone 39, 40
Roots 14, 21, 24, 25, 30, 31, 36, 38, 43
Roots, aerial 96, 97
Roots, anchoring 25, 71
Roots, bloated 42, 43
Roots, brittle 42, 43
Roots, feeding 25, 31, 71
Roots, fine 29, 31
Roots, invisible 16, 25
Roots, thick 31
Roots, visible 25, 44, 71
Rose fertiliser 65
Rot 34, 47, 48, 99
Rubbish 14
Russell lupins 8
Russell, George 8
Rust 34, 71, 84, 85, 86, 87, 88, 96

Sale, conditions of 7
Salts 66
Sand 11, 13, 15, 16, 17, 46, 47, 48, 56, 70, 80
Saprophytes 12
Scales 74
Scarifying 55
Scars 73
Sciarid flies 12, 81
Scion 59, 60, 61
Scorched foliage 21, 66, 67, 76
Scotch tape 60
Scrubbing pots 20
Seashore sand 15
Seaweed 44
Seed bed 24
Seed sowing 13, 56
Seedling blight 64
Seedlings 24, 26, 55, 56, 57
Seeds 14, 37, 48, 50, 52, 54, 81
Self-pollination 51, 52
Self-watering 69, 70
Sellotape 59
Shading 35, 45, 67, 72
Sheep manure 11

Shock 12, 30
Showing 5, 21, 54
Shrews 80, 81
Shrews, common 80
Shrews, pigmy 80
Side shoots 56
'Silver Kewense' 34
Slugs 77, 80, 81
Smoke 105
Smoke, tobacco 102
Smokes 45, 75, 77, 81
Smoking 102
Snails 77, 80
Soapsuds 76
Sodium nitrate 83
Soil 16, 17, 21, 30, 56
Soil ball(s) 15, 28, 29, 30, 31, 68, 69, 72, 73
Soil base 16
Soil grains 16
Soil heating cables 47, 48
Soil particles 16
Soil thermostat 47, 48
Soil-less composts 8, 12, 40, 41, 56
Solanum family 82
Solanum tuberosum 1
Solid fuel 105
Soot water 65
Sowing seed 13, 56
Species 50, 51
Spiders 80
Spores 34, 84, 85, 88
Spots, necrotic 65
Spray(s) (ing) 75, 77, 88, 96
Spraying 24
Stamens 51, 52
Starvation 12, 22
Stem rot 20, 82
Stem rot, bacterial 82
Sterilisation 11, 14, 15, 39
Sterilisation, chemical 14
Sterilisation, partial 14
Stigma 51, 52, 53
Stipules 37, 72, 88
Stock plants 13, 59, 60
Stoma (stomata) 87
Stones 14
'Stradt Bern' 59
Straw 11
Stringer, Reverend Stanley 7, 9, 50, 52
Style 51, 52
Succulent growth 64
Sugar 11
Sugar water 65
Sulphate of potash 13
Sulphur 64, 101, 102, 105
Sun rooms 100
Sunlight 8, 60, 67
'Sunstar' 50
Superphosphate of lime 13

Supplementary feeding 12
Surgical knife 37, 55, 59
Swann-Morton 59
Sycamore 78
Systemic disease 87
Systemic insecticides 45, 75, 76, 77

Tape, adhesive 60, 61, 62
Tape, Scotch 60
'Tapestry' 50
Tea leaves 11
Tea, cold 65
Temperatures 8, 46, 47, 49, 51, 56, 75
Tepid (or lukewarm) water 24, 25, 26, 28, 31
Terracotta pots 19
Test tubes 43, 44
Thermo-plastics 19
Thermogem 109
Thermostat, air 46, 104
Thermostat, soil 47, 48
Thrips 76
Thrower, Percy 8, 102
Time switch 48
Toads 80
Tobacco virus 82
Tomato 3, 82
Tomato ringspot virus 82
Top watering 67, 68
Town gas 100, 103
Trace elements 64
Trailing geraniums 5
Transpiration 35, 39, 45, 46, 60, 61, 67, 71, 72
Transport pots 23
Traps 77, 78
Tray rooted cuttings 44
Trays, multipot 26
Trays, plastic 50
Trough, balcony 8

U.C. Composts 11, 15, 16, 41
Underground union 36
University of California 11, 55, 83
Unsterilised knives 39
Unsterilised soil 15
'Urchin' 34
Urine 65

Vacapots 49, 55
Varieties, new 50
Vascular wilt 82
'Vega' 7
Vegetative cuttings 33, 35
Ventilation 8, 33, 34, 35, 55, 84, 88, 100, 101, 102, 103, 105, 108, 110

Vermiculite 16, 40
Vertical cuts 29
Verticillium albo-atrum 83
Verticillium wilt 83
Virus, crinkle 82
Virus, net 84
Virus, tobacco 82
Virus, tomato ringspot 82
Viruses 39, 45, 73, 75, 81, 82, 83, 84
Visible roots 25, 44, 71
Visual examination 16

Wasps 76
Water (lukewarm or tepid) 24, 25, 26, 28, 31
Water heaters, gas 100
Water retention 12, 16
Watering 12, 16, 19, 20, 21, 30, 31, 63, 66,
    70, 71, 72, 100
Watering, automatic 12, 20
Watering, bottom 67, 68
Watering, over 20, 21, 22, 71, 72
Watering, self 69, 70
Watering, top 67, 68

Weed seeds 14, 15
Weight 19
Well dressing 9
Wells, Bill 50
'Wells, Grace' 50
White Mesh' 82
Whitefly 45, 76, 77, 83
Wilting 60, 82
Wilting cuttings 40
Window boxes 8
Windowsills 34, 103
Wire, low voltage 47
Wood, ripe 38
Wooden greenhouses 108
Woodlice 80
Worms 14, 15, 17, 30, 80
Wreaths 9

Xanthomonas pelargonii 82

Zinc 64
Zonal pelargonium 5